D1345741

THE ROAD TO EUROPEAN MONETARY UNION

The Road to European Monetary Union

André Szász
former Executive Director
Dutch Central Bank

© André Szász 1999

All rights reserved. No reproduction, copy or transmission of this publication may be made without written permission.

No paragraph of this publication may be reproduced, copied or transmitted save with written permission or in accordance with the provisions of the Copyright, Designs and Patents Act 1988, or under the terms of any licence permitting limited copying issued by the Copyright Licensing Agency, 90 Tottenham Court Road, London W1T 4LP.

Any person who does any unauthorised act in relation to this publication may be liable to criminal prosecution and civil claims for damages.

The author has asserted his right to be identified as the author of this work in accordance with the Copyright, Designs and Patents Act 1988.

Published by
PALGRAVE MACMILLAN
Houndmills, Basingstoke, Hampshire RG21 6XS and
175 Fifth Avenue, New York, N. Y. 10010
Companies and representatives throughout the world

PALGRAVE MACMILLAN is the global academic imprint of the Palgrave Macmillan division of St. Martin's Press, LLC and of Palgrave Macmillan Ltd. Macmillan® is a registered trademark in the United States, United Kingdom and other countries. Palgrave is a registered trademark in the European Union and other countries.

Outside North America
ISBN-13: 978–0–333–74973–9

Inside North America
ISBN 978-0–312–21873–7

This book is printed on paper suitable for recycling and made from fully managed and sustained forest sources. Logging, pulping and manufacturing processes are expected to conform to the environmental regulations of the country of origin.

A catalogue record for this book is available from the British Library.

Library of Congress Catalog Card Number: 98–40521

Contents

Contents

Introduction

From a distance it looked like a riot. As my car approached the end of the Rue Froissart in Brussels I could see a crowd in front of the building where the secretive Monetary Committee – as the press invariably called it – of the European Community used to meet. Glaring lights in the gathering dusk indicated television crews. Cameras flashed. As soon as I got out of the car and tried to cross the short distance to the entrance I was completely hemmed in, and questions were shouted from the blinding lights. 'Why have you come?' 'What will the meeting be about?' 'How long will it last?' Of course they knew perfectly well what the meeting was about. That was why they were here. It was Wednesday evening 16 September 1992, soon to be dubbed 'Black Wednesday'. Only hours earlier, sterling, after intense speculation involving billions of dollars, had been pushed out of the Exchange Rate Mechanism of the European Monetary System. We had been summoned to pick up the pieces. Everyone knew it, yet this was not what I said. Our Committee's chairman never ceased to warn us not to talk to the press. When he sat in the chair behind the large round table with his back to the window and a pile of press cuttings in front of him, containing – I suppose – our earlier indiscretions, which he looked at balefully but refrained from reading out, he always reminded me of my school teacher many years ago. Saddened rather than angered by his pupils' misbehaviour, he would exhort us to be more discreet next time, and give the only acceptable answer to questions from the press: 'No comment! No comment! No comment!' And so – just before security finally came to my rescue and escorted me to the entrance – when again they asked what we were going to discuss, I replied: 'International monetary questions!'

International monetary questions are supposed to be rather esoteric. So they are, so far as their technical aspects are concerned. But the intense press coverage and wild headlines on occasions such as this revealed another side to it, that of high political drama. The link between these two sides is the subject of this book.

My theme is European monetary integration and its political background. European integration is about politics, often dealt with at the highest political level. It was on that highest level that monetary issues were pushed to the forefront of the integration process. Why monetary issues became so important is one of the questions to be discussed. Monetary issues are power issues. A related subject is how decisions are made. The initiative came from the summit. But though Heads of State or Government can take initiatives, they cannot implement. For that they need the monetary authorities: Finance Ministers and their close collaborators on the one hand, central banks on the other. In some countries, central banks have their own policy responsibility: the legal obligation to maintain the value of the currency. Their views are taken seriously by the public and thus also by politicians, and cannot simply be brushed aside. The difference between Germany and France in this respect is a thread that runs through this book.

At a more general level, writing about European monetary integration means writing about French–German relations. These relations are regarded by each as a cornerstone of its foreign policy. Both are convinced that good relations between them are crucial for stability in Europe. Both believe that these relations have to be part of a European framework. In order to be acceptable to France, this framework has to contain monetary arrangements, as it is in the monetary domain that Germany has become increasingly powerful since the late 1960s.

In tracing the development of European monetary integration from its origin in the 1960s to the eve of the establishment of Monetary Union, I present just one view. This view is inevitably coloured by the fact that I was personally involved in these issues as a central banker for more than thirty years, in particular after I became a member of the Executive Board of the Nederlandsche Bank in 1973, and, as such, a member of the Monetary Committee of the European Communities (I had been an Alternate for a few years before that) and the Deputy of the Dutch Central Bank's President in the Committee of Central Bank Governors. But these are not memoirs. Occasionally, I draw on personal experiences in order to illustrate a point, or the ambience, or just to enliven what might otherwise become a dreary tale. My teaching experience taught me that this helps listeners – or readers – to endure the rest. I can only hope that in doing so I have neither violated the code of discretion to which former central bankers are expected to adhere, nor offended anyone.

My purpose in writing this book on what seems to be the eve of the establishment of Monetary Union is to help provide an answer to the question: why are we doing this? I try to make it clear that Monetary Union is a major political enterprise. As such, it is inevitably based on compromises and contradictions. I am not arguing for or against it. As a former central banker, I cannot help being aware of the risks. But there are also risks, having created such strong expectations if it is not done. And there are opportunities, too, provided we know what we are doing.

I wish to express my appreciation to the Nederlandsche Bank for the facilities generously put at my disposal after my retirement. I thank my long-suffering secretary during so many years, Marijke Winter, for her patience in typing and correcting draft after draft. Many thanks go to Macmillan for editing the typescript and in particular for correcting my English. Finally, once again I am deeply indebted to Henk Boot. Time and again, as so often in the past when the events described in this book unfolded, we analysed together the motives and intentions of the main players in European monetary diplomacy. His suggestions and his comments on my successive drafts were invaluable to me in writing this book.

ANDRÉ SZÁSZ

1 The Political Background to European Integration

Political motives dominated European integration from the start. An overriding motive was the determination to prevent another war between Germany and France. Three wars had taken place within a century, at ever decreasing intervals. The firm intention to render further wars impossible inspired six European countries – France, Germany, Italy and the Benelux countries – to single out the two sectors of national economies then indispensable for waging war, the coal and steel sectors, and to subordinate them in a European Coal and Steel Community to a High Authority, which was intended to be supranational. As French Foreign Minister Robert Schumann, after whom the project was named, put it in May 1950: 'The common production thus established will make it plain that any war between France and Germany becomes not only unthinkable, but materially impossible.'[1]

The threat of Soviet expansion made post-war European rearmament inevitable, including that of the German Federal Republic. In order to make German rearmament acceptable to Germany's western neighbours, especially France, French Prime Minister René Pléven proposed to put it in the context of a European Defence Community. In a statement in the French Parliament on 24 October 1950, Pléven proposed the creation 'of a European army under the political institutions of a United Europe', a fully integrated European force under the responsibility of a European Defence Minister and overseen by an assembly on the model of the European Coal and Steel Community that was being set up at the same time.[2] This was a major step towards Political Union. However, although like the Coal and Steel Community this was a French proposal, motivated by the widely shared desire in France to integrate the German army and thus prevent it from ever becoming a threat again, there was also much opposition to doing the same with the French army, which stood as a symbol of recovered national liberty. The European Defence Community was rejected by the French Parliament on 30 August 1954, with the Gaullist

Deputies striking up La Marseillaise when the result of the vote was announced.

1.1   THE ECONOMIC ROAD

With the rejection of the European Defence Community by the French Parliament, the direct approach towards European political integration was obstructed. After a period of despondency, it was more or less generally accepted that the time was not right for integration in the domain of security and foreign policy. Instead, the Benelux countries now proposed steps towards economic integration. With the European Defence Community stillborn, a European Economic Community with supranational elements might yet lead to eventual political integration. The new approach was endorsed by the Foreign Ministers of the ECSC, who at a conference in Messina on 1–2 June 1955 stated that 'the time has come to make a fresh advance towards the building of Europe. They are of the opinion that this must be achieved, first of all, in the economic field.'[3] Negotiations, however, soon ran into difficulties. The European Economic Community might well have been postponed indefinitely, had not political events intervened.

1.2   THE IMPACT OF THE SUEZ CRISIS

In 1956, following the nationalisation of the Suez Canal by Egypt's President Gamal Abdel Nasser, Britain and France staged a joint military intervention. The intervention turned into a political disaster. This was mainly due to opposition on the part of the United States, who had not been consulted and who resented the action particularly as it coincided with the Soviet invasion of Hungary. Threats by the Soviet Union, exploiting the diversion from its own embarrassing military action, looked even more menacing since the western alliance was in disarray. The Suez Crisis, signalling the end of Britain's and France's status as global powers, had a traumatic effect on both countries. But their reactions were totally different.

Throughout Britain there was at first a wave of anti-American feeling. President Eisenhower's appearance on newsreels was hissed in cinemas. Strong pressure on sterling, an important factor in forcing the United Kingdom to terminate military action when France still wanted to continue, was attributed by the UK government to American encouragement. Though there is no evidence for this, American refusal to help – and even to endorse British efforts to obtain finance from the International Monetary Fund – was in itself bad enough, and must have influenced the market. In a paper of 28 December 1956, Anthony Eden, shortly before resigning as Prime Minister, assessed the lessons of Suez. He called for a review of British world position, noting that 'the consequence of this examination may be to determine us to work more closely with Europe . . .' A remark in the next sentence proved almost prophetic: '(t)he timing and the conviction of our approach may be decisive in their influence on those with whom we plan to work.'[4] But in the end, notably after Eden had been succeeded by Harold Macmillan, Britain's choice was not for intensified cooperation with Europe but for restoring the 'special relationship' with the United States. W. Scott Lucas writes in his study on the Suez Crisis:

> To restore the Anglo-American 'alliance', Britain paid the price of permanent subservience to American policy. . . In 1957, Macmillan effectively promised Eisenhower that Britain no longer retained her right to defy the United States in the implementation of her foreign policy. 'Alliance' had been restored, but Britain was a junior partner dependent of American benevolence.[5]

This may be exaggerated. But Britain's choice did imply that its future foreign policy would defer to the United States.

But not France! Here too resentment was strong against the United States for abandoning its allies and putting pressure on them, and added to this was resentment against Britain for giving in and leaving France no choice but to do likewise.[6] Yet it led to a determination to never again be so dependent, and certainly not on the Anglo-Saxons. To that end, three conclusions were reached.

The first was for France to proceed with its efforts to create its own nuclear armament, the *force de frappe*.[7] In military terms, this would make France less dependent on the American nuclear deterrent, that had – rightly or wrongly – been seen as unreliable during the Suez Crisis. Later, during De Gaulle's presidency, the General's doubts whether the United States would be ready to face an all-out nuclear war to defend Europe would play an important role in his policies. Politically, becoming a nuclear power would to some extent compensate for the loss of world power status was evident after the Suez Crisis.

The second conclusion was to intensify relations with the German Federal Republic. Logical under the circumstances, it was facilitated by the fact that Chancellor Konrad Adenauer showed much more understanding of the Suez interventions than did the United States.

Third, and linked to the second, was the decision to accelerate negotiations on the European Economic Community. According to Robert Marjolin, who negotiated for France and subsequently was to become one of the first two French members of the European Commission, there was considerable opposition in France against establishing a common market in which French industry would be exposed to German competition. The stance of French officialdom, where protectionism was deeply entrenched, was particularly negative, and the list of French demands and reservations was endless. According to Marjolin, the breakthrough in the negotiations came as a result of the intervention of French Prime Minister Guy Mollet, who wanted to conclude the treaty in order to 'erase, or at least to lessen, the humiliation that France had just suffered from the Suez affair' in November 1956.[8] German Chancellor Adenauer, who had demonstrated his solidarity by visiting his French counterpart in Paris in the midst of the Suez Crisis, welcomed the reorientation in French policy and contributed to it by major concessions on his part.[9]

The sterling crisis, and the United States' refusal not only to help, but also to allow Britain to draw on the IMF, has been mentioned as a major form of pressure to force Britain, and consequently France, to give in. Concerning international monetary policy Britain and France also drew different lessons for the future. Macmillan, then Chancellor of the Exchequer, says in his memoirs 'the obstruction (of the British drawing on the IMF) . . . was not so easy to forgive.' It was 'a breach of the spirit, and even of the letter under which the Fund is supposed to operate. It was a form of pressure which seemed altogether unworthy.' Once the action was over, the US was prepared to help: 'It was, of course, a little wounding to feel that we were to be given a "reward" for our submission to American pressure. Nevertheless, I was not foolish enough to refuse.' Rather, he now began 'the difficult task of re-establishing the old relations, without loss of dignity or retraction of our own positions, but with full sincerity and, happily, with full success.'[10]

In the years to come, sterling would remain a source of concern, at times even agony. One reason was that the monetary authorities of a number of countries still kept an important part of their international reserves in sterling, and these sterling balances constituted a potential threat to the pound's exchange rate and to British international reserves. This remainder of sterling's role as a reserve currency contributed to making British monetary interests identical to those of the United States. Thus in international monetary affairs the British position would closely follow the American line. Not so France. As with its strategic and foreign policy, so in its international monetary policy opposing US domination would become one of its main themes.

1.3 ASSESSMENT

The European Community's history, a later German Chancellor (Willy Brandt) would write in his memoirs, is a history of its crises. The choice for the economic approach resulted from a crisis, caused by the rejection of the European Defence Community by the French Parliament. The Suez Crisis contributed to its implementation.

The Suez Crisis was instrumental in causing a reorientation of French policy.[11] In order to break out of its resulting political isolation, France turned to the European Economic Community and to a privileged partnership with Germany. With Germany responding, these decisions set the pattern for the remainder of the century.

Equally decisive for future developments was Britain's decision not to turn to Europe. Its choice may have been inspired by a combination of reasons: a traditional policy avoiding too close ties with the Continent, the Commonwealth that still played a role during this period, the still recent memory of its glorious role in the Second World War won in close alliance with the United States. Whatever the reasons, it was not until five years later that it first applied for membership of the European Communities. By then it had become clear that they had become an economic success and there was a danger that, in view of that success, America might base its alliance strategy around the EEC rather than Britain.[12] But by that time admission required the consensus of the founding fathers of the European Communities, and France would not forget Britain's earlier choice: 'He who will not when he may, when he will, he shall have Nay.'[13]

Just as France did not forget the consequences of US domination and drew its own conclusions for its future strategic and foreign policies, so it also did in its monetary policies. Here, too, Europe would have to provide the means.

2 The Rome Treaty (1958) and the Barre Plans (1968–9)

The Treaty establishing the European Economic Community was signed in Rome on 25 March 1957, and came into force on 1 January 1958. In three respects, it was the result of compromises.

- The European Economic Community was more than a customs union but less than an economic union. In addition to the Common Market establishing free circulation of goods, services and, to some extent, capital, it established common policies, but only for certain sectors.
- Its Community institutions and procedures went beyond intra-governmental cooperation but it was less than supranational.
- Notwithstanding the political considerations set out in the previous chapter, the EEC was only acceptable to France because the Common Market was balanced by a Common Agricultural Policy (CAP). As Robert Marjolin wrote:

> Rightly or wrongly, the French government was convinced that without a European farm policy the Treaty of Rome would be heavily weighted against France and in favour of the industrial states in the north of the Community, especially Germany.[1]

This perceived balance of interests played an important role in French attitudes in the years to come.

2.1 IMBALANCES IN THE TREATY

The European Economic Community was based on the Common Market. But it was more than that. In a number of sectors, among them agriculture, the Treaty established common policies to be decided upon at the Community level. Regarding general economic, financial and monetary policies, however, the constraints on national policies introduced by the Treaty were far less strict.

The Treaty obliged member states to ensure balance of payments equilibrium, high employment and price stability, and coordination of their economic policies in order to attain these aims. They had to regard their conjunctural policies and exchange rate policies as matters of common interest. But though they had to consult each other and to coordinate their policies, in practice these were no more than declarations of intent. In the uneasy triangle of balance of payments equilibrium, high employment and price stability they could, and did, set their own priorities. As a result, their economies diverged, and their exchange rate relations came under pressure.

2.2   CAP AND A COMMON CURRENCY

In March 1961 economic discrepancies resulted in a revaluation of the Deutsche mark and the Dutch guilder. This contributed to convincing the European Commission that there was an inconsistency between the common agricultural policy (CAP) and the autonomy of member countries' general economic and monetary policy. Less than five years after the Rome Treaty came into force, in a memorandum of 31 October 1962 the Commission argued that exchange rates between members had to be permanently fixed, apart from very limited adjustments, since large adjustments could imperil common agricultural prices and thus the Common Market itself. In an article published on 1 January 1965 Commissioner Robert Marjolin stated:

> The only way to assure the maintenance of the common agricultural prices, without major crises, is to fix exchange rates, a *de facto* fixation which will soon have to become a *de jure* fixation in order to establish and maintain the necessary confidence. Thus, Monetary Union has ceased to be a dream or even a project of which realisation is uncertain. It has become an inevitable obligation. It will be achieved by the adoption of rules and norms that apply to the totality of the economic action of the Member States.[2]

I was then a young economist at the Nederlandsche Bank's Research Department. The Bank's President, Marius Holtrop, alarmed by newspaper reports about Marjolin's intended proposals, asked for further information. When he had read the article, he returned my cover note on which he had scrawled: 'Pep talk!' Nor did Dutch Finance Minister Johannes Witteveen take it seriously. Replying to questions in Parliament he argued that a single currency would amount to member states giving each other a blank cheque. Obviously, this would only be acceptable in case of far-reaching integration of economic and budgetary policies as well. A single currency would therefore be only conceivable as the final piece of full European integration. Such far-reaching proposals were not being considered at the time (1965).[3] Yet only four years later they would be, and at the highest political level!

2.3   ECONOMISTS AND MONETARISTS

In the debate between 'economists' and 'monetarists' that was enfolding in this period, the view of the Dutch monetary authorities was typical of the 'economist' view.[4] The 'monetarists' (not to be confused with followers of Milton Friedman and the Chicago School) wanted to give priority to integration in the monetary sphere, believing that since the issues relating to this were more 'technical' it would be easier to achieve than integration of budgetary policies, which went to the core of sovereignty and was therefore politically far more sensitive. Once achieved, monetary integration was expected to 'spill over' and force integration in other domains.

The 'economists' opposed monetary integration in isolation. They argued that it could only take place in parallel with economic integration, or even that it could only complete the latter: in this form, the view was often referred to as 'crowning theory'.

Germany and the Netherlands represented the 'economist' view. The 'monetarist' view was particularly strong in the European Commission, and was supported by most member countries, France in particular, though in the French case the desire to focus on monetary integration was not necessarily based on the hope that this would force integration in other domains.

Dutch Central Bank President Holtrop warned against the 'monetarist' approach at an early stage. In an article published in 1956, Holtrop discussed the Spaak Report on which the Rome Treaty was to be based. He deplored what he saw as a tendency in the report to fail to appreciate the role of balance of payments deficits as a warning signal of excessively expansionist domestic policies (which was even more true then than today, international capital flows being widely regulated). The report, he wrote, tended to see deficits as merely a troublesome phenomenon, standing in the way of continued expansion. In reality, no phenomenon played a more valuable role in combating inflation, and should consequently be more appreciated, than the balance of payments deficit. It is like the pain that signals illness before it is too late for treatment.[5]

Thus Holtrop saw little merit in the ideas starting to surface in the early 1960s of replacing national currencies with a European one, thereby eliminating the disciplinary effect of balance of payments deficits on budgetary and other policies. In an article published in 1963 he argued that monetary integration could not precede economic and political integration but could only follow it, describing money as 'an attribute of sovereignty'.[6] His reaction to Marjolin's article in 1965 was therefore understandable.

With hindsight, Marjolin himself came to the conclusion that it was not realistic to expect CAP to have the 'spill-over effect' as he called it to produce a European currency. Nor was it really imperative to save CAP, despite all the problems caused by exchange rate adjustments. Oddly, in his memoirs published in 1986, Marjolin not only failed to mention his article published twenty years earlier, but he also claimed that he had never shared those views, attributing them to Commission President Walter Hallstein. He called it a 'fundamental error' to think that governments

> could be constrained to take crucial decisions involving relinquishments of sovereignty, simply because an 'inner logic' (meaning the theory of chain reaction or the spill-over effect), the reality of which is moreover debatable, left it no other alternative.

In discussing subsequent efforts to attain Economic and Monetary Union he regarded the chief reason for failure 'the absence of any real understanding of what was involved.' He argued that

> the notion of an Economic and Monetary Union was closer to that of a Political Union, federation or confederation, than to the notion of a customs union. Practically identical, in fact, to a Political Union, it would have to include a European political power, a Community budget, and an integrated system of cen-

tral banks. All this would require profound changes for which the member countries were obviously not ready.[7]

In this, of course, he was right. But these insights only came later.

2.4 THE BARRE PLANS

During the second half of the 1960s the economies of the member states continued to diverge. The differences were accentuated by global balance of payments disequilibria. In November 1967 the British government was forced to devalue sterling. The United States dollar was under heavy pressure and US gold reserves were dwindling. The central banks participating in the Gold Pool, instituted in November 1961 by the Group of Ten industrial countries with the intention to prevent an increase of the price in the gold market, were forced to intervene; the Gold Pool was finally abolished in March 1968. All this made exchange rate adjustments within the Community more likely.

It was in these circumstances that Marjolin's compatriot and successor, Raymond Barre, proposed to the Council of Finance Ministers during a meeting on 26–27 February 1968, a 'Monetary Plan of Action for the Community'. This memorandum contained the following proposals:

- Member States should declare that exchange rates would be adjusted only with mutual prior consent (in a summary published in 1969 this was replaced by 'mutual consultation').
- The fluctuation margins should be eliminated.
- A system of mutual assistance should be established.
- A single European unit of account should be established.

These proposals were justified by refering to the progress in the construction of the European Economic Community that called for greater monetary solidarity between member countries, a need further increased by existing international monetary uncertainty. This would allow the Community to play its proper international role.

The Monetary Committee of the EC was asked to study these proposals. Here the German and Dutch members argued that such a one-sided monetary approach made no sense. In an interim report dated 8 January 1969 the Committee stated that a close

coordination confined to monetary policies would have no prospect of being durable so long as both budgetary policies as well as
the development of prices and incomes were not integrated in this
effort to increase coordination. 'There is, therefore, no reason to
believe that progress in coordination confined to the monetary sector
will be sufficient or even possible if not accompanied by progress
in the other sectors.'[8]

This stance of the Monetary Committee resulted in new Commission proposals on 12 February 1969 that were less one-sided.
These proposals, which became known as the Barre Plan, formed
the basis of the decisions taken at the summit in The Hague on 1
and 2 December 1969.

2.5 ASSESSMENT

The European Economic Community as envisaged in the Rome
Treaty in 1958 did not comprise monetary integration.

– Member States' monetary obligations did not go beyond coordinating their monetary policies.
– The obligation to liberalise capital movements was limited 'to
   the extent necessary to ensure the proper functioning of the
   Commom Market' (Article 67).

However, the issue of monetary integration came up in the early
1960s, never to disappear. There were three reasons for raising the
issue.

– In view of the lack of effective economic coordination between
   member states, exchange rate adjustments could be expected, and
   these would disturb CAP. For the European Commission, this
   was an argument to push for a single currency. Understandably,
   this was not taken seriously. A single currency, with its far-reaching
   implications, would not be introduced for 'technical' reasons alone.
   True, in view of the political importance France attached to CAP,
   if the latter were really endangered this would have had political
   consequences, though not necessarily in the form of a single currency. As it was, other solutions were found for the problem,
   and Marjolin, who raised it in the first place, later preferred to
   forget that he did.

- Monetary integration was regarded as 'technical' and easier to achieve than budgetary integration, which was seen as going to the core of sovereignty and was therefore politically far more sensitive. Once achieved, it was expected to force integration in other domains. For the European Commission and its services this was no doubt an important motive. Since it was unlikely to appeal to De Gaulle's France, they stressed CAP instead.

- The third, and probably politically most important, reason is linked to the issue of the sharing of the burden of balance of payments adjustments. The German mark and, to a lesser extent, the Dutch guilder, were emerging as strong currencies, due at least in part to relatively strict domestic policies. This periodically posed the problem of how to share the burden between surplus and deficit countries. Monetary integration, eliminating balance of payments constraints, would have been one way to solve the issue under the slogan of 'monetary solidarity'. It was to this that Dutch Finance Minister Johannes Witteveen alluded when referring to a single currency as a blank cheque between member states. Nederlandsche Bank President Marius Holtrop used another image when posing the question: whether the ant could be expected to put its stored resources at the disposal of the cricket.[9]

Monetary arrangements determine how deficit and surplus countries share the burden of adjustment. France wanted European arrangements that would enable it to pursue relatively expansionist policies without being constrained by balance of payments deficits. This implied arrangements that would oblige the Federal Republic of Germany to pursue more expansionist policies than it would have preferred. Germany gave a considerably higher priority to price stability than did France, and any other EEC country for that matter. German policies reflected a deep-seated, historically motivated fear of inflation on the part of the German public. The independent central Bank, the Deutsche Bundesbank, with stability of the currency as its main objective enshrined in law, reflected this attitude. The German monetary authorities resisted international monetary arrangements that would force them to pursue policies endangering price stability.

The issue of monetary integration was therefore to a large extent a power struggle between France, supported by most EEC countries and by the European Commission, and Germany, supported by the Netherlands. In this struggle Germany, with its increasing economic and monetary strength, had the *status quo* on its side. It was France and the others that wanted to change existing arrangements and were therefore *demandeur*. Had the struggle been confined to the monetary domain, there would have been no reason to expect a constant search for compromises. But monetary events never take place in isolation. They are influenced by political developments, and influence those in turn. Political considerations induced the Federal Republic to search for ways of meeting French demands on the basis of the revised Barre Plan, as will be discussed in the next chapter.

3 Economic and Monetary Union: The Hague Summit of 1969

On 1 and 2 December 1969 the Heads of Government, or in the French case the Head of State, of the six member states of the European Communities convened in The Hague at the joint initiative of the new German Chancellor, Willy Brandt, and the French President, Georges Pompidou, who earlier that year had succeeded General De Gaulle. At the meeting it was agreed to deepen and to widen the European Communities.

- Deepening meant the establishment of Economic and Monetary Union. In paragraph 8 of the final communiqué released after the meeting they announced that 'they have agreed that on the basis of the memorandum presented by the Commission on 12 February 1969 and in close collaboration with the Commission a plan by stages should be drawn up by the Council during 1970 with a view to the creation of an Economic and Monetary Union. The development of monetary cooperation should be based on the harmonisation of economic policies. They have agreed that the possibility should be examined of setting up a European Reserve Fund, to which a common economic and monetary policy would lead.'[1]
- Widening implied that France was prepared to withdraw the veto to British entry that General De Gaulle had first publicly announced in 1963.

In order to understand the background to these decisions we have to explore the monetary upheavals and political tensions that had emerged in the years preceding the summit, developments that reflected a shift in the balance of economic power both in transatlantic relations and within Europe. The factors leading to the summit in The Hague can be summarised under three headings:

15

- Tensions in the international monetary system;
- Tensions within the European Economic Community;
- East–West relations and Germany's new *Ostpolitik*.

3.1 TENSIONS IN THE INTERNATIONAL MONETARY SYSTEM

During the 1960s, the Bretton Woods system of stable exchange rates on a global scale was still in force. The system was based on a gold-dollar standard. The dollar, though unlike gold it was not mentioned in the Articles of Agreement of the International Monetary Fund, played a central role as a reserve asset and as the main intervention currency. It did so due to the size of the US economy and of US markets, and the relative prosperity in the United States in a world impoverished by war. In terms of the Articles of Agreement, the role of the dollar followed from the fact that the US monetary authorities were the only ones that freely bought and sold gold. The other member countries, not having assumed this obligation, had to ensure that rates for exchange transactions within their territories did not differ more from parity than one per cent. In practice, they implemented this obligation only against the dollar, buying or selling dollars against their own currency. As a result, exchange rates between other currencies than the dollar – the cross-rates – were also stable against each other, though the deviation from parity could be twice that permitted against the dollar.

It was up to countries buying dollars to decide whether to hold these dollars in their reserves or to convert them into gold at the expense of the US gold reserves. Dollar assets were interest bearing but lacked a gold value guarantee, while with gold it was the other way round. By converting dollars into gold if the dollar holder felt US policies were being too expansionary and the value of the dollar in terms of gold became uncertain as a result, the dollar holders – creditors of the United States – could exert a certain disciplinary pressure on US domestic policies. In the gold-dollar standard, the United States ensured the link between gold and dollars, and the other countries ensured stable exchange rates between the dollar and their own currency. As long as countries buying dollars in the market were genuinely free to decide whether to hold these dollars in their reserves or to convert them into gold, the system was a true gold-dollar standard. When in the course of the 1960s converting dollars became increasingly problematic, because it might shake the system and because the US authorities, unwilling to adjust their policies, put pressure on the creditors to hold on to the dollars the system obliged them to buy, the system began to develop into something different: a dollar standard, in which US policy decisions taken on the basis of domestic considerations without regard to external repercussions determined the size of global monetary reserves and thus the monetary policy stance in the system as a whole. In the prevailing inflationary climate this caused widespread misgivings.

During the greater part of the post-war period the United States' balance of payments had been in deficit. Initially the European countries welcomed the corresponding increase of their depleted reserves that enabled them to restore convertibility of their currencies in 1958. When this continued, however, aggravated by the Vietnam war, and when in the mid 1960s US debts to official holders started to exceed US gold reserves, this could not but cast doubt on the American ability to convert dollars into gold, a cornerstone of the Bretton Woods system. Confidence in the dollar was bound to be affected.

In 1963 the US authorities, in an effort to meet the concerns of their foreign creditors, took the initiative to commit a study of the international monetary system.[2] As far as the United States was concerned, the objective of the study was not a drastic reform of the system. They wished the dollar to remain the main reserve currency, and to that end they wanted to ensure tranquillity in the system. They would have preferred to discuss these issues, not within a group of industrial countries, but in a body of broader composition in which they expected their views would be more widely supported.[3] Most creditor countries, however, preferred a group composed of the countries that had earlier showed themselves able and willing to supply the IMF with additional liquidity if necessary (a necessity that might follow from a need for the United States to draw on the IMF). The fact that their preference prevailed indicates the shift that had taken place in the balance of power since the Bretton Woods system had been established. At that time, discussions had been dominated by the key currency countries, the US and the UK, and the views of the US had been decisive. By this time the other industrial countries, the continental European ones among them, being the US' major creditors, played an important role in the discussion that took place in the Group of Ten. This shift in the balance of power was brought home dramatically to me during the first ministerial meeting I ever attended – the Group of Ten Meeting in Stockholm in March 1968, where the agreement to establish Special Drawing Rights (SDR's) in the International Monetary Fund was reached. The ministers and governors of the EC countries, disagreeing among themselves, asked for a recess and withdrew. We lesser folks remained in the meeting room, waiting for the result. But not just us. At the deserted conference table US Secretary of the Treasury Henry Fowler sat by himself, soon to be joined by the UK Chancellor of the Exchequer Roy Jenkins. Those two lonely figures sitting side by side, representing the countries that had dominated the Bretton Woods Conference, who were now waiting for the outcome of the EC caucus, vividly illustrated the shift in the balance that had taken place.[4]

This shift in the balance was reflected in the outcome of the discussions. The EC countries argued in favour of a system that would no longer depend on the US for the supply of reserves. Moreover, they insisted that if a mechanism was to be set up inside the International Monetary Fund to supply international reserves, the EC countries should be able to block a decision to create reserves. The next step was to change the voting procedures in the decision-making on important existing IMF activities, giving the EC a veto here too. To that end, the majority required for certain decisions was raised to 85 per cent, ensuring that both the United States and the EC could block the decisions, assuming the latter adopted a common position.

These changes in IMF voting arrangements, which were meant to reflect the EC's increased economic and monetary weight relative to the US' earlier dominant position, came about at French insistence. For France, since General De Gaulle had come to power in 1958, international monetary policy was basically foreign policy by other means. The objective of its foreign policy was to reject subordination to the policy decisions of others, whether in the military domain (NATO) or in the international monetary system (IMF). In both, the United States had a dominant position. This frequently brought about confrontation with the United States. Whereas normally in this confrontation with a superpower France could hardly hope to bring to bear more than its nuisance value in foreign policy, the situation was different in the international monetary domain. Here the United States had become vulnerable as a result of its growing balance of payments deficits. Not only France, but other

European countries also resented the development of the international monetary system into a dollar standard. In the case of France, however, what rankled was not only the monetary aspect but also the fact that the dollar's international position enabled the United States to pursue its hegemonical policy and finance its military expenditure abroad.[5]

In the international monetary discussions the United States found itself on the defensive. General De Gaulle was quick to recognise the possibilities this offered for his foreign policy. Though the General tended to regard economics, in former British Prime Minister Harold Wilson's words, as 'quartermaster stuff', he was aware that 'battles have been won by aggressive and far-sighted quartermasters'.[6] But he also realised that France's chances of successfully confronting the United States alone were limited, even in the international monetary sphere. This would be different if the EC countries were to act in unison. France therefore attached great importance to coordinating the EC countries' views and actions in the international monetary discussions. It also tried to bring about a common policy regarding the dollar and repeatedly made technical and institutional proposals to create what was called a 'European monetary personality'. Getting Germany, with its increasing monetary weight, behind France in its policies regarding the dollar was the main objective of these efforts.

Germany found itself in a delicate position. Politically it was dependent on the United States, who were the guarantors of the freedom of West Berlin. The maintenance of an American military presence in the Federal Republic itself was crucial for its security. Germany was therefore loath to exploit the weakness caused by US balance of payments deficits which could – as the American authorities did not hesitate to point out – be attributed in part to US military expenditure abroad. Thus, while President De Gaulle instructed the Banque de France to convert its dollar holdings into gold in order to put pressure on the United States, Bundesbank President Karl Blessing in a letter to his US counterpart Martin on 30 March 1967 gave the assurance that Germany would continue to refrain from doing so, thus contributing to the development of the Bretton Woods system into a dollar standard. Nevertheless, the increasing foreign exchange inflows in Germany that were in large part the counterpart of US balance of payments deficits meant a continuous inflationary pressure that made the German monetary authorities restive.

Since US balance of payments deficits continued and even increased, contrary to US assurances based on hope rather than action, the sustainability of the Bretton Woods system became increasingly uncertain. A suspension of interventions in dollars by EC countries became a possibility. As a result their currencies would float not only against the dollar, but also against each other – causing considerable problems due to their economic interdependence – unless new arrangements were made to prevent this. Such arrangements, as the difficulties in the Bretton Woods system were amply demonstrating, could not be restricted to mutual intervention obligations but would also have to impose constraints on domestic policies in order to be durable.

These international monetary developments formed the background to the decision to adopt Economic and Monetary Union as a common objective, which was taken in December 1969 by the European Heads of State or Government. During the discussions in the preceding years on the reform of the international monetary system a common aim had emerged in the European countries to make monetary developments less dependent on US policy decisions, though the motives were not identical: in Germany the emphasis was on concern about the import of inflation, in France political considerations prevailed. There was a growing awareness in Europe that the Bretton Woods system of global par values might not be sustained, in which case the EC countries with their interdependent economies would have to develop monetary arrangements of their own. There were also voices, in France in particular, that wanted to change the international system in order to make it reflect the change in the balance of economic power in transatlantic relations, enabling them to share in what they saw as the benefits of a reserve currency.[7] But these considerations would not have been sufficient reason to want to merge national currencies into a common European one, with its far-reaching implications. For that, political motives were decisive.

3.2 TENSIONS WITHIN THE EUROPEAN COMMUNITY

While the balance was shifting from the key currency countries to the European Economic Community, there was also a shift in the balance of power within the Community from France to the Federal Republic of Germany. In the early 1950s France came to realise the importance of not repeating the tragic mistakes committed after the First World War. Some form of French–German partnership in a European context was a condition for stability and peace in Europe. Unfortunately, while the French agreed among themselves that this was true, they could not agree on the form it should take.

General De Gaulle, who came to power in May 1958, accepted the Rome Treaty that had come into force at the beginning of that year, though he fiercely rejected the European Commission's aspirations of being recognised as a political body. The General also attached great importance to increasing political cooperation on foreign policy and defence between the EC countries. He and his ministers often referred to this objective as political union. But though he pursued common policies and common action, these were to be based on close and permanent coordination between governments, without decision-making by *quelque construction apatride*, some stateless construction. The EC countries should at all times remain themselves, and this certainly applied to France. Being itself meant having its own policies and having its own means to carry them out. He accepted the necessity of close cooperation with the United States in view of the menace of Soviet expansion. But this cooperation should never take the form of subordination, neither in foreign policy and defence, nor in the economic and monetary sphere.[8] Hence the US dominated NATO should be reformed, and hence the role of gold should be enhanced at the expense of the dollar.

It was on the basis of this philosophy that France proposed intensified political cooperation between EC countries. To this end proposals were elaborated under the chairmanship of Christian Fouchet. German Chancellor Konrad Adenauer agreed, but the Benelux countries, the Netherlands in particular, objected, and prevented their realisation in April 1962. The main reason for this was their reluctance to participate in political cooperation under De Gaulle's leadership.[9] Under these circumstances, President De Gaulle and Chancellor Adenauer agreed that their two countries should proceed on the basis of a bilateral treaty between France and Germany that would provide for close and permanent cooperation. The Treaty was signed at the Elysée Palace in Paris on 22 January 1963.

While the two countries saw themselves as the core of any future European political cooperation, France regarded itself as the senior partner because of its status as one of the allies who had won the war, as well as being one of the occupying powers in Germany, and also in the process of becoming a nuclear power. Adenauer tacitly accepted this relationship, taking care never to move too far out of line with the French.[10] But the balance of power between the two countries was changing. This was reflected in an increasing restiveness in Germany regarding French aspirations. As Adenauer's last Foreign Minister Gerhard Schröder remarked in private: 'We are not suited for the role of junior partner.'[11]

An early symptom of the change was the controversy that arose around the ratification of the Elysée Treaty. De Gaulle's attitude regarding the United States and NATO was causing concern in Germany. Moreover, he had put Adenauer in an embarrassing position when, having made negotiations between the Community and Britain increasingly difficult in the preceding months, he publicly rejected British participation in the EC during a highly publicised press conference just one week before the Treaty was signed. This was bound to create the impression that Germany, by proceeding with the conclusion of the Treaty regardless, agreed with De Gaulle's position. In the end the German Bundestag agreed to ratify the Treaty on 8 May 1963 but adopted a unilateral statement in the form of a preamble, stating in effect that the Treaty did not change relations with the United States and NATO and had no bearing on the prospects of British participation. This flew in the face of De Gaulle's perception of the partnership. It is said that 'General De Gaulle's great ambition, that of a Europe based on German support for French policy, came to an end on 8 May.'[12] No wonder he was upset by what he called *cet horrible chapeau* (that horrible preamble).[13] According to his close collaborator Michel Debré he deeply resented the Bundestag's action.[14] This was confirmed by the German side: Hermann Kusterer, Adenauer's personal interpreter, who participated in the two statesmen's confidential conversations, observes that for De Gaulle the Bundestag's declaration was 'a punch in the stomach' and that hereafter disillusion set in.[15]

A number of spectacular actions on De Gaulle's part contributed to the estrangement, actions that in his view were vital to his vision of Europe, but with which Germany, and all other EC countries, openly disagreed.

- Following De Gaulle's well-publicised press conference just a week before the Elysée Treaty was signed, vetoing British entry into the EC (a timing most embarrassing to Adenauer, and an important factor contributing to the adoption of the preamble by the Bundestag) negotiations between the United Kingdom and the EC were broken off on 29 January as a result of French pressure.

– At the beginning of July 1965, France forced a show-down in the EC by no longer participating in its work – the 'empty-chair policy' – until on 29 January 1966 in Luxemburg it was agreed to disagree: majority voting contained in the Rome Treaty was not to be applied if a country deemed that its major interests were involved.

– On 7 March 1966 France announced its withdrawal from the military structure of NATO.

Thus, already during Adenauer's last year as German Federal Chancellor, but in particular under his successors – Ludwig Erhard from 1963 and Kurt Georg Kiesinger from 1966 – relations between Germany and France lost their earlier cordiality. They became strained in 1968. Germany's increasing economic power, combined with the effects of the 'events of May', the student revolt in May 1968 that almost toppled De Gaulle and induced the French Government to follow expansionist policies, contributed to exchange rate tensions. Germany and France disagreed on who should do what to restore equilibrium. In November a Group of Ten meeting was called in Bonn to deal with the problem. Then Bundesbank Vice President Otmar Emminger, who called this the most unpleasant monetary conference he ever attended, writes in his memoirs that in the view of the Bundesbank a combined German revaluation and French devaluation would have been the only real solution. According to him Banque de France Governor Jacques Brunet agreed with this view, and such a combined operation might have been acceptable to the French government as well.[16] But the German Economics and Finance Ministers opposed any revaluation of the German mark; the former, Karl Schiller, for fear of strangling the economic upswing that was taking place, while Finance Minister Franz-Joseph Strauss passionately argued that this would merely be a concession to De Gaulle's nationalist sensitivities.[17] Instead, the German government decided on an alternative measure in the form of foreign trade levies, this in their view had the advantage that it could easily be abolished when circumstances changed. In order to thwart any further pressure to revalue, they announced this measure in public at the outset of the conference, thus presenting it as a *fait accompli*, not only excluding a revaluation but also making it impossible to present even the levies as part of a package deal agreed upon at the meeting.

What was no doubt clumsy conduct on the part of the German government was widely regarded in international press reports as indication of a new assertiveness reflecting Germany's return to the international stage as a major economic power. German comments expressed satisfaction about the international role the German mark now played, and there was some gloating over the triumphalist attitude of the German ministers at the conference, against which Vice Chancellor Brandt later warned his countrymen. The only possible outcome now seemed to be a French devaluation. At the Bonn meeting, French Finance Minister François-Xavier Ortoli felt he had no choice but to agree to a French devaluation in the order of 10 per cent, an outcome that inevitably became widely known right away. But General De Gaulle, whose distaste for this measure could only have been further increased by the German Government's behaviour, decided – supported by his Prime Minister Maurice Couve de Murville and by Raymond Barre – to disavow him after all, defying both Germany and the market. To everyone's stupefaction he announced that the franc's parity would remain unchanged. By this time, the Monetary Committee of the EC had been convoked for an emergency session on 24 November in Paris to deal with the French devaluation that had been, we all thought, agreed upon at the Group of Ten Meeting in Bonn. Having arrived in Paris on the previous evening, I was sitting in one of the pavement cafés at the Place Trocadéro for a nightcap when a newsvendor appeared with the late edition. In dazed disbelief I read the headline: COUP DE THEATRE! LE GENERAL DIT NON![18]

De Gaulle resented Germany's refusal to revalue the German mark, thus trying to force his hand to devalue the franc. For him, the strong franc of the Fifth Republic – as opposed to the series of devaluations under the Fourth – was both a symbol of the success of his administration and a tool in his policy regarding the United States. As Michel Debré, at that time Foreign Minister, later put it: 'For an administration that had proclaimed that a solid currency was one of the conditions for diplomatic independence ... (a devaluation) would indeed be a heavy blow.'[19] Hence the resentment against Germany that had, in French eyes, put France in this humiliating position: 'the strength of the mark permitted

Germany for the first time in November 1968 to speak with a very loud voice. This strength ensured it of the economic supremacy that made it the master of Europe for a very long time.'[20] Looking back, Debré did not mince words when giving his opinion about the Germans:

'I know the Germans sufficiently to be aware that they abuse their power as soon as they are in a position to do so.'[21] It was therefore with grim satisfaction that he noted the reaction once the General had decided not to devalue after all: 'The stupefaction is general and the surprise total, especially in Germany where the Government had already announced the French devaluation.' He adds – what irony – that De Gaulle received a telegram with congratulations from US President Lyndon Johnson.[22]

When De Gaulle resigned in a huff after an unfavourable outcome of a referendum in April 1969, the franc once again came under pressure and was finally devalued by his successor Pompidou in August 1969. Meanwhile in Germany a public revaluation debate unfolded, with the Minister of Economics Schiller (together with the Bundesbank) now in favour and the Minister of Finance Strauss still against, and with capital inflows the inevitable result. The currency thus became an issue in the election campaign. Finally the new Government under Chancellor Willy Brandt decided to revalue the German mark by 8.5 per cent on 24 October, the par value having been suspended earlier by the outgoing Government. By the time Brandt became Chancellor the episode had neither improved relations between the two countries, nor the atmosphere within the European Economic Community.

3.3 BRANDT'S NEW *OSTPOLITIK*

The European Community's history, Brandt wrote in his memoirs, is a history of its crises. When assuming the position of Federal Chancellor in October 1969 'I was confronted with one of the crises without end, and not the easiest one.'[23] Restoring relations was the first priority of the new Social Democrat–Liberal coalition. Doing so was a prerequisite for one of the most important initiatives the Government was planning: its new *Ostpolitik*, a policy to normalise relations with Eastern Europe. A central part of this policy was to establish relations between the two Germanies, the Federal Republic of Germany and the German Democratic Republic, without abandoning the former's ultimate aim of reunification.

In his monumental *White House Years* Henry Kissinger, President Nixon's Assistant for National Security Affairs at the time, describes what he calls the central problem of the Federal Republic's foreign policy. Any West German Government, he writes, was bound to avow the goal of German reunification, but this was unachievable without a massive collapse of Soviet power. The Federal Republic could not simply wait for that; it needed some plausible concept for dealing with a divided Germany. Throughout the fifties and sixties successive governments had attempted to resolve this dilemma by ostracising the East German regime. But by 1970 more and more countries were recognising East Germany in defiance of Bonn's threat to cut off relations (the Hallstein Doctrine). The policy increasingly ran the risk of backfiring; it threatened to isolate Bonn rather than East Germany. By the seventies the Adenauer policies on reunification were bound to bring the Federal Republic into increasing conflict with both allies and the non-aligned.[24]

The 'Grand Coalition' of the Christian Democrats and Social Democrats in which Kiesinger was Chancellor and Willy Brandt Vice Chancellor and Foreign Minister had tried to improve relations with the East, but because it lacked an agreed view its progress was necessarily limited. A breakthrough was only to come after the new coalition under Brandt assumed office.[25] But in order to give a chance to the new policy towards the East, Bonn had to secure and reinforce its relations with the West. There were three reasons for this.

First, Brandt's government could only hope to attain a satisfactory result in its negotiations with the Soviet Union if it was clearly seen to negotiate as part of the West. Its chief negotiator, Egon Bahr, later wrote how important it had been in the negotiations that the Federal Republic had the backing of NATO.[26] This could be extended to mean being part of the western world, in particular, part of an integrating Western Europe.

Secondly, and linked to the first point, Brandt's new government could not possibly overlook the fact that its intentions for a new *Ostpolitik* were causing serious misgivings with its western allies, both in Europe and on the other side of the Atlantic. As Kissinger put it:

It seemed to me that Brandt's new *Ostpolitik* ... could in less scrupulous hands turn into a new form of classic German nationalism. From Bismarck to Rapallo it was the essence of Germany's nationalist foreign policy to manoeuvre freely between East and West. By contrast, American (and German) policy since the 1940s had been to ground the Federal Republic firmly in the West, in the Atlantic Alliance and then the European Community.[27]

The State Department, in an assessment of the new coalition's likely foreign policy, argued that it 'could not pursue simultaneously active policies toward East Germany and integration of the Federal Republic into Western Europe.' Kissinger shared this concern.[28] In retrospect Kissinger admitted that for the Brandt Government the new *Ostpolitik* was absolutely essential, but added that he did not see it that way at the time.[29] According to Kissinger, his misgivings were shared by both the French and the British.[30] As far as the French were concerned, this is borne out by Eric Roussel's biography of Georges Pompidou. Pompidou watched German *Ostpolitik* with strong reservations which he maintained even after the so-called Eastern Treaties (*Ostverträge*) had been concluded. In September 1970 the President summarised his objections: Brandt had made formidable concessions. Germany now acted on its own without asking anyone for permission. And the Soviet Union now had it in its grip. On another occasion he argued that sooner or later the Soviet Union and the United States would agree among themselves, with Europe being squeezed in between. Therefore 'Germany should be linked to Europe in such a way that it could no longer cut loose.'[31]

Last but not least, there was strong opposition to the new *Ostpolitik* within Germany itself. According to Gerhard Stoltenberg (later to become Kohl's first Finance Minister) discussions on this policy resulted in a polarisation not known since the establishment of the Federal Republic.[32] Even if the negotiations were to succeed, it was far from certain whether there would be a majority in Parliament required to approve the resulting Eastern Treaties. The attitude of Germany's western partners could make the difference.

For these reasons, it was imperative for the Brandt Government to take steps to repair the growing resentment and suspicion and to remove any doubt whether it was pursuing its *Ostpolitik* as part of the West. Stagnation in western european integration had to be replaced by a new dynamism. In his memoirs Brandt leaves no doubt about the link. When visiting Paris in 1971 he took the occasion to react to assertions in the French press that Germany was not really interested in Economic and Monetary Union, and merely wanted a free hand in the East: 'In reality we wanted progress in the West – precisely also because of our *Ostpolitik*.'[33]

By agreeing to the establishment of Economic and Monetary Union and proposing the creation of a European Reserve Fund, Brandt opened up perspectives that could not fail to appeal to France.

- It would meet concerns caused by the *Ostpolitik*, since EMU would link the Federal Republic to Western Europe 'in such a way that it could no longer cut loose', as Pompidou put it.
- By offering to start a process that would in time merge the German mark into a European currency, Germany indicated that it did not intend to use the strength of its currency to obtain economic supremacy and become the master of Europe, as Debré and others feared.
- European monetary arrangements would make it easier to establish common European monetary policies regarding the United States.

Starting a process of 'deepening' would, however, only be part, of the effort to imbue European integration with a new dynamism. 'Widening' the European Communities was the other part. De Gaulle's veto of British entry had strained relations since 1963. According to Kissinger, Pompidou told the Americans during a visit to the United States about his concerns regarding the *Ostpolitik*, averring that it was fear of a resurgent Germany that had caused him to reverse De Gaulle's opposition to Britain's entry. Brandt himself did what he could to bring about this change in French policy, arguing that whoever was concerned that Germany's increased economic strength was threatening the balance within the Community should be in favour of widening it, if only for that reason.[34] Even more important, he reassured Pompidou during the Summit Meeting in The Hague regarding the financing of the CAP in a widened EC, essential for French domestic reasons.[35]

3.4 ASSESSMENT

In view of (West) Germany's geographical position in the centre of Europe, both in relation to its size and its history, any major

German approach to the East was bound to cause grave misgivings in the West. The political balance in Europe was felt to be at stake. Germany could not allow these misgivings to persist. It had no interest in endangering the political balance and the action causing the misgivings might well prove self-defeating if Germany's western partners were not to some extent reassured. This was the problem facing Willy Brandt's government in 1969 (as it also faced his successors two decades later). The solution was to balance the initiative to the East with a renewed dynamism in the West (as its successors did two decades later).

Why the stress on monetary integration? Because international monetary issues were playing an important role as a result of the shift in the transatlantic balance as well as in the balance within the EEC. The change in the transatlantic balance was reflected in a spluttering of the Bretton Woods system. Its breakdown affected the EEC and called for European positions and solutions. The shift in the balance within the EEC was reflected in an increasing strength of the German mark, threatening French–German relations, the core of European integration. European integration in turn formed the framework in which French–German cooperation had to develop.

For the Federal Republic, *Ostpolitik* was of vital importance. It could only succeed with western, including French, acceptance and support. In the monetary domain, due to its increasing strength, Germany had something to offer to get that support. In the short run, this paid off. When the leader of the Christian Democrat opposition in the Bundestag, Rainer Barzel, told Pompidou that his party intended to vote against the eastern treaties, the French President – despite his own misgivings – discouraged him from doing so. In the end the opposition abstained, and the treaties were passed.[36]

To take the initiative to establish Economic and Monetary Union is one thing, to implement it another. The first, only the Heads of State or Government can do. To implement it, they need others. And once political considerations and decisions are translated into monetary action, the latter is subject to the forces and constraints prevailing in the monetary sphere.

4 The Werner Report (1970)

Soon after the summit in The Hague, the Council of the European Communities decided to set up a committee under the chairmanship of the Luxemburg Prime Minister Pierre Werner and consisting of the chairmen of various committees 'to prepare a report containing an analysis of the different suggestions and making it possible to identify the basic issues for a realisation by stages of Economic and Monetary Union in the Community.'[1] As cynics put it, now that the Heads of Government had decided to establish Economic and Monetary Union, a committee was necessary to find out what it was.

The final report of the Werner Committee was published in October 1970. Though it presented a plan to be realised in stages, it focused on the first and the final stage, leaving the intermediate stages largely open. Its conclusions were in essence approved, although in a watered-down form, in a resolution of the Council and of the representatives of the governments of the member states on 22 March 1971 concerning the attainment by stages of Economic and Monetary Union in the Community.[2]

4.1 MONETARY UNION

Though the Heads of State or Government had established Economic and Monetary Union as an objective in their communiqué issued in The Hague, the communiqué gave no indication of what was meant by Monetary Union. The Werner Report defined it as an area with a single currency and a centralised monetary policy. This definition was approved in the Council resolution, which stated that the Community would

(f)orm a single currency area within the international system, characterised by the total and irreversible convertibility of currencies, the elimination of margins of fluctuation of exchange

30

rates, the irrevocable locking of parities – all of which are essential preconditions for the creation of a single currency – and including a Community organisation of the central banks.

It was implicit in both the report and the resolution that the Community organisation of the central banks would pursue the centralised monetary policy required, but neither its relations to the political authorities (i.e. the extent of its dependence or independence) nor its policy priorities were defined. The resolution merely stated: 'The Community organisation of the central banks shall, within its field of responsibility, assist in achieving stability and growth within the Community.'

Thus no choice was made between the widely diverging models existing in the Community, with the Deutsche Bundesbank at one extreme with its far-reaching independence and its obligation to pursue the stability of the currency (interpreted as price stability), and, at the other, central banks that were dependent on government policies and had no priorities specified by law.

4.2 ECONOMIC UNION

The communiqué of The Hague did not define Economic Union any more than it did Monetary Union. It did, however, contain the sentence 'The development of monetary cooperation should be based on the harmonisation of economic policies.' Though strictly speaking this sentence concerned development towards EMU rather than EMU itself, it could be read to imply that Monetary Union should be based on the harmonisation of economic policies. The Werner Committee now took a great step beyond the harmonisation of economic policies, giving a definition of Economic Union that entailed a large measure of centralisation. Here, too, the resolution in essence followed the report, stating that the Community was to

(p)ossess such powers and responsibilities in economic and monetary matters as will enable its institutions to administer the Union. To this end the requisite decisions on economic policy shall be taken at the Community level and the necessary powers shall be conferred upon the institutions of the Community.

The resolution then mentioned specific policy areas, and stated:

as regards budgetary policy proper, the margins within which the essential elements of public budgets as a whole should lie, in particular the variation of their amount, and the size, mode of financing and use of balances, shall be determined at Community level.

Perhaps the most marked difference between the report and the resolution was that the former contained references to the institutional form of centralisation of non-monetary as well as monetary policies. It stated the need for 'a decision centre for economic policy' as well as for a Community System of central banks. The resolution did not mention such a decision centre. It did, however, say:

Powers and responsibilities shall be distributed between Community institutions on the one hand and Member States on the other in accordance with what is necessary for the cohesion of the Union and for the effectiveness of Community action... Community policies pursued within the framework of the Economic and Monetary Union shall be subject to debate and control by the European Parliament.

4.3   POLITICAL UNION

In the view expressed both in the report and in the resolution, Economic and Monetary Union thus implied on the one hand a single currency and a common monetary policy pursued at the Community level, and on the other hand economic, and in particular budgetary, policies for which the essential decisions determining the policy stance were also taken at the Community level. Though the report was more explicit than the resolution on what Community level meant, both stated that Community policies would be subject to control by the European Parliament.

Since budgetary policies go to the heart of national sovereignty, this implied that Economic and Monetary Union was a step in the direction of Political Union. Once again, the report was explicit where the resolution was not:

These transfers of responsibility represent a process of fundamental political significance that implies the progressive development of political cooperation. Economic and Monetary Union thus appears as leaven for the development of Political Union, which in the long run it will be unable to do without.

4.4 FIRST STAGE

According to the report the first stage would be mainly character-ised by intensified coordination. The main specific proposal, of which no mention had been made in the communiqué of The Hague, was of a monetary nature. It was proposed that from the start of the first stage member countries would 'as an experiment' reduce the fluctuation margins between their currency to less than what resulted from their fluctuation margins against the US dollar. The technical details of this proposal were set out in an annexe to the report. This was a paper written by an expert committee of the Commit-tee of EC Central Bank Governors under the chairmanship of its President, the Belgian Central Bank Governor Hubert Ansiaux. In accordance with this proposal, the resolution stated that

(t)he Council and the Member States shall invite the central banks of Member States, from the beginning of the first stage and on an experimental basis, to hold exchange rate fluctuations between the currencies of Member States within margins narrower than those resulting from the application of the margins in force for the US dollar, by means of concerted action with respect to that currency.

It added that 'depending on the circumstances and on the results obtained in the harmonisation of economic policies, further measures may be taken'. The resolution also stated that 'the Community shall progressively adopt common standpoints in monetary relations with third countries and with international organisations.' Finally it asked the competent committees

to draw up, in close collaboration and by 30 June 1972 at the latest, a report on the organisation, functions and statutes of a European Monetary Cooperation Fund, to be integrated at a later stage into the Community organisation of central banks. . . . . with a view to the possible establishment of this Fund during the first stage, if the results obtained in reducing margins and aligning economic policies so justify.

4.5   ASSESSMENT

When Heads of State or Government announced the establishment in stages of Economic and Monetary Union, this did not mean that they had in mind a precise concept of what should be established. Even if some of them had, it did not mean they all agreed. Subsequently, the negotiators faced three fundamental disagreements.

– What priority was to be given to price stability in the EMU and during the development towards EMU. This disagreement was implicit rather than explicit; it was expressed in the negotiators' institutional preferences.
– Supranational or intergovernmental arrangements. Since De Gaulle's departure France's opposition to supranational arrangements had become less strident, opposition still remained, whereas the other members of the Community of Six were more or less in favour, as was the Commission.
– The different views between 'monetarists' and 'economists' (see 2.3). This difference focused on the sequence of integration, though it also concerned the final stage.

The Werner Report and the 1971 resolution were compromises between 'two basic positions which, in the final analysis, are very difficult to reconcile' as Hans Tietmeyer, himself an alternate member of the Werner Committee at the time, later put it.[3] They were compromises not in the sense that member states resolved their differences by meeting each other on intermediate positions, but rather that they agreed on documents which they felt left them free to continue to push for their own preference. Both the report and the resolution acknowledged that a single currency required the transfer of decision-making on the main elements of national budgets to the Community level. This reflected the German and Dutch position; without it, German agreement would have been unlikely. The compromise lay in what was left open, and in the priority monetary issues were given in practice.

Concerning the issues left open, the following points were conspicuous for their absence.

– The controversial issue of what priority price stability should have was not tackled. The position of the Community organisation on the central banks was left entirely open, including its mandate, competences and relation to politics.

- Though the need to determine the main elements of budgetary policy at the Community level was acknowledged, the resolution avoided any reference to the institutional implications, deleting even the description 'decision centre of economic policy' which, though vague, suggested it would not be purely intergovernmental.
- In the resolution there was no mention of Treaty amendment, though any substantial transfer of competence would obviously require new Treaty provisions.

Thus at that time member states did not envisage entering into any precise treaty obligations regarding the substance of Economic and Monetary Union. Since the establishment of EMU was impossible without first concluding a treaty to that end, this illustrated the fact that what some member states were interested in was not the final stage of EMU. These member states, notably France, were interested in early action in the monetary field, which Germany would not have agreed to had it not been presented as steps towards Economic and Monetary Union: the establishment of a European exchange rate arrangement, the 'snake', and a European Reserve Fund.

5 The Snake (1972–8)

The resolution of the Council and the governments of 22 March 1971 – adopting the proposal made in the Werner Report – invited central banks, from the beginning of stage 1 and on an experimental basis, to hold exchange rate fluctuations between currencies of member states within margins narrower than those resulting from the application of the margins in force for the dollar.

Member states were, of course, aware that exchange rate stability – let alone development in the direction of the permanent fixation of parities – required economic convergence as well as monetary arrangements. Yet, unlike the latter, where formal obligations were entered into, the paragraphs in the resolution dealing with coordination of economic policies did not go beyond intentions. Doing so would have implied real constraints on national autonomy. Moreover, it would have posed the question of how the burden of adjustment would have to be shared over deficit and surplus countries, and on this issue disagreements in the snake turned out to be hardly less than in the Bretton Woods system.

5.1 THE SNAKE IN THE TUNNEL

'In order to reinforce the solidarity in the Community regarding foreign exchange', the report of the Werner Committee proposed that, from the beginning of the first stage and on an experimental basis, exchange rate fluctuations between Community currencies should be held within margins narrower than those resulting from the application of the margins in force for the dollar (at this time, the Bretton Woods system still existed). When depicted in a graph, this narrow band writhed like a snake through the wider band, or tunnel, observed against the dollar. Hence, the arrangement was soon generally referred to as 'the snake in the tunnel', or just 'the snake'. Initially this proposal was controversial within the Committee because the German and Dutch members opposed it. The Committee found a way through by posing a number of questions related to the issue to the Committee of Central Bank Governors, which was justified since technical issues were involved.[1] The Governors entrusted the study to a group of experts, in which I was one of the Dutch representatives. The group was chaired by the President of the Committee of Governors himself, Belgian Central Bank Governor Hubert Ansiaux. This was unusual and probably motivated by his intention to quell all opposition and objections coming from mere experts. This he did, complete with tantrums if deemed necessary. The Dutch members saw little point in the proposal, which they regarded as a purely symbolic step towards a single currency, so long as no actual steps were taken. The narrowing of margins would merely limit the scope for interest rate differences between member states and thus hamper monetary policies. But they found themselves in a rather awkward position when they disagreed with the chairman but did not wish to endanger relations between the two central banks. Often their German colleagues privately agreed with them, but the Bundesbank took the position that the narrowing of margins was a political decision which it did not wish to oppose. Thus, in the end, it was only the Nederlandsche Bank that expressed reservations to the report, arguing that the narrowing of margins should not precede economic convergence, but follow it.[2] In formulating these reservations, we met some opposition from – of all people – our Bundesbank counterparts. They protested that we could not use arguments with which they agreed for a minority position which they did not share! In the end this problem was solved, and a sentence was included stating that reduction of the margins was based on the assumption that in parallel sufficient progress would be realised in the gradual convergence of economic policies. This was henceforth referred to as 'parallelism'.

5.2 MOMENT OF TRUTH

Before the plans to narrow the fluctuation bands between EC currencies could be put into effect, Germany felt compelled to float the German mark in the face of huge liquidity inflows. On 6 May 1971 the German members of the Monetary Committee indicated that Germany would have to cease interventions in the exchange markets in order to stem the capital inflows that bloated domestic liquidity. In the following days the German authorities tried to persuade their partners to float together against the dollar within widened margins, offering them credits if necessary. This was rejected by France and Italy. On 9 May Germany therefore announced its decision to let the German mark float on its own, a decision followed by the Dutch authorities for the guilder. Three months later, on 15 August, US President Richard Nixon announced his decision to terminate the dollar's convertibility into gold. According to the IMF Articles of Agreement the US authorities now found themselves under the same obligation as other IMF members to intervene in the exchange market to stabilise their exchange rate. This they ignored.

The EC countries other than Germany and the Netherlands now had a choice between continuing unilaterally to buy dollars they could no longer convert, or let their currency float. A renewed initiative to organise joint floating, this time taken by the Benelux countries, met with no success. In the absence of an exchange rate arrangement regarding the dollar, exchange rate arrangements within Europe seemed to become more necessary than before, but were also more difficult to achieve. They were more necessary because individual countries' competitive position is less affected if their currency appreciates only against the dollar and not against the currencies of their main trading partners. They were more difficult to achieve because differences in economic fundamentals and in policy priorities now became more evident and stood in the way of joint floating against the dollar.

Whereas for Germany the unfavourable impact of the appreciation against the dollar on its competitive position would have been mitigated by joint floating with its main trading partners, for France and Italy joint floating meant a deterioration of their competitive position due to the German mark's strength, which they were not prepared to accept. Already in May, when France and Italy had first rejected a joint float, Dutch Finance Minister Johannes Witteveen had pointed to this weakness when explaining events to the Dutch Parliament. He referred to the differences in economic development as well as in policy priorities:

> This becomes clear at such critical moments and when we are faced with such difficult decisions. It is the moment of truth; it is no longer theoretical musings about how nice it all can be. One has to make a choice. And then it became clear that in France and Italy combating inflation becomes somewhat less important when there is some worry that a slight rise in the common exchange

rate might endanger economic expansion ... or cause some unemployment.[3]

It was only when the global system of stable exchange rates had been temporarily restored following the Smithsonian Agreement of December 1971 that the European snake could be introduced. Thus it was 'the snake in the tunnel' that entered into force on 10 April 1972, the snake being margins of 2.25 per cent between participating European currencies and the tunnel the margin each participating European country observed between its currency and the US dollar. On 19 March 1973 it was decided to let the dollar float and therefore the tunnel ceased to exist. Even before that date, the number of EC countries participating in the snake had started to diminish.

5.3 SNAKE AND MINI-SNAKE

The British terminated their participation on 23 June 1972. In March 1973, when the final demise of the Bretton Woods system was imminent and European countries explored the possibility of floating jointly against the dollar, Chancellor of the Exchequer Tony Barber went through the motions of participating in this exploration. But the conditions he attached to renewed British participation (interest-free credit for unlimited amounts and unlimited duration) were such that the other European countries considered it an attempt to disguise a refusal to participate by shifting the blame on to others. This inspired some of his colleagues to similar antics. Thus, German Finance Minister Helmut Schmidt elaborated on how generous he would have been to make British participation possible, agreeing to endow the European Fund for Monetary Cooperation with capital of its own, contributing to guarantee sterling balances, adding however after each item that, alas! it was not to be, since he had understood from Chancellor Barber that this was not enough.[4]

Italy was next to leave the snake on 12 February 1973, after unsuccessful efforts to weaken the settlement arrangements following interventions in participants' currencies. Then, on 19 January 1974, the French authorities announced their decision to suspend participation and let the franc float on an experimental basis for a period of six months. Germany, the Benelux countries and Denmark, after an emergency meeting on 21 January 1974 which was preceded by discussions of the Benelux countries, announced their decision to continue the arrangement. The non-EC countries Sweden and Norway, which had earlier linked their currencies to the snake, continued to do so.

France's departure from the snake – following that of Italy – weakened its 'Community character'. From then on, its informal nature was stressed. At ministerial meetings this was reflected in the absence of representatives of the Commission, and by the absence of translation: all participants spoke English. Things changed the moment France resumed its participation. French Minister of Finance Jean-Pierre Fourcade informed his colleagues on the morning of 10 July 1975 that the French decision would be published in the afternoon. He stressed that he regarded the snake as a Community mechanism, and the wish to 'strengthen the mechanisms of the Economic and Monetary Union' was stated as the motive for the French decision in the press release published (in French) after the meeting.

The French authorities attached considerable political importance to their renewed participation in the snake.

This was illustrated by a small incident. When they returned to the snake the French authorities, in accordance with existing IMF arrangements, informed the Fund of this change in France's exchange rate arrangements. The IMF Executive Board's usual practice was to take note of such changes, but in this case France insisted that the Executive Board not confine itself to taking note of the decision, but should welcome it. When this desire was not supported by all the other EC countries, Minister of Finance Fourcade took the trouble to write to his EC colleagues complaining of their lack of support.[5]

As mentioned earlier, the French government took the occasion of its renewed participation to emphasise the Community character of the snake. In doing so, it did not confine itself to declarations. Before France's re-entry, Switzerland had approached the members of the snake in order to explore the possibility of association with it, in a similar way to the other non-EC members, Sweden and Norway. Ministers of Finance and Central Bank Governors of the snake countries, after a meeting with their Swiss counterparts in September, stated that in principle they were in favour of Swiss association.[6] The French government, however, soon made clear its opposition in the discussions that followed, and the participating countries were therefore obliged to announce on 15 December 1975 that no final decision could be made on this issue due to a lack of unanimity. Though France did not give any clear arguments for its position, there can be little doubt that it feared association by an important non-EC currency like the Swiss franc would detract from the snake's EC character. No less important, it would increase the hard currency element in the arrangement.[7] In the eyes of the French government these objections outweighed the benefits of association with Switzerland which were stressed by the other participants, viz that it would contribute to the snake's international position and thus to global exchange rate stability.[8]

France continued its efforts to make the snake more 'symmetrical'. Even while outside the arrangement it had made proposals with the aim of shifting the burden of adjustment to surplus countries. Thus, Minister Fourcade made several proposals in a paper dated 16 September 1974 which he introduced in his capacity as chairman of the Council.[9] The proposals were referred to as '*relance monétaire européenne*'. Key elements they contained were as follows:

- The existing unit of account should be replaced by a new one consisting of a basket of member currencies.
- A new exchange rate arrangement should replace the existing one. Existing bilateral intervention obligations should be replaced by intervention points expressed in this unit of account.
- A 'Communitary level of the dollar' (*niveau communautaire du dollar*) should be established.
- Both the margins with the unit of account and the level of the dollar should be kept secret.

These proposals were unacceptable to the members of the snake at the time because of their technical complexity, because most did not believe margins could be both effective and remain secret, and because of the intended weakening of discipline. They would resurface four years later when the EMS replaced the snake.

5.4 ONCE AGAIN FRENCH PROBLEMS

In March 1976, the French franc found itself once again under heavy pressure due in part to a considerable deterioration of the current account of its balance of payments. Valéry Giscard d'Estaing, who had been Minister of Finance when the franc left the snake in 1974, had as President arranged its return at the old central rate. He now had to decide how to face the renewed pressure. In his memoirs he is as reticent about the decision-making on this second occasion as he is explicit about the earlier decision. At that time, he visited President Pompidou in his weekend house, and described at some length both its interior and the President's weekend outfit (he was wearing a marine-blue pullover and an open shirt) as well as the conversation, which he quotes directly. The choice was between two options which Giscard put to the Head of State. One was to continue interventions and have to resort to international credit, the second was to leave the snake and let the franc float freely. Giscard confines his description of the decision-making in March 1976 to two sentences: 'I found myself before the same choice I had presented to President Pompidou at the time, and I reached the same conclusion. We did not want to exhaust our reserves in order to stay within the fixed margin: on 15 March 1976 the franc left the snake for good'.[10]

Continuing to lose reserves financed by borrowing was, of course, no option in the long run. The real alternatives for France to floating were apparently too unpalatable to contemplate even in retrospect.

- If France was to stay in the snake with a central rate unchanged, it would have to adjust its domestic economic policies to improve its balance of payments and tighten its monetary policy to stem the outflow of funds. In effect, this meant adopting priority for price stability as the Germans had done: inflation in 1975 had been 12 per cent, twice that of Germany. For this, the time was not yet right. Moreover, though Giscard fails to mention that too, the March 1976 crisis coincided with local elections that did not go well for him, making a policy change even more awkward.
- A second option was to stay in the snake but to devalue, implying less domestic adjustment but more loss of face. In 1974 this possibility was not even discussed with the partners. At that time it was far from certain that they would be willing and able to continue the arrangement after France had left. This may have clinched the argument in favour of leaving the snake, rather than devaluing. In 1976 it was almost certain that the snake would again continue without France. Therefore, given the importance of the snake for France as discussed above, France would have

preferred to stay in. But in order to mitigate the loss of face associated with a devaluation, Minister Fourcade insisted on making it part of a general realignment in which not only France devalued against the German mark but all the others did so as well, be it with a smaller percentage than France. The others, notably the Dutch, did not see why they should devalue their currency against the German mark just to suit French presentational requirements, though in the end they were prepared to accept a devaluation of two per cent.

– But at this point Fourcade – who had apparently been on the telephone to Paris, where the election results were sinking in – informed his bewildered colleagues that France had decided to leave the snake. He read out a brief statement, the punch line of which was that Germany had been helpful but the others had not. This he repeated several times in the same words (apparently dictated from Paris) to various questions posed during the brief discussion that followed.[11] After the meeting he told the waiting press that, though now floating, the franc's value would be kept close to the snake 'as long as it still exists'. One could not help feeling that he would not mind if France's departure would trigger the snake's demise. During the days that followed, an acrimonious exchange of views took place between ministers in the form of press comments. Dutch Minister of Finance Wim Duisenberg, stung by Fourcade's criticism of unhelpfulness, told the press that his government would have been prepared to accept a devaluation of two per cent against the German mark. At this, the guilder promptly took a dive, illustrating that exchange rates do not lend themselves to megaphone diplomacy.[12] It was on this note that French participation in the snake came to an end.

5.5 ASSESSMENT

No reasons were given when central banks were invited to hold exchange rate fluctuations between currencies of member states within margins narrower than those resulting from the application of the margins in force for the dollar, at least not explicitly.

– The Werner Report, in point 7 of its conclusions, merely stated that this should be done in order to reinforce solidarity in the

Community where foreign exchange was concerned.

– The reduction of margins was presented implicitly in the 1971 resolution as a first step towards their elimination, and thus pointed in the direction of the establishment of a single currency. The Council mentioned the intention of further successive reductions in the future, 'depending on circumstances and on the results obtained in the harmonisation of economic policies'. It was thus a symbolic step towards EMU.

– There was also a link with the intention to 'progressively adopt common standpoints in monetary relations with third countries and with international organisations', as stated in the paragraph immediately preceding the one about the reduction of margins. A common policy regarding the dollar first comes to mind, the more so since it was explicitly stated that the reduction of margins was to be effected by means of concerted action with respect to the dollar.

France, in particular, pursued two objectives in the snake:

– In stressing its 'European' character and referring to it as Europe's 'monetary identity', it argued that the arrangement required solidarity between member states, entitling deficit countries to expect surplus countries to assume a greater part of the burden of adjustment. The insistence on a more 'symmetrical' system was to be a constant theme in the years to come, to be reflected in an insistence on flexible settlement and credit arrangements.

– In requiring – if only for technical reasons – concerted action with respect to the dollar, the arrangement was expected to stimulate the establishment of coordinated policies regarding the dollar and the United States.

The system was designed to coexist with, or rather to function within, the Bretton Woods system. But technically it could also replace the latter. This happened when the dollar was floated in March 1973. A fundamental difference now emerged between, on the one hand, France, supported by a number of other countries and the Commission, and, on the other hand, Germany and the Netherlands. France stressed the system's European character whenever it was in a position to do so. Germany and the Netherlands tended to regard it first as a system of stable but adjustable exchange rates on a regional scale, and encouraged non-EC countries to participate. Settlement and credit arrangements should be strict in order to foster monetary discipline. Soon this regional exchange rate arrangement reflected the same tensions that had earlier plagued the global system, resulting from different policy priorities and disagreements on the sharing of the burden of adjustment.

Personally, I was not surprised. It was what I had tried to warn against when drafting the minority view in the Ansiaux Paper annexed to the Werner Report. Yet, looking back, I feel that I have been too negative. In an article on the reduction of margins I concluded that the reduction would only make sense as part of an effective programme to establish a single European currency, an objective requiring first of all a better policy coordination.[13] With hindsight I believe that the interdependent EC economies required an exchange rate arrangement in view of the Bretton Woods system's likely demise, even in the absence of the objective of a single currency. And I would now attach more importance to the political aspect of monetary cooperation in Europe than I did then.

6 The European Monetary Cooperation Fund

In addition to the reduction of fluctuation margins between Community currencies, the 1971 resolution announced the early establishment of a European Monetary Cooperation Fund 'to be integrated at a later stage into the Community organisation of central banks.' While the reduction of fluctuation margins had not been mentioned at the summit in The Hague in December 1969 but only came up in the Werner Committee, the examination of a 'European Reserve Fund' was announced in the Hague communiqué. The initiative came from Germany's new Chancellor Willy Brandt. In his memoirs he says the offer he made was important,

> encouraged by Jean Monnet and admonished to extreme caution by the technical departments concerned ... As soon as the conditions would be met, we would be ready to collaborate to establish such a tool for common policy and to establish its modalities. We would be prepared to transfer a certain part of our reserves to the Fund and to accept common management of these reserves, together with the corresponding part of the reserves transferred by our partners.[1]

6.1 SHIFT IN PURPOSE AND TIMING

From Brandt's memoirs it is clear that what he had in mind was an eventual (partial) pooling of the participating central banks' reserves. Though he was vague on the timing, the final communiqué issued after the summit in The Hague was more precise when referring to a Fund 'to which a common economic and monetary policy would lead'. This indicated its establishment at a relatively late stage of the process, when common economic and monetary policies would already be in place.[2]

In the proposals contained in the Werner Report there was a shift both in the Fund's purpose and in its timing. It was no longer called the European Reserve Fund but the European Monetary Cooperation Fund, and it was linked to the proposed reduction of fluctuation margins. In as far as the intervention techniques would function satisfactorily and sufficient economic convergence could be realised, the Fund could already be established in the first stage, and in any case that should be the case in the course of the second stage. The Fund should absorb the proposed credit mechanisms. As progress was made towards the realisation of EMU, the Fund should become an institution charged with the management of reserves at the Community level so as to become integrated in the final stage into the Community System of Central Banks that would then be created.

On the basis of these proposals, the 1971 ministerial resolution invited the Monetary Committee and the Committee of Governors to draw up a report

> on the organisation, functions and statutes of a European Monetary Cooperation Fund, to be integrated at a later stage into the Community Organisation of the central banks provided for in Section I(2), with a view to the possible establishment of this Fund during the first stage, if the results obtained in reducing margins and aligning economic policies so justify.

The deadline for the report was 'by 30 June 1972 at the latest'. It soon became clear that the exchange rate mechanism (the snake) to which the Fund was now linked would not start to function as foreseen; in fact it only did so in April 1972. Thus the report obviously could neither make any judgement on its satisfactory functioning, nor on progress in economic convergence, on which the Fund's establishment was to be conditional.

6.2 CONTROVERSIES

In these circumstances, controversies could only be expected. The first confrontation took place in a working group established by the two committees, in which I represented the Nederlandsche Bank; it reported on 1 June 1972. Here it became clear that for some member countries the Fund's purpose remained a gradual pooling of reserves. Now that the establishment of the Fund had been brought forward so much, this was not acceptable to the Bundesbank representatives, supported by the Dutch. In their view, the Fund's task at this stage should not go beyond coordinating participating central banks' policies. The majority argued with some plausibility that for this one did not need a Fund. An awkward situation arose. There was political agreement on the early establishment of a Fund, but not on what it should do. In the end we settled on a number of very limited technical tasks, mainly the management of the credit mechanisms and the multilateralisation of positions resulting from interventions in Community currencies. The latter was my proposal, but inexperienced as I was I tabled it too soon, so that initially it was rejected by all. In this way I learned the importance of timing in negotiations: compromises should only be proposed once the meeting is weary enough to welcome a way out of the impasse.

The European Monetary Cooperation Fund remained a source for controversy even after its establishment. During the talks on the Funds' tasks the European Commission and its services, as was usual in monetary matters, had supported the French position. But the Commission also had other fish to fry. Both the snake and the new Fund were established on the basis of arrangements between the central banks concerned, outside the Rome Treaty. This bothered the Commission and it insisted that the Fund be established by Council regulation. The central banks – perhaps regarding this insistence as no more than a reflection of bureaucratic instincts never entirely absent in Brussels – in the end acquiesced that, parallel to their own agreements, there should be a Council regulation establishing the Fund.[3] Once it was issued, however, the services of the Commission informed the surprised central banks that as a result the Fund now was no longer based on Central Bank agreements but had become part of Community legislation.[4] This meant that any change in what was basically an arrangement between central banks now depended on Council decisions made on the proposal of the Commission, with central banks merely in an advisory role. Moreover, the statutes of the Fund, that were annexed to the regulation, stipulated that the Fund's Board of Governors was to act 'in accordance with such directives as the Council may adopt acting unanimously on a proposal from the Commission.'

From the point of view of a Central Bank like the Bundesbank, not subject to political directives from its own government, this was a potential threat to its independence, or at least a potential shift in the existing checks and balances. Central banks in practice drew two conclusions from this experience. One was to be weary and on the look-out for ulterior motives whenever the Commission would make proposals in their sphere of competence in the future. Furthermore, they firmly resisted the Commission's pressure to emphasise the role of the Fund at the expense of the Committee of Governors. Thus all policy issues were exclusively discussed on the basis of the agenda of the Committee of Governors at their monthly meeting in Basle. At the end of the meeting, the Committee converted itself into the Board of Governors of the European Monetary Cooperation Fund. During the concluding minutes the chairman read out the formal agenda over the buzz of conversation while all were busy packing their bags and nobody paid attention. The Fund's tasks were confined to purely administrative matters: it was in fact no Fund at all but a book-keeping agency, virtually run as a sub-section of the Bank for International Settlements (BIS) in Basle.

The aura of unreality surrounding the Fund was further enhanced following a decision of the governments in 1965, according to which all financial institutions of the Community had to be based in Luxemburg as compensation for the loss of the European Parliament to Strasbourg. On the basis of that decision, the governments decided that the Fund should be located in Luxemburg and that the meetings of the Board of Governors generally would take place there.[5] The Governors had no intention of travelling monthly to Luxemburg for the sake of a few minutes' meeting. But the Luxemburg government clung tenaciously to its claim, and in order to appease it, a name-plate of the Fund was fixed at the entrance of an office building in the centre of the city. For a while even a number of rooms was vacated on one of the upper floors, waiting for the Fund to arrive. And on one occasion the Governors, yielding to Luxemburg's insistence, did come to have a look, after they had completed their meetings in Basle. They trooped silently through the bare rooms, accompanied by their chattering Luxemburg hosts who, seemingly unaware of the visitors' manifest lack of enthusiasm, cheerfully acted as guides, pointing out the sights below.

6.3 ASSESSMENT

Willy Brandt was right to call his proposal for the eventual establishment of a European Reserve Fund important. It should be remembered that in 1969 there were serious concerns in France as well as elsewhere about Germany's re-emergence as an economic power. Introducing the prospect of an eventual pooling of reserves was a major part of his efforts to mend French–German relations by reassuring French fears of German monetary strength.

Once the German Chancellor had made this important, though of course conditional, opening at the highest political level, discussions shifted to the Werner Committee and the Council. Here what was a major concession on Brandt's part became a point of departure for further negotiations. The discussions resulted, step by step, in a Fund to be established not towards the end of the process of integration, as intended by Brandt, but at its beginning, and not dependent on whether the results obtained in aligning economic policies justified its early establishment, as the Council resolution had stated. Moreover, as a result of the Commission's action, the Fund was drawn into the orbit of existing Community legislation and procedure, and thus subject to political instructions.

Pooling reserves once Monetary Union has been, or is about to be, established is, of course, entirely different from doing so at the start of a process that may take decades. The former is an obvious thing to do, the latter was unacceptable to the Bundesbank as long as there was no Treaty or law to enforce it. At the political level, the others had forced the issue by bringing the Fund's establishment forward in time and subjecting the Fund to Council decisions. The Bundesbank, supported by the Nederlandsche Bank, reacted by making sure that the Fund's tasks would be reduced to purely administrative matters.

7 The Making of the European Monetary System (1978)[1]

In the second half of the 1970s little remained of the initiative taken by Willy Brandt at the turn of the decade to repair French–German relations and to get European integration moving again:

- Economic and Monetary Union, although originally intended to have been established within a decade and should by this time have been nearing its completion, was rarely mentioned again.
- The European Reserve Fund, into which (part of) the participating central banks' international reserves were to be pooled, had actually taken the form of a European Monetary Cooperation Fund that was in fact merely a book-keeping agency.
- The snake, the only proposal in the Werner Report that was realised, had shrunk into a mini-snake that France had for the second time, and now definitively, felt compelled to leave in March 1976.

This state of affairs mirrored a general stagnation in the process of European integration, often referred to as eurosclerosis. Both France and Germany had reason to be dissatisfied with this situation. Common monetary decision-making, to which France attached so much importance both in the interests of its diplomacy and in that of its domestic economy, seemed to have moved out of reach. Since it was German concessions that were required, there was little France could do about it. For Germany, too, the situation was unsatisfactory. Progress towards European political integration had been a key element of German foreign policy since Adenauer's days. But in an atmosphere of general stagnation in the Community, with France not participating in European monetary cooperation, this was not attainable.

7.1 TRANSATLANTIC TENSIONS

In 1974, Willy Brandt was succeeded as Chancellor by Helmut Schmidt, former Defence Minister and former Finance Minister. Schmidt soon became increasingly unhappy with the policies of the new US administration under Jimmy Carter. This applied both to US economic and security policies. US economic policy resulted in a considerable depreciation of the dollar against the currencies of the other industrial countries, aggravated by a number of speeches in the first half of 1977 by Secretary of the Treasury Michael Blumenthal and other high US officials who – whatever the intention may have been – in effect 'talked down' the dollar. This caused increasing worries on the part of the German government regarding Germany's competitive position, and was a strong incentive to try to expand the existing block floating by encouraging other countries, in particular Germany's most important trade partner France, to rejoin the snake. But Schmidt's concern was not confined to economics. He was dismayed by what he considered to be the Carter administration's unpredictable security policy ('He has no notion of strategy' he commented to Giscard)[2], in particular after he had pushed through in his own party, at considerable political cost, the acceptance of the neutron weapon, only to see it abruptly abandoned by the US President. This induced Schmidt to seek closer European cooperation in the realm of defence, but such development required that monetary cooperation should be restored first. In Giscard's words: 'The money (EMS) was mainly my idea. Defence was that of Chancellor Schmidt.'[3]

Thus political considerations were the basis for the monetary initiatives in 1978, as had been the case in 1969. The reasons for establishing the European Monetary System went far beyond the merits of an exchange rate arrangement, both for Helmut Schmidt and for Valéry Giscard d'Estaing. As the latter put it in an interview with German journalists, the EMS 'is about something else than just a currency agreement: it is a new stage in the organisation of Europe.[4]

7.2 THE EXCHANGE RATE MECHANISM

For France, whatever importance it attached to a European exchange rate mechanism, a simple return to the snake after two spectacular failures was out of the question. As Giscard put it in his memoirs: 'One had to find a different formula' (*'Il faut imaginer une autre formule.'*)[5] Any arrangement in which it could participate had to be different, and look different, from the snake. In particular, its technical arrangements concerning intervention and settlement obligations had to be such as to ensure a more 'symmetric' sharing of the burden of adjustment between surplus and deficit countries than had been the case in the snake. As far as intervention obligations were concerned, what France had in mind was in essence the system proposed in September 1974 by Finance Minister Fourcade, and rejected by Germany and other participants of the snake at the time (see 5.3). France also demanded an effective pooling of reserves in a genuine European Monetary Fund.

The intervention system in the snake was based on what came to be called the parity grid. Each participating currency had a central rate against each other participant; based on the central rate was an upper and lower limit (or intervention point) at which intervention was obligatory.[6] Central banks that were obliged to support their currency could obtain the necessary foreign exchange from the Central Bank of the strong currency. The debts thus incurred had to be settled. As a result, interventions were reflected in changes in official reserves. Surplus countries tended to regard this as the mechanism that ensured the disciplinary effect of the exchange rate mechanism. Deficit countries complained that this was one-sided, 'asymmetrical'. They lost reserves and, since that could not go on indefinitely, were obliged to take deflationary measures, while – so they argued – the surplus countries could accumulate reserves indefinitely without being obliged to do anything to adjust their surpluses.

The intervention mechanism proposed by France was designed to meet the view of the deficit countries. The parity grid existing in the snake was to be replaced by central rates and intervention points expressed not in each other but in a common unit of account, the ECU. All participating currencies were to be represented in the ECU, weighted on the basis of the economic significance of the country concerned. The ECU itself would not be traded and would not have a market value of its own; its market value could be calculated at any time on the basis of the exchange rate of each currency in its composition. While in the parity grid the intervention points were always reached by at least two currencies simultaneously, this was not necessarily the case in the new system that was proposed. Therefore, if a currency reached its intervention point the question of which currency the Central Bank concerned had to buy (or to sell) was open. This technical change was expected to result in a change in burden sharing:

- the new system was expected to be more flexible than the parity grid: if a majority of currencies depreciated, so would the ECU. Thus the majority of currencies would have to be supported at a later moment and at a lower point than under the parity grid;
- it was expected that under the new system it would be the German mark that would appreciate against the ECU. Since it would not be clear which currency the Bundesbank would have to buy, it could be expected to buy dollars;
- if the Bundesbank would, however, buy participating currencies, even though these did not need to be directly supported, there would be no case for insisting on settlement. The countries concerned were 'innocent debtors'.

In as far as the proposed system would result in the Bundesbank systematically buying dollars and stabilising the dollar–German mark rate, this would tend to strengthen the competitive position of the weaker EMS countries. If Germany would prefer to buy weak EMS currencies, their reserve losses would be less than under the parity grid, and so would be the pressure on them to adjust. The surplus country would under all circumstances undergo the inflationary effect of the inflows, and be under pressure to adjust.

7.3   THE EUROPEAN MONETARY FUND

In addition to the proposed change in intervention obligations, France demanded that the existing European Monetary Cooperation Fund be replaced by a genuine Fund, referred to as European Monetary Fund. As mentioned earlier, the existing EMCF was destined to be integrated at a later stage into a Community organisation of central banks. Accordingly, its present limited tasks were exclusively tasks in the competence of central banks. This was not to be the case with the Fund that was to replace the existing EMCF. What France had in mind was a kind of 'European IMF' with a mixture of tasks, some of which were central banks' tasks, but others not, for instance the determination of policy conditions to be attached to credits to be granted by the Fund. The latter would be a task comparable to that of the Washington-based IMF, in which governments, and not central banks, were ultimately responsible for decision-making. This was likely to affect the position of central banks, notably the Bundesbank.

France insisted on a considerable expansion of the existing credit mechanisms. These were not only to be administered by the new Fund but to be integrated into it. The Fund was to be enabled to grant credit – both for short and medium duration – by creating reserve assets to be held by participating central banks and to be used by them for settlements: the ECU. The ECU, in addition to being a unit of account, was thus to perform three important functions in the new exchange rate mechanism if designed according to French intentions:

– it was to determine the intervention obligations of participating central banks, making these less strict than had been the case in the snake;
– it was to be a reserve asset that could be created by a new European Monetary Fund, alleviating the settlement burden of deficit countries;
– it was to be a highly visible mark pointing to the difference between the old snake and the new system. In order to enhance this effect Giscard proposed to call the unit of account henceforth 'European Currency Unit' but to refer to it by its first letters, making it ECU, the name of an old French coin.

7.4 SCHMIDT'S PROBLEM AND SOLUTION

Even when he was Finance Minister in Willy Brandt's Cabinet, Helmut Schmidt attached great importance to monetary cooperation with France; when France first left the snake, he announced at a mini-snake meeting that he would do his utmost to ensure its return before leaving office.[7] As Federal Chancellor, his concern was the continuity of German foreign policy as a whole, and as he says in his memoirs, 'Currency policy (*Währungspolitik*) is (also) foreign policy.'[8] France's second and final departure from the snake was therefore also a foreign policy problem, compounded by what he repeatedly refers to as US President Carter's unpredictability. He therefore regarded France's renewed participation in an exchange rate arrangement as a political necessity and a precondition for further integration, notably in the military and in the political domain. It must have become clear to him soon after his informal consultations with Giscard on the subject, started towards the end of 1977[9], that France would only consider renewed participation on the basis of its own demands set out above. This posed a problem. France's approach was a purely monetarist one: specific and far-reaching monetary obligations were not paralleled by anything beyond good intentions regarding economic policy. Acceptance by Germany would mean a complete reversal of the economist line consistently taken until then by the German monetary authorities, including Helmut Schmidt himself when Finance Minister.[10] This was a price he was prepared to pay. It was most unlikely, however, that the same would apply to German officialdom and in particular to the Bundesbank. Schmidt's solution was to keep them out of the proceedings as long as he could. Obviously at some point their involvement was unavoidable, but before that he wanted the Heads of State or Government to approve the plan in principle, thus creating a *fait accompli* and a political momentum which German officials would not be able to resist. Since this implied that his foreign counterparts were not to be allowed to involve their experts either before signing on the dotted line, this required bulldozer tactics. To this, his personality (his nickname was *Schmidt Schnautze*, Schmidt the lip) was well suited.

7.5   CONFRONTING THE PARTNERS

Once Schmidt and Giscard were agreed, their next step was to present their scheme to the partners. British Prime Minister James Callaghan enjoyed special treatment. Though British participation was not essential for the scheme, Schmidt in particular attached importance to it. Thus, in telephone conversations with Schmidt and with Giscard Callaghan was informed that a monetary initiative was in the offing, and it was intended to initiate him into the details before the others during a breakfast with both in Copenhagen on 8 April 1978 when a European summit was being held there. During the first day of the summit, on 7 April, the subject did not arise, but in the evening 'Schmidt, whether through boredom or for some other reason, had completely changed his mind, his plan, or his tactics . . . and after only a very few preliminary words proceeded to spill the whole beans.'[11] The next morning, during breakfast, Callaghan was invited to send a representative to a small circle consisting of personal representatives of Schmidt and Giscard to further elaborate the scheme. At the same time the Committees who were responsible for this in the Community were also invited to discuss the issue but they were groping in the dark. The participation of the countries belonging to the snake, in contrast to that of Britain, was of course crucial. But Schmidt took this for granted, concluding that they did not necessitate any particular courtesy. When the scheme was sprung on their mainly unsuspecting and largely uncomprehending heads of government, even Schmidt noted that some of them showed signs of irritation at being taken by surprise. Understandably, not having been Finance Ministers as was the case with Schmidt, Giscard, Callaghan and Jenkins (these were the only ones taking part in the discussion, according to Jenkins' diary) the others felt rather out of their depth. I suppose that Schmidt's somewhat rambling, wide-sweeping style of exposition – which I had had occasion to observe when he was Minister of Finance – did not help matters. No wonder that the first reports that now started to penetrate to Finance Ministers and central banks were rather confused. I witnessed this first-hand when replacing President Zijlstra at a routine ministerial meeting of the snake countries on 17 April in Luxemburg. Towards the end of the meeting the question came up, as usual, whether to issue a public statement. If so, should it refer to the Copenhagen Summit, and what could it say about it? German Finance Minister Matthöfer had the answer: 'We don't know what the Prime Ministers said in Copenhagen, but we agree with them!' No statement was issued. On this same occasion, Dutch Finance Minister Frans Andriessen told me that the only thing he had been able to find out from Prime Minister van Agt about the Copenhagen Summit was that Schmidt had been 'very active'.[12]

It was Schmidt's and Giscard's intention to build up sufficient political momentum to enable Schmidt, who would chair the next summit in Bremen on 6–7 July 1978, to push through the scheme's main features. Only after that would 'the experts', as Schmidt condescendingly referred to the ministries concerned and the central banks, be let in on the issue to further develop its technical details, which would be on the basis already fixed at the summit. Until then, his aim was to keep the pressure up and 'the experts' out. This attitude, however, could not be fully maintained, and Schmidt and Giscard felt compelled to send their personal representatives to the various countries in order to give them a general picture of what would be on the agenda at the summit.

In Bremen, British Prime Minister Callaghan made it clear that Britain would not join the new scheme, at least not at the outset. In his memoirs he indicates that he regarded it as too much of a German mark zone, in which 'the strong Deutschemark would have the effect of tugging sterling upwards with deflationary consequences to our economy, unless long-term credit was absolutely unlimited.' No less importantly, '(m)any people in the Labour Party remained suspicious of what they thought was too close an entanglement with Europe.'[13] The others were put under strong pressure. For instance, Schmidt took some time to soothe Dutch Prime Minister van Agt's bruised feelings at the high-handed treatment the latter felt he had received, but when van Agt argued he could not commit himself definitively on the technical issues since he could not judge the implications, he was told that if that was the case he should not have become a Prime Minister![14]

7.6 BACK TO THE SNAKE

The statement released after the Bremen Summit – which became known as 'Annex to the Conclusions of the Presidency of the European Council'[15] – gave the impression that the main features of the European Monetary System had been fixed by the heads of government. It stated:

- that the ECU was to be at the centre of the system, suggesting (though admittedly not spelling out) that the intervention obligations would be based on it;
- that ECUs would be created not only against dollars and gold, which was merely asset substitution, but also against member currencies. This would have been reserve creation and seemed to point to a role of the European Monetary Fund – which was to replace the existing EMCF within two years – that was comparable to that of the IMF.

In actual fact, these main controversial issues remained open at Bremen. As Peter Ludlow commented: Prime Ministers can initiate, but they can only partially implement.[16] Full involvement of all concerned could no longer be postponed. Two factors in particular determined further developments.

First, public opinion in Germany reacted sceptically to the scheme. In particular, the CDU/CSU opposition in parliament and notably its leaders, Helmut Kohl and Franz-Joseph Strauss, were negative. Since Schmidt's coalition partner, the FDP, was also sceptical, Schmidt could no longer afford to ignore the Bundesbank.

Second, in the discussions that followed, the Bundesbank made it clear where it would draw the line. It was prepared to go quite far in enlarging the existing credit mechanisms, though not in putting the emphasis so one-sidedly on unconditional credit as some would have liked. But it firmly opposed an intervention system that would endanger its grip on the money supply. Initially, Germany had been sympathetic towards an intervention scheme based on the ECU. When Schmidt's personal representative Horst Schulmann visited The Hague on 29 June as part of the preparation of the Bremen Summit, he told Dutch officials that Germany saw political advantages in such a system, though it was not quite sure about its technical feasibility. Now the German stance hardened and Germany insisted on continuing the parity grid system.

During the negotiations, the Bundesbank was strongly supported by the Nederlandsche Bank. The Dutch shared the Bundesbank's objections against the policy motives behind the ECU scheme, namely, shifting the burden of adjustment to surplus countries. They feared that a system biased against Germany would in time reduce Germany's willingness to continue the system, putting its durability in doubt. They also felt that a scheme so technically complex as the one proposed would lack credibility in the markets. Finally, they wanted a system that could easily continue to function even if some participants withdrew, as had been the case with the snake. Not all these arguments could be fully spelled out, of course, but a practical consideration could be stressed: if markets concluded that as a result of the negotiations relations between the currencies of the snake participants would change, currency turbulence would be likely. On this the monetary authorities of all snake participants agreed. Initially their idea was to continue the snake within a more general system of the EMS, but this would have caused both technical and political problems.

In the end, Schmidt felt obliged to make it clear to Giscard at a meeting in Aachen on 14–15 September that Germany could not agree after all to a system that was not based on the parity grid as in the snake. Giscard went along on this basis, accepting that Schmidt had no choice, and also because by now the process had too much political momentum to be stopped. This outcome was presented with as much face saving as possible.

– It was announced that the system would be reviewed within six months.
– Central rates would be expressed in ECUs.
– A formula was introduced, called the 'divergence indicator', based on the calculation of participating currencies' ECU rate. If on this basis a currency became 'divergent' the country concerned was presumed to take action, though no automatic policy measures were agreed.

Regarding the European Monetary Fund, which according to the Bremen statement was to be established within two years, it was decided to leave its nature and tasks open for the moment, merely stating that it would entail 'the full utilisation of the ECU as a reserve asset and a means of settlement'. It would be 'based on adequate legislation at the Community as well as the national level' which was code for amending the Rome Treaty.[17] The European Monetary Fund was never established.

7.7   SCHMIDT AND GISCARD

Earlier in this chapter I stated that for France a simple return to the snake after two spectacular failures was out of the question. Any arrangement in which it could participate had to be different, and look different, from the snake. Everything possible was done to make the European Monetary System, as finally agreed, look different from the snake. But in essence it was not. The exchange rate mechanism was exactly the same. The genuine Fund that was to replace the existing one was never established. And though the ECU was proclaimed to be at the centre of the system, the ECU as agreed was as far removed from the ECU France intended as was the existing Fund from the one that was to replace it. Given the strength of Giscard's feelings on the issue, and given Schmidt's readiness to meet them, this may seem a surprising outcome. But it was precisely Schmidt's readiness to meet French requirements that enabled Giscard to accept in the end a result that was so different from what was intended. This paradox is due to the special relationship they had established.

For Helmut Schmidt, France was the key to further European integration that was of vital interest to Germany. Therefore he felt that Germany should defer to French requirements whenever possible.[18] Not since Adenauer had a German Chancellor gone so far in this respect. But whereas Adenauer felt he had no choice given the weakness of the German position at the time, Schmidt felt he could afford it, given his position of strength. This induced him, when both were still Finance Ministers, to develop a close personal relationship with his French counterpart, investing in it whatever tact he possessed.

In those days, I was occasionally in a position to observe the two, and I was struck by the combination of the friendship they flaunted and the rivalry they apparently could not help engaging in. Both were showmen. They knew that whoever arrived last at ministerial meetings made the most dramatic entry, drawing away the mass of photographers from their colleagues. Schmidt and Giscard invariably arrived last. Between them, they seemed to be involved in a contest which, as far as I can recall, Giscard always won. How exactly it was done I do not know. It was rumoured that both were sitting in their respective delegation rooms in the building, sending out spies to the meeting room from time to time to find out whether the other had given up. In time, we tended to look at it as a race between the two, ending in a photo-finish. Whatever the truth, the fact is that everybody was kept waiting, including their colleagues, sometimes for a considerable time. Observing this lack of consideration meeting after meeting I sometimes could not help feeling that their manners left something to be desired, however different they were. Giscard had a haughty, languid, quasi-aristocratic air. Schmidt had a bluntness that, combined with a sharp voice and an abrupt manner of speech, had earned him the nickname Schmidt the Lip (*Schmidt Schnautze*).

A minor incident during one of the meetings illustrates this impression. Giscard was speaking, in French of course, when suddenly, in the midst of his speech, Schmidt – sitting opposite – ripped off his earphones and threw them clattering on to the table, shouting loudly '*Diese Übersetzung ist miserabel, ich verstehe kein Wort!*' (This translation is worthless, I don't understand a single word!) Giscard, in some consternation, broke off his speech in mid-sentence and reached for his earphones, holding them to one ear to hear the translation of what Schmidt had been shouting. This was no doubt faithfully supplied by the long-suffering interpreters. Giscard, carefully putting down his earphones, resumed his speech by expressing his gratitude to his colleague Schmidt for the fact that, finding it incomprehensible, he blamed the interpreters and not the original. This caused a ripple of laughter around the table, and Schmidt rather ungraciously put on his earphones again to find out what the amusement was about.[19] Their partnership was demonstrated not only by the fact that they sometimes withdrew to a corner to converse with each other while a lesser colleague was speaking, but also they seemed to flaunt their friendship by referring to one another by their first names. This was only just coming into fashion between ministers and was put down to their showmanship. Soon it was extended to all ministers, even newcomers. When Wim Duisenberg attended his first ministerial meeting after becoming Dutch Finance Minister, Schmidt sent one of his underlings to the Dutch delegation to inquire what his first name was. In time the habit spread to the Deputies and even to Central Bankers, though there was something artificial in hearing German Central Bankers address their foreign counterparts with their first names and each other with *Sie* and *Herr*. Schmidt and Giscard apparently kept up the habit of keeping others waiting after they became heads of government. In his diary Roy Jenkins, writing about the Copenhagen Summit, wonders how Giscard managed to arrive last at the meeting when his plane had touched down before Schmidt's. He speculates that, somewhere on the way from the airport, he had had his car tucked away in a side road, waiting to see Schmidt go past.[20]

7.8 ASSESSMENT

There are striking similarities between events of 1969, leading to the adoption of EMU as a common objective, and those in 1978, leading to the establishment of the EMS. On both occasions an initiative was needed to get the stagnating process of European integration moving again. On both occasions the initiatives had to be of a monetary character, but the motives for taking them were largely political, as was their final objective. Since the initiative on both occasions were aimed primarily at monetary integration, it was German concessions that were required. These were both times held out by the then German Federal Chancellor to meet French demands, but on each occasion he failed to deliver in the end. Yet on both occasions the purpose was met since the process of integration started to move forward again for a while.

It is not widely realised to what extent the EMS as finally agreed differed from what was first proposed. As a result there exists a fairly general misconception about the attitude of central banks, in particular the Bundesbank, regarding the EMS. There is a widely-held belief that the Bundesbank opposed the establishment of the EMS and only yielded to heavy pressure by Chancellor Schmidt, who threatened to enforce acceptance by changing the law. As we have seen, this is not what happened. What the Bundesbank opposed, strongly and effectively supported by the Nederlandsche Bank, was not the EMS as such but the plan to replace the simple and tested intervention mechanism existing in the snake by a highly complicated and hardly viable political concoction based on the ECU. Given the political support the Bundesbank enjoyed on this issue, Schmidt would not have been in a position to force the Bank to accept it, had he tried. In view of the scepticism regarding the EMS prevailing in Germany he needed the Bank's support, which he obtained by finally opting for the mechanism that existed in the snake, and getting Giscard to accept it too. In addition, the Bundesbank received the assurance of the Federal Government that it would be entitled to cease interventions if these would endanger stability in Germany.[21] What contributed to the misconceptions regarding the Central Banks' attitude concerning the EMS, apart from the fact that the technicalities involved were little understood, is that neither the politicians nor the central banks had any interest in emphasising in public the difference between what was originally proposed and what was finally agreed.

It was no mean accomplishment on the part of Helmut Schmidt to get France to accept in the end an arrangement that was also acceptable in Germany. It is sad therefore that, though he claims that he and Giscard managed to achieve all that mattered, Schmidt sounds so bitter in his memoirs about those whom he feels stood in his way, like the Economics Minister, Count Lambsdorff, and in particular his collaborators in the Economics Ministry, who (he writes) could be expected to mobilise parliamentary and press opposition. Could the bitter memory of later events, leading to the termination of his chancellorship, have played a role?[22] He refers scathingly to the 'gentlemen of the Bundesbank' who regarded themselves as 'the guardians of the grail of stability'. More generally, he pours scorn on 'the experts' who clothed their opposition in the guise of expertise which in reality was based on political prejudice. To quote David Marsh on Helmut Schmidt: 'One of his favourite terms of intellectual abuse is to call a person "an expert", meaning that the unfortunate myopic cannot see the strategic wood for the trees.'[23] As one who closely followed events at the time, I cannot help feeling that he is sometimes less than fair. No doubt he is justified in claiming that his efforts to establish the EMS were of a highly political nature based on an overall strategy.[24] But he fails to realise that – as pointed out earlier – once political initiatives are translated into monetary action, this is inevitably subject to the forces and constraints prevailing in that domain. Schmidt gave priority to his political objectives and was prepared to accept considerable monetary risks.[25] He was ready to accept on Germany's behalf additional intervention obligations without insisting on any budgetary constraints. He was willing to establish a European Monetary Fund with monetary policy competences without insisting on safeguards regarding its autonomy. But he could not find the necessary support for this in Germany.

The merits of Schmidt and Giscard in getting the process of integration moving again are by no means reduced by the fact that they could only conclude an agreement by leaving the controversial issues largely unsolved, substituting dates for substance:

- The intervention mechanism was to be reviewed in six months' time.
- This also applied to the ECU, and notably to the limits to the obligation for creditor central banks to accept them in settlement.
- The nature of the European Monetary Fund was left entirely open, only the fact that it would be established within two years was agreed.
- There were no obligations at all concerning economic policies. Here Schmidt made it clear that he put his entire trust in Giscard's policy intentions.[26] This trust was misplaced, since Giscard was soon to be replaced by Mitterrand.

Participants entered into the European Monetary System in 1979 without having either a common strategy or common tactics. They did not agree on priorities for their domestic policies or on constraints to these policies; there were no common guidelines comparable to the convergence criteria in the Maastricht Treaty a decade later. Nor did they agree on 'rules of the game' in managing the EMS. They did not even seriously try to reach prior agreement on these issues. Had they tried, they would have failed. The EMS would not have started. This was politically unacceptable to German Chancellor Helmut Schmidt. The alternative was starting the EMS without prior agreement on these issues and running the risk of failure. This was Schmidt's choice, either because he underestimated the risk of failure and its political implications, or because he believed that once the EMS was working, the risk of failure would be a sufficient deterrent to make participants reach an agreement which had earlier been impossible. Perhaps it was a mixture of both.

The objective of the EMS was the creation of a zone of monetary stability in Europe. Though this was not spelled out, it suggested an exchange rate arrangement rather than Economic and Monetary Union, an objective that was not mentioned. Yet it is likely that once the system was in place the integration process was meant to be extended beyond an exchange rate arrangement, and even beyond the economic and monetary sphere. Schmidt expected to use the momentum created to establish a closer cooperation with France in defence, once Giscard d'Estaing was re-elected. This was not to be.

8 The Working of the European Monetary System in the Period 1979–87

After last minute delays due to domestic problems in France, the European Monetary System went into operation on 13 March 1979. Soon the sceptics' misgivings seemed justified: at times the system appeared to hover on the verge of a breakup, at other times what was intended to be a zone of monetary stability in Europe seemed to develop into a crawling peg. Market turbulence and payments imbalances induced participants to continue their disputes concerning the 'asymmetry' in sharing the burden of adjustment that could not be solved during the making of the EMS. Yet in the end the system endured, though not undamaged.

This chapter will concentrate on the influence of market developments on the working of the EMS and on relations between participants. The working of the EMS in the period 1979–91 can be subdivided into three stages:

1979–83: The early years were a turbulent period in which underlying policies diverged, almost leading to a break-up of the system or at least to a repetition of what had happened to the snake.

1983–7: In contrast to the snake, France in the end did not leave the EMS but adjusted its underlying policies. This was a necessary but not a sufficient condition to stabilise the system. Market confidence takes time to be established and requires clear evidence that the authorities give priority to exchange rate stability over domestic objectives. Evidence of this was lacking. The authorities tended to yield to market pressure and adjusted exchange rates even in the absence of fundamental disequilibria, and the system seemed to develop into a crawling peg. This danger was averted when the monetary authorities of participating countries concluded an understanding on mutually consistent tactics that became known as the Basle–Nyborg agreement.

1988–91: There followed a period of five years with virtually no exchange rate realignments. Since inflation rates, however, continued to diverge, this protracted period of tranquillity turned out to have a price.

It is the first two episodes that will be discussed here.

8.1   1979–83: CRISIS

In Bremen and Brussels in 1978, Heads of Governments had gone into considerable detail where the monetary arrangements of the EMS were concerned, but regarding convergence of economic policy they had confined themselves to expressing good intentions. As mentioned earlier, German Chancellor Helmut Schmidt put his confidence in the continuing presidency of Giscard d'Estaing. The latter, however, soon lost the presidency to François Mitterrand. When unemployment in Europe increased in the early eighties, under the influence of the second oil shock, Mitterrand's socialist government pursued expansionary policies. France's inflation rate exceeded that of Germany, its balance of payments worsened, and once again the franc came under pressure.

Generalised realignments took place on 23 September 1979, on 4 October 1981, and again on 12 June 1982. On these occasions the French franc was devalued against the German mark with 2 per cent, 8.5 per cent and 10 per cent respectively. In addition, the Italian lira was devalued in March 1981 and the Belgian franc, followed by the Danish crown, in February 1982. The frequency and cumulative size of these adjustments in such a short period did not bode well for the new system. Then came March 1983.

By this time, it was fairly obvious that the system could not continue in this way. Within President Mitterrand's government, which consisted of socialist and communist ministers under Prime Minister Mauroy, a sharp division emerged between left-wing members who wished to continue expansionist policies and leave the EMS to render that possible, and those who wanted to cut back the budget deficit and stay in the EMS. It was President Mitterrand who had to decide which course to follow. A picture of the struggle for Mitterrand's ear during the first months of 1983, as well as of the president's vacillations, emerges from his Adviser Jacques Attali's diary.[1] The main proponent of France staying in the EMS and of an adjustment of domestic policies was Finance Minister Jacques Delors. Delors had to fight on two fronts. On the one hand, he had to fight his domestic adversaries, on the other hand, his German counterparts in order to get Germany to accept a larger part of the burden of adjustment. This goes some way to explain his public posturing. Especially during the course of February and March 1983 the French Minister of Finance started to engage in megaphone diplomacy, making public statements suggesting that the franc's exchange rate was correct but that the German mark was undervalued, that it was now up to the Germans to act as good Europeans and take measures, if not revaluing then lowering interest rates, and that if they failed to understand this they were 'playing with fire'.[2] Such statements did little to calm the markets. When in March 1993, just a week after the fourth anniversary of the EMS, the by now inevitable ministerial meeting took place to discuss once again an exchange rate adjustment, Jacques Delors did what he could to dramatise events, leaving the meeting to return briefly to Paris, which according to Attali's journal surprised even President Mitterrand.[3] After a weekend of bickering that continued into Monday, so that central banks were obliged to suspend interventions, ministers finally reached an understanding which in effect implied another 8 per cent devaluation of the French franc against the German mark. By now expectations regarding the EMS' future were bleak. Yet a change was now taking place in French official thinking. Its first signs could be detected when President Mitterrand indicated on television on 23 March why he had decided that France would stay in the EMS, and explained why the franc had been devalued. Concerning the first point, he said:

> We did not, and do not, want to isolate France from the Community of which we benefit (*dont nous sommes partie prenante*), separate it from the movement that will make this Europe at last one of the greatest players in the world, just as we did not and do not want, whatever reservations we may have, to distance ourselves from the alliance on which our security partly rests.

With hindsight, one can state that Mitterrand's decision in 1983 to keep France in the EMS was a choice for Europe: in the years that followed, European integration became one of the central objectives of his presidency.[4]

Regarding the exchange rate, only a few days earlier, just before the realignment, Finance Minister Delors had been quoted in the press:

> It is up to the Germans to take a decision. I hope they will do what is necessary to hold the EMS together ... When a currency goes too far out of line, it is up to it to make an effort. That is the philosophy of the EMS.[5]

Now the President of the republic declared:

> It is a law from which no one can escape: a country whose price increase exceeds that of its neighbours is condemned to devalue in one way or another. That is the truth. I have to tell you this without looking for false excuses.[6]

8.2 BASLE–NYBORG

For some time after the 1983 realignment, currency markets remained calm. The French government had adjusted its policies, giving increased priority to price stability. This was reflected in a reduced inflation differential with Germany.

Table 1 Private consumption deflators

| | Average annual percentage changes | |
	1981–3	1986–8
Germany	5	1
France	11	3

Source: *OECD Economic Outlook*, 51, June 1992

For this conversion, the French authorities expected a rapid reward in the form of reduced interest rate differentials between France and Germany. The market, however, is not that easily convinced, either by official statements or by genuine conversions, as long as it is not convincingly demonstrated that these endure in the face of adversity.

On 6 April 1986 the new French Finance Minister Edouard Balladur, citing recurrent speculation about the franc, insisted on a realignment; the adjustment agreed upon in Ootmarsum, the Netherlands, implied a 6 per cent devaluation of the French franc against the German mark and the guilder. Members of the Monetary Committee felt that something had to change in the management of the EMS. The first of a series of fairly fundamental discussions on the working of the EMS took place in the Committee in Brussels on 12 June 1986 under the chairmanship of Hans Tietmeyer.

I had been asked to produce a paper to prepare the discussion.[7] The reason for asking me was probably a letter sent three years earlier by the Dutch members of the Committee to the then chairman, Michel Camdessus.[8] In the beginning of 1983 I was seriously worried about the direction in which the EMS was developing, with its frequent generalised realignments. One might wonder whether an exchange rate arrangement with such frequent adjustments, exceeding what was justified by fundamentals, made economic sense. Moreover, seen with specific Dutch interests in mind, we had to face the fact that the Dutch had been forced, against their will, to accept a devaluation of the guilder against the German mark in the realignment of 1979, and this would soon be followed by another devaluation in the realignment of 1983. In our letter we proposed that 'the Monetary Committee should give more priority to discuss the question whether ... monetary policy could and should not do more to ensure the proper functioning of the system.'[9] At the time the letter had little impact, but three years later it was apparently remembered. In my spoken introduction to the paper I stated that even if exchange rates reflected competitive positions it was essential that they were properly defended if under pressure. The crucial rule should be to give the markets the experience that taking speculative positions was costly, risky and not profitable. This meant that in the short run monetary policy had to give a high priority to exchange rate considerations, implying interest rate increases at an early stage, before speculation got out of hand. The fluctuation margins should be better utilised in order to introduce a two-way risk. And if central rate adjustments were justified, their size should be so moderate that they could largely be absorbed in the fluctuation margins, so that market rates would not necessarily reflect the adjustment, and thus there would be little profit. This, of course, supposed that inflation differentials were moderate. In the discussion that followed, the main opposition came from my French Treasury colleague Daniel Lebègue. He pointed out that an early increase of interest rates, as I advocated, implied accepting German policies as given; he understood that smaller countries did this, but was not prepared to do so himself. A better utilisation of the fluctuation margins meant in practice that a currency under pressure should not be defended in the upper part of the band, as France had done on a number of occasions, but instead be allowed to depreciate and then be defended. But this depreciation, Lebègue argued, was itself likely to fuel speculation. As far as the size of devaluations was concerned, he rejected any prior constraints. The fundamental objection was the first one. In effect it meant the rejection, on the basis of political considerations, of a German mark bloc. Thus this first round was hardly encouraging, although this is often the case in first rounds of this sort.

Then in December 1986 currency turmoil started again, leading to a realignment in January 1987, only nine months after the previous one. (In between, in August 1986, an Irish devaluation had taken place.) Given the moderate inflation differentials and the short interval between the two realignments, it was clear that only speculation and not fundamentals were the reason of this adjustment. Its size was limited: the French franc (and other currencies) devalued against the German mark and guilder by 3 per cent, but it came after the 6 per cent devaluation of the previous year. Moreover, the decision was only reached after much bickering that immediately found its way into publicity which politicised and dramatised the meeting. The problem was that Belgium insisted on a middle position (i.e. devaluing less against the German mark than France), spotlighting the fact that what the French and others did was in fact devaluing, while the Belgian government no doubt hoped it would appear that Belgium, being in the middle, 'did nothing'. A 'compromise proposal' of the Belgian chairman Mark Eyskens to present the adjustments as differentiated 'revaluations' by all against an imaginary zero point was not acceptable, not because it was economically absurd but because it did not solve the political problem caused by presenting three groups.[10]

A realignment that was not justified by fundamentals, but caused exclusively by speculation, could only convince the market that this was how the authorities would react to the next attack, creating self-fulfilling expectations, and causing doubt whether the EMS could be maintained in this way. In official circles there were two kinds of reactions. One came from Belgian Finance Minister Mark Eyskens. Having himself done much to dramatise the January decision, he now proposed in an interview with AP–Dow Jones published on 9 March to empower central banks to decide on small 'technical' realignments in order 'to make it unnecessary for Finance Ministers to confront each other so often on such a politically sensitive issue.' Most central banks were sceptical, realising that this would not necessarily 'depoliticise' realignments but rather politicise relations between central banks.

They realised that what was really needed was not a change in decision-making on these frequent realignments but a change in the management of the EMS in order to reduce their frequency. It was becoming increasingly clear that currency speculation could not be dealt with exclusively by interventions but that additional measures were required to make speculation more costly and risky. The question was how to achieve this. French Finance Minister Edouard Balladur, at a ministerial lunch on 9 February, and in an interview with *Le Monde* that appeared the next day, announced a French memorandum to be discussed in the Monetary Committee, of which he summarised the contents on both occasions. The memorandum, in which, as Dutch Finance Minister Ruding commented, 'a number of old French hobby horses were running round', was then duly submitted. It focused on the need to establish a common policy regarding the dollar and the yen, proposed activation of the divergence indicator that had been agreed upon when the EMS was established but played no role in policies, as well as intensified coordination of interventions in the exchange markets and readiness of EC central banks to hold each other's currencies in their reserves. (I shall come back to these issues in the next chapter.)

Discussions on what was referred to as 'the strengthening of the EMS' now evolved both in the Monetary Committee and in the Committee of Governors in Basle. Deputy Director of the Nederlandsche Bank Henk Boot, recording central bankers' discussions in Basle on 9 and 10 March, noted that the French seemed to feel 'curiously helpless' once speculation was gathering speed, taking the view that in that case realignments, even if not justified by fundamentals, would be better if they took place quickly. Their position seemed to be that exchange rate stability could only be maintained if large reserves and credit facilities were disposable, not so much to be used but to deter speculation. Yet their main point was that the Bundesbank should bear the brunt of maintaining central rates by contributing to coordinate intervention and to a common policy regarding the dollar.[11]

This was not acceptable to the Bundesbank since it felt it might lose control over money supply and be seriously hampered in its policy of maintaining price stability. However, everyone concerned realised that if nothing changed the EMS could not be maintained, notwithstanding improved fundamentals.

The solution was a compromise. Agreement was reached along the lines discussed earlier at the meeting of the Monetary Committee on 12 June 1986. At the same time, agreement was reached on a number of technical changes regarding interventions and settlements, though nothing comparable to what had been demanded earlier. Once this was agreed by the Governors in Basle on 8 September, the package was presented to the Ministers of Finance who, together with the Governors, met on 13 September in Nyborg, Denmark.

Following the Nyborg ministerial meeting, the Committee of Governors issued a press communiqué on 18 September summarising the measures on which the Governors had agreed at their meeting on 8 September. The communiqué first enumerated the technical measures that were agreed: extension of the interval between intervention and settlements, and the doubling of the ceiling under which renewal of financial operations was automatic. It stated that though in the case of intramarginal interventions there was no automatic access to existing financing facilities, there was to be a presumption that intramarginal interventions agreed to by the Central Bank issuing the intervention currency would qualify for such financing, up to certain limits. The further enhancement of the official ECU was announced. The communiqué then went on to state, that

(t)hese measures form part of a comprehensive strategy to foster exchange rate cohesion within the EMS. The Governors are convinced that greater exchange rate stability depends on all Member States achieving, through their economic and monetary policies, sufficient convergence towards internal stability. In the light of this basic understanding they have agreed in particular to exploit the scope for a more active, flexible and concerted use of the instruments available, namely exchange rate movements within the fluctuation band, interest rates and interventions.

The public discussion that followed focused almost exclusively on the technical changes. The German press in particular was critical regarding the concessions made by the Bundesbank. President Pöhl had defended the measures at a press conference on 14 September, indicating that the Bundesbank would not agree to a change in the balance between financing and adjustment, and would reject 'salami tactics', implying that further concessions were not to be made. The 'comprehensive strategy', the rules of behaviour that were agreed upon, was scarcely mentioned. Yet it was this that contributed to the absence of realignments in the period that followed, lasting until 1992.

8.3 ASSESSMENT

Participants entered into the European Monetary System in 1979 without having either a common strategy or common tactics. As a result, the first years were critical for the EMS, and 1983 was even one of crisis, in which the system hovered on the brink of failure. It was only then that something approaching priority for price stability comparable to that in Germany started to emerge in France, although initially for external rather than for internal reasons.

Views on sharing the burden of adjustment, however, continued to diverge, and with it views on the role of monetary policies in managing the EMS, and on rules of conduct more generally. It was only the continued frequency of realignment that finally forced participants to agree on the necessity of such rules. This, referred to as a 'comprehensive strategy' in the central banks' press communiqué, was in my view the real significance of the Basle–Nyborg agreement.

When central banks later referred to Basle–Nyborg, it was these rules they had in mind. This is illustrated, for instance, by a report of the Committee of Governors published after the 1992 currency crisis which will be discussed later. Paragraph 2, entitled 'The desirable mix of the Basle–Nyborg instruments' refers to these rules, after having stated that the recent EMS crisis had 'confirmed that interventions alone – whether intramarginal or at the margin – have a limited effectiveness in containing tensions and may even exacerbate them.'[12]

The changes in technical arrangements that formed part of the Basle–Nyborg package attracted much attention in 1978.[13] Their principal significance, however, was to make the rules of conduct acceptable to France.[14] France accepted the compromise because it realised that it was doubtful whether the EMS could be sustained if realignments continued with the same frequency. Perhaps even more important, a policy change was now taking place in France requiring a higher priority for price stability as well as for exchange rate stability. But France continued to object to German primacy in monetary policy. Its acceptance of the Basle–Nyborg rules of conduct was therefore ambiguous. In particular, though accepting that the early increase of interest rate differentials was essential to prevent the development of currency crises, in practice it would insist that France should not increase its interest rates when under pressure, but the Germans should cut theirs.

For some time the French authorities continued to hope that by introducing technical changes in the exchange rate mechanism they could bring about a gradual shift in the sharing of the burden of adjustment. But the reaction to the technical part of the Basle–Nyborg package in German public opinion made it clear that no further major concessions on the part of the Bundesbank could be expected in this domain. If France wanted to find a way of influencing German monetary policy in order to achieve a shift in the sharing of the burden of adjustment, it had to try a different tack.

9 Promoting the ECU

The first nine years of the EMS, the period 1979–87, consisted of a series of currency crises forcing exchange rate realignments. They reflected fundamental differences in view and in interests regarding the sharing of the burden of adjustment between surplus and deficit countries, which resulted from different priorities in domestic policies. Earlier, these differences had compelled France to leave the snake twice. When the snake was replaced by the EMS, France tried to ensure that the ECU would play a central role in the new system, both in rendering the burden sharing more 'symmetrical' and in presenting the EMS as more 'European' and French-inspired, and thus less of a German mark zone. As was described in chapter 7, these efforts failed in the end due to opposition by the Bundesbank, supported by the Nederlandsche Bank. The EMS therefore started with the main controversies unresolved. In the years that followed, France – supported by a number of other countries as well as by the European Commission – tried to achieve its objective of a more 'symmetrical' burden sharing by proposing to gradually expand the role of the ECU. To this end, periodic – preferably annual – 'packages' of technical proposals were to be introduced, presented as technical improvements that would also have the political advantage of maintaining the momentum of integration. Each package by itself would change little in the functioning of the system, but the total effect was to be a shift in the burden sharing at the expense of the strong currency countries, notably Germany:

- Initially, the proposals concentrated on the creation of ECUs. It was proposed to reform the existing European Monetary Cooperation Fund into a more genuine Fund, enabled to create ECUs in extending credit to deficit countries.
- Soon, the emphasis shifted to the acceptance of ECUs by surplus countries. It was proposed to eliminate the existing limitations to the obligation to accept ECUs in settlement of claims resulting from interventions.

9.1　THE FUND

As discussed earlier, the establishment of a genuine European Fund, with its own resources and thus being able to decide on the granting of credit to Member States (and eventually to intervene in the exchange market) had been an important French objective for a number of years. The Resolution of the European Council of 5 December 1978 appeared to open the perspective of such a Fund being established within two years of the EMS coming into force, but at the same time it created a formidable obstacle: the requirement that it should be based on 'adequate legislation at the Community as well as the national level', i.e., a change in the Treaty. Once discussions on the Treaty change started, it would become obvious that views on the nature and tasks of the Fund – deliberately left open in 1978 – widely diverged. In due course it became clear that there was considerable reluctance to pursue this objective. This was the case not only in the strong currency countries, but also in France. As mentioned earlier, it had been decided in 1978 to create ECUs by depositing 20 per cent of member countries' dollar and gold reserves with the EMCF. For the time being, this transfer of dollars and gold from national central banks to the Fund had been given the form of three months swaps that were each time automatically renewed. Introducing the final system would require genuine transfer of ownership. Parting with 20 per cent of French gold reserves, however, ran into domestic opposition. France, therefore, no longer insisted on the implementation of this proposition. Instead, it started to search for ways of achieving the objectives it originally had with the European Monetary Fund without necessarily establishing the EMF itself. To this end the French authorities and the European Commission proposed consolidating the existing credit mechanisms into a single system, referred to as *'méchanisme renové'*, within the existing European Monetary Cooperation Fund. Credits would be granted in newly created ECU's which would be undistinguishable from ECUs created against gold and dollars. This idea, which was put forward in particular by then Vice-Governor of the Banque de France De la Genière, was in line with the intentions behind the proposals made in Bremen a year earlier.

The Bundesbank and the Nederlandsche Bank rejected this proposal. Its effect, the Dutch argued, would be to transfer liquidity-creating powers from national central banks to an institution at the Community level. This would require a Treaty provision establishing checks and balances on a Community level comparable to those existing nationally in the relations between central banks and governments.[1]

9.2   ACCEPTANCE LIMITS

The objective the French authorities had in mind in proposing to transform the European Fund into a liquidity-creating institution could only be achieved, if the liquidity it created – the ECU – were accepted in settlement without limits by central banks of participating countries. As related earlier, the role finally allotted to the ECU when the EMS came into force was far more limited than France had envisaged earlier, when the Bremen annexe stated that the ECU would be at the centre of the system. This not only applied to its role in defining intervention obligations, but also to its creation against member currencies. The European Council Resolution of 5 December 1978 stated that the final system would entail 'the full utilisation of the ECU as a reserve asset and a means of settlement'.[2] As long as the final system was not established, however, the Bundesbank and the Nederlandsche Bank insisted that creditors would not be obliged to accept ECUs in settlement for more than 50 per cent of their outstanding claims resulting from interventions.

France only acquiesced in this acceptance limit (as it was called) with the greatest reluctance, and subject to an early revision of the settlements rules; Finance Minister Monory argued that it detracted from the ECU's role.[3] The French believed it made the ECU inferior to the dollar, and thus unable to compete with it. From the start, France consistently tried to achieve the abolition of the acceptance limits, supported by most member states and above all by the European Commission. The Bundesbank, and especially the Nederlandsche Bank, refused to yield. They felt they could not discount the possibility that sooner or later ECUs would be created against national currencies, much as they opposed this. In that case acceptance limits in their view would be indispensable. They argued that creditors were free to accept ECUs in settlement in excess of the acceptance limits on a voluntary basis, as indeed they did. Obliging them to do so was another matter, and hardly a way to make the ECU more attractive. In one of our many discussions on the subject in the Monetary Committee I drew the analogy with the wonderful Brussels restaurants that had not acquired their Michelin stars by forcing the food down their customers' throats. In addition to promoting the use of the ECU by elimination of the acceptance limits, France – supported by most other countries and by the Commission – tried to make the ECU's acceptance for the settlement of intramarginal interventions obligatory in the same way as for interventions at the margin. This, too, was rejected by the Bundesbank. Intramarginal interventions by other central banks usually took place in German marks already in their possession; the Bundesbank thus was not directly involved, and for the German money market it had no expansionary effect but merely meant that one German mark holder was replaced by another. Involving the Bundesbank by obliging it to accept ECUs would mean making the market more liquid.

In other ways, too, France and others tried to promote the use of the ECU. When, in addition to the 'official ECU' created against dollars and gold held in official reserves, the private sector also started to create ECU's and this 'private ECU' market soon developed fast, efforts concentrated on linking the two ECUs. This was also resisted by the two creditor central banks.

There was a tendency on the part of the proponents of expanding the role of the ECU not to engage in discussions on the reasons why the ECU's role should be promoted. The fact that this had been announced by the European Council in Bremen and Brussels was, for them, sufficient reason. In as far as they did explain, three arguments were clear:

– The ECU was considered as a symbol of European monetary integration. Or, as Vice-President of the European Commission François-Xavier Ortoli put it in a more flowery though less articulate way: 'The extension of the use of the ECU is a privileged means of reinforcing European monetary identity'[4]
– It was argued that the use of the ECU would spread the effect of capital movements over all EC currencies and thus make the EMS less vulnerable to speculation.
– There was a view that the ECU would help the EC countries to pursue a common policy against the dollar.

It should be noted that at this stage the ECU was not seen by France as an asset that would replace national currencies, but rather as an international reserve asset. Thus replacing national currencies was not mentioned by French Finance Minister Delors when he said in an interview in March 1982:

> First of all, it is necessary to use the European Currency Unit more often in transactions between our countries, as well as in our lending an borrowing abroad. We must see to it that the ECU becomes, little by little, a transaction and reserve currency. Secondly, we must consult one another more often about monetary policy. And finally, we must adopt a common stance with regard to the dollar and the yen. As an indefatigable pilgrim of the European concept, I have been working on these three elements since arriving at the Ministry.[5]

It was only at a later stage, when Monetary Union re-emerged as a policy objective, that the ECU was to take the place of national currencies.

9.3   NEGOTIATIONS

In 1982 and 1984 two main rounds of negotiations took place on technical proposals to modify arrangements concerning the EMS. The Ecofin Council agreed on 14 December 1981 that the Commission was to make proposals to improve the existing mechanisms without starting the so-called institutional stage (which according to the European Council Resolution of 5 December 1978 would have had to start not later than two years after the start of the EMS). After preliminary discussions, the Commission presented its proposals in the form of a draft Council Resolution on 10 March 1982. The most controversial elements were the abolition of the existing acceptance limit of 50 per cent, and additional obligations for surplus countries to put their currencies at the disposal of deficit countries for intramarginal interventions. In addition to their objections against the substance of these proposals, the Bundesbank and the Nederlandsche Bank resented the fact that they were presented in the form of a draft Council Resolution, implying that these issues – which in their countries were their responsibility – were to be decided by the Council. The Commission was of course aware of these sensitivities. Its attitude reflected the view – prevalent at this time, in particular within the services of the Commission – that the EMS, attributed to an important extent to Commission President Roy Jenkins' initiative, had been forced through by the German and French governments over the opposition of the Bundesbank in particular. This process, it was felt, should be repeated.

The Bundesbank for its part, though of course aware that it had succeeded in drastically altering the original proposals regarding the EMS, hesitated to risk a head-on confrontation, and explored the scope for compromises without making concessions that would endanger its grip on the money supply in Germany. The Nederlandsche Bank did what it could to stiffen the Bundesbank's resolve. We opposed a 'symmetrical' system on principle since its disciplinary effect would then largely be lost, and the system would in our view lose much of its sense. We also believed that if the Bundesbank would yield, its participation would become increasingly reluctant, endangering the system's durability. We feared that any additional 'flexibility' forced on the Bundesbank would result in less flexibility on its part, probably at our expense, in issues where its discretion remained. This concern soon turned out to be justified.

A second round of negotiations took place in 1984. To the surprise of most participants, they learned at the Ecofin Council Meeting on 12 May 1984 that Bundesbank President Pöhl was prepared to accept the abolition of the acceptance limit for ECUs in its existing form, provided the payment ratio of 50 per cent would be replaced by acceptance limits in the form of absolute amounts per creditor central bank. This the Bundesbank had bilaterally agreed with the Banque de France, who no doubt regarded it as a first step towards the complete abolition of acceptance limits. The Bundesbank subsequently explained to the Nederlandsche Bank that its main reason for agreeing had been that it was reluctant to be the Central Bank that always said no. Moreover, absolute limits would provide an even better safeguard against excessive ECU holdings. Keeping the existing payments ratio was also acceptable, but in that case it would be the others, not the Bundesbank, who rejected new proposals! As it turned out, all other central banks rejected this joint French–German proposal. They would – with the exception of the Dutch – have welcomed the complete abolition of acceptance limits. But absolute limits as now proposed meant that once the German limit had been reached, there would be an obligation for other central banks to accept ECUs even in the absence of reserve inflows. This required complicated designation arrangements comparable to those existing in the IMF for SDRs. Under the circumstances, the majority preferred to retain the existing payments ratio, but to seek additional flexibility in a different way: obliging creditor countries to accept ECUs in settlement for intramarginal interventions in the same way as for obligatory interventions.

This came as an unpleasant surprise to the Bundesbank. Once again it found itself obliged to reject a majority proposal, this time without Dutch support. Soon my counterpart Leonhard Gleske was on the telephone, explaining unhappily that until then the Bundesbank – as I was aware – had been flexible in agreeing to intramarginal interventions since as long as the Bundesbank was not directly involved there was no liquidity effect in the market, but merely creditor substitution. This would change if intramarginal intervention would automatically involve the Bundesbank; in that case it would become more reluctant to agree to such interventions. Under the circumstances he felt the best thing would be to leave the existing arrangements unchanged. I asked him whether that would be his position at the next meeting, but he said he could not do that since the Bundesbank had agreed with the Banque de France to propose a change; in that case, I said, I was afraid I could not help him.[6] In the end, a 'package' concerning the ECU was agreed upon in early 1985 under the Dutch chairmanship of the Committee of Governors, in which the payments ratio remained unchanged but some flexibility was introduced regarding the use of ECU in other ways.

9.4 ASSESSMENT

As discussed earlier (7.4), for France the EMS had to be different, and to look different, from the snake it had felt compelled to leave twice. France should be able to determine its own policy priorities, and not be placed in a position where the resulting reserve losses would force it either to adopt the German priorities or to leave the system. This did not mean that it rejected external discipline altogether. But the burden of adjustment should also be borne by the main creditor country, Germany. Moreover, French public opinion would find discipline more acceptable if it was imposed, not by what was regarded as a German mark bloc, but by a genuine European system in which French influence was as noticeable as

German. It was this objective that France, supported by other EC countries and by the Commission, tried to achieve, first at the making of the EMS in 1978, and, when this had largely failed, in later years in the form of technical proposals.

Promoting the ECU was central to achieving this objective. Creating ECUs on behalf of deficit countries would mitigate the pressure of reserve losses and shift the burden of adjustment to surplus countries, provided these were obliged to accept ECUs without limits; elimination of all obstacles existing in this respect was therefore a first priority. In time the development of a genuine ECU market would open up entirely new vistas, enabling an ECU-creating Fund to buy dollars and thus make the EMS less dependent on the Bundesbank's dollar policy.

In addition, urging the promotion of the ECU seemed good tactics. Since the establishment of the EMS, the ECU had been associated with further European integration, even though there had been no mention of developing it into a single currency; in fact, France – the ECU's spiritual parent – did not envisage that at all until a later stage. All governments had accepted the formula that the ECU should be at the centre of the EMS (Bremen, 6–7 July 1978) and that the final system would entail its full utilisation as a reserve asset and a means of settlement (Brussels, 5 December 1978), so the creditor countries could be asked to honour their commitment and thus maintain the momentum of integration instead of belatedly raising the question why the ECU should be promoted.

As a result, the Bundesbank and the Nederlandsche Bank soon found themselves permanently on the defensive. The Bundesbank, in particular, felt it was in an awkward position. It was publicly presented as the main obstacle to further European integration, always saying no to everything that was proposed; in reality, it strongly argued in favour of the only thing that in its view would really lead to integration, i.e. economic convergence, but this had less public appeal than the promotion of the ECU. Remembering the Schmidt–Giscard initiative, the Bundesbank was concerned it would find itself in a similar situation, possibly leading to a confrontation with its own Government. The Nederlandsche Bank was worried that the Bundesbank would make concessions, either forced by its government or in order to avoid being forced. The long-term result would not be more, but less, flexibility. The French–German proposal to replace the payment ratio by absolute creditor limits, interrupting our normally close cooperation with the Bundesbank, illustrated the situation that might emerge if we could not break out of this defensive position. This experience further stimulated us to take a more offensive stance. In face of the repeated proposals requiring the strong currency countries to accept additional obligations, we felt we should raise the issue of existing obligations which we respected but which many others, including the European Commission, simply ignored: capital liberalisation.

10 The Single European Act (1985–6)

In the mid-1980s, the atmosphere of stagnation in European integration gave way to a renewed dynamism. In June 1984 the European Council set up a committee, the Dooge Committee, which was to make proposals for improving integration, including political cooperation. In its report the committee made proposals for amending the Rome Treaty in order to improve decision-making in the Community. The European Commission in June 1985 published a White Paper containing proposals for the completion of the internal market. In September of that year, the first meeting took place of the Intergovernmental Conference which was to negotiate a change in the Treaty, leading to the Single European Act that was to come into effect on 1 January 1987.

These developments coincided with the accession, on 1 January 1985, of Jacques Delors to the presidency of the European Commission. He soon turned out to be a major dynamic force in the integration process. Like his predecessors, Delors attached great importance to monetary integration as an engine of European integration. Unlike them, however, he tried to strike a more balanced note. Until then the European Commission seemed to take the view that progress could only be achieved by getting the Bundesbank overruled by the German government, as it felt had been the case in 1978 when the EMS was created. The creditor central banks, on their part, felt that the Commission neither understood nor sympathised with the checks and balances between central banks and governments prevailing in their countries, which they regarded as essential in order to preserve the value of the currency. They had come to identify proposals for monetary integration with monetary laxity. Delors, in his inaugural address to the European Parliament in January 1985, set out to reassure them: 'What a triumph if the Community could demonstrate that monetary stringency and the fight against unemployment could go hand-in-hand.' In the months that followed, he tried to help the then chairman of the Committee of EC Governors, Wim Duisenberg, to find solutions for a 'package' of proposals to promote the ECU discussed in the previous chapter; more generally he explored the possibilities of cooperating with the creditor central banks. In this context, he soon recognised the opportunities offered by focusing on capital liberalisation, a topic invoked by the Bundesbank and the Nederlandsche Bank but long neglected in Brussels. On the other hand, and more in line with his predecessors' tradition, he also tried to force the pace of monetary integration by proposing Treaty amendments that would have affected central bank autonomy. While the new approach turned out to be surprisingly successful, the old one was not. This experience was not lost on Delors.

10.1   CAPITAL LIBERALISATION[1]

Capital liberalisation was one of the early successes of the European Economic Community. It is true that the Rome Treaty, in Article 67.1, obliged member states to abolish capital restrictions only 'to the extent necessary to ensure the proper functioning of the Common Market', but in practice this was interpreted widely, and a good deal of attention was devoted in the early years to capital liberalisation. The atmosphere changed when France, due to pressure on the franc following the students' revolt in May 1968, reintroduced capital restrictions. It did so with the consent of the European Commission, having recourse to the safeguard clauses contained in the Treaty. These safeguard clauses were meant to be temporary, but the Commission chose not to attach a time limit. Thus President Duisenberg remarked in a speech he gave in Berlin in early 1985 that the French exemption

> had been in force without interruption since 1968, when De Gaulle's France got into trouble because of the students' revolt. One should assume that the specific circumstances justifying it at the time have changed since then (and I do not only mean that those students have hopefully graduated by now).[2]

Duisenberg's remark was not just meant to enliven his speech, but was part of a line taken since 1982 by the Dutch monetary authorities. It was our reaction to pressure from the Commission, largely instigated by the French, to promote the ECU. The proposals invariably entailed additional obligations for the creditor central banks. Our reply was to raise the issue of existing obligations which we respected but which France, and others, did not. In the middle of March 1982 Dutch Finance Minister Fons van der Stee proposed in an Ecofin meeting reconsidering capital liberalisation, not confining it to ECU-denominated capital as the Commission wished. As a follow-up, I asked for the matter to be put on the agenda of the Monetary Committee in July, proposing among other things to reinstate the regular annual examination of the use of capital restrictions, as provided for in the First Capital Directive of 1960 and in the statute of the Monetary Committee, a task that had for many years been ignored. We also wanted to limit the duration of exemptions, in accordance with the rules. These proposals were supported by other countries that had themselves liberalised capital. Germany hoped that liberalisation would strengthen market forces and would thus put pressure on governments to follow stability oriented policies which in its view was the real condition for further integration. For the United Kingdom the latter was not a motive, but capital liberalisation fitted well in its concept of Europe as one market without barriers where economic development was fostered by the free play of market forces. The main opposition came from France. The Commission usually followed the French lead in such matters, and thus the Dutch initiative was initially given a frosty reception.

Attitudes gradually started to change in 1983. France, having made its choice in March to remain in the EMS, began to adjust its policies. With Finance Minister Jacques Delors as one of its main architects it embarked on a strategy that implied the opening-up of markets with the aim of enforcing rationalisation upon the French industry through the forces of competition. Accordingly, it modified its until then reticent attitude towards capital liberalisation. In the wake of the French reorientation a change of heart gradually occurred in the Commission's thinking, the more so since its attitude had come under criticism by the Court of Justice and the European Parliament.

Thus by the time Delors assumed the EC Presidency in January 1985 capital liberalisation was already on the political agenda. That same month Nederlandsche Bank President Wim Duisenberg gave his speech in Berlin quoted above. During the months that followed the Germans intensified the pressure. Finance Minister Gerhard Stoltenberg stated in March that 'a further strengthening of the EMS (meaning technical changes proposed by the Commission and backed by France) is absurd as long as there is no further liberalisation of capital movements.'[3] Bundesbank Director Leonnard Gleske made similar remarks in April.[4]

What Delors did was to adopt the issue and carry it forward. As a first step the Commission, in response to pressure in the Monetary Committee, agreed that exemptions would be monitored more strictly and that their duration would be limited in time. Next, it linked capital liberalisation to the completion of the internal market. In its meeting on 3 and 4 December 1984 the European Council had agreed that steps should be taken to complete the internal market, but without further specification. Delors now came forward with a plan to stimulate integration by focusing on the internal market. At its March 1985 meeting the European Council further specified this goal by setting 1992 as target date, and the Commission published a White Book in June with proposals to that end. In the White Book the complete liberalisation of capital movements was contained as an essential ingredient of the internal market.

Completion of the internal market required an amendment of the Rome Treaty. To that end, the Single European Act was prepared. The Commission proposed that in this Act the definition of the internal market would also encompass the free movement of capital, and that the obligation to liberalise should no longer – as was the case in Article 67 of the Rome Treaty – be limited 'to the extent necessary to ensure the proper functioning of the Common Market.' Member states did not adopt this proposal. But after the Single European Act had been adopted in December 1985 and signed in February 1986, Delors returned to the theme.

In May 1986, the Commission presented a programme to fully liberalise capital movements in two stages. This coincided with a substantial relaxation of foreign exchange controls in France where a deregulation and liberalisation process was being pursued. France's changing attitude was not without influence on other countries that still maintained capital restrictions, and as a result the Commission programme amending the 1960 Directive regarding capital liberalisation was agreed in November, and came into force in March 1987.

10.2   A 'MONETARY DIMENSION' IN THE TREATY

The first impression creditor central banks had after Delors' accession to the presidency of the European Commission was that he would be more open to cooperation with them, and less inclined to try to get them overruled by their own governments, than his predecessors. In consulting Wim Duisenberg, President of the Committee of EC Central Bank Governors, on the prospects of the package of measures to promote the use of the ECU then under discussion in Basle, Delors assured him during a lunch on 6 March 1985 that in the future the Commission would not make proposals on issues within the central banks' competence, and would not repeat what he called his predecessor Thorn's 'mistake' of proposing Council resolutions in this sphere (see 9.3).

However, Delors made it clear right from the start of his presidency that in his efforts to endow the integration process with a new momentum, monetary issues would be given a high priority. In his inaugural speech to the European Parliament, he stressed in particular the strengthening of the European Monetary System and the extension of the role of the ECU:

> The reasoning behind his suggestion was that the burden placed on the dollar is too great: a Community currency would enable central banks to diversify their reserves.' He asked the Parliament if the Community would not then be in a stronger position 'to ask Japan to take its share of the load and persuade the US to introduce the internal discipline which would make for relative stability on foreign exchanges.[5]

In the course of 1985, preparations took place for the Intergovernmental Conference that was to establish the Single European Act. Though the subject matter of the negotiations was not monetary issues, the European Commission wished to take this opportunity to insert what was referred to as a 'monetary dimension' into the Treaty. In this context, three issues can be distinguished:

– There was a wish to include Economic and Monetary Union in the Treaty as an objective.
– There was a desire to incorporate the European Monetary System and the ECU in the Treaty.

– There was discussion on the applicability of Article 235 of the Treaty to monetary issues. This article enabled the Council, provided it was unanimous, to take measures necessary to realise the objectives of the Treaty in cases that the Treaty did not provide the authority necessary.

Economic and Monetary Union had been an objective of the European Community since its announcement in the communiqué of the Conference of the Heads of State or Government on 1 and 2 December 1969 in The Hague, and it had been confirmed at their conference, attended by the new members, the United Kingdom, Denmark and Ireland, on 19–21 October 1972 in Paris. This was not, however, mentioned in the Treaty, and the Commission wished to use this first major revision of the Rome Treaty to make EMU an objective.

The intention to incorporate a 'monetary dimension' in the Treaty met two kinds of objections. The United Kingdom objected to any mention of monetary matters, since it was fundamentally opposed to Economic and Monetary Union, notwithstanding the 1972 declaration. In this general rejection it was supported only by Denmark. The Bundesbank and the Nederlandsche Bank, in line with their governments' position, accepted the objective of Economic and Monetary Union, as well as its incorporation in the Treaty. They were concerned, however, about the legal implications that a monetary article drafted in general terms might turn out to have for central bank autonomy, recalling that after the Council – at the insistence of the Commission – had adopted a directive in 1973 relating to the European Monetary Cooperation Fund, the Commission took the view that as a consequence the Fund was now subject to Community rules (see 6.2). The Commission's next step, the creditor central banks feared at the time, might well be to try to convert the snake arrangement, based on agreements between central banks, into something subject to decision-making according to Community rules, i.e. Council decisions made at the proposal of the Commission.

Should the EMS and the ECU be mentioned in the Treaty in an unspecified way, the Bundesbank and the Nederlandsche Bank felt that the Commission might again take the view that as a result this had now become subject to Community procedures. For the Bundesbank, subjecting its foreign exchange policy to Community decision-making even prior to the start of EMU, with its concomitant safeguards, would have been unthinkable, and the Nederlandsche Bank fully agreed.

Neither the Bundesbank nor the Nederlandsche Bank opposed Economic and Monetary Union, as stated earlier. They felt strongly, however, that central bank autonomy as they knew it should be preserved, both during the development towards EMU and after it took effect. This implied that if their competence, or part of it, were to be transferred to the Community level, this could only be done on the basis of adequate legislation, which would mean amending the Treaty in which the checks and balances between central banks and governments were spelled out, as was the case in their national legislation. In terms of the Rome Treaty, this meant that changes affecting the competence of national central banks could only take place on the basis of Article 236, containing the procedure for amending the Treaty, not on the basis of Article 235, which enabled the Council, provided it was unanimous, to take measures necessary to realise the objectives of the Treaty in cases where the Treaty did not provide the authority necessary.

Delors ignored this view. He set forth his intentions in general terms at an informal meeting in Luxemburg on 20–21 September. Capital liberalisation increases international monetary interdependence; on the basis of that reasoning, Delors linked the issue of capital liberalisation with that of incorporating a monetary dimension in the Treaty, arguing that the former required an adequate legal framework. That framework should incorporate the European Monetary System, it should contribute to the internal stability of the Community, it should confirm the autonomy of the monetary institutions and should be based on the principle of progressive integration.[6] As a next step he circulated a draft in the form of a proposed extension of Article 107 of the Rome Treaty. This article originally stated that member countries regarded their exchange rate policy as a matter of common interest. Delors' draft would incorporate the EMS in the article. It stated that the European Monetary Cooperation Fund 'enjoys the autonomy necessary for the performance of its tasks' and added that this Fund would be replaced, 'at the appropriate moment, by a European Monetary Fund which will enjoy institutional autonomy.' This, the draft stipulated, could be decided on a proposal from the Commission by the Council, acting unanimously. In other words, no further change of the Treaty would be required.[7]

To state in general terms that a Central Bank is autonomous is, by itself, meaningless. In this respect, the essence lies in the detail. The European Fund's competence would have to be spelled out in the Treaty, just as national central banks' competences are spelled out in national legislation. The Nederlandsche Bank and the Bundesbank had strong objections against Delors' proposal which they set out in letters to their governments on 1 November 1985 and 8 November 1985 respectively.

10.3   THE LUXEMBURG EUROPEAN COUNCIL

The issue was to be decided at the Luxemburg European Council that started on 2 December 1985 in Luxemburg. At this, Britain was both against introducing a monetary dimension in the Treaty and against incorporating EMU as an objective. On the latter point it soon found itself isolated, apart from Danish support. As Margaret Thatcher put it in her memoirs:

> We in the British delegation were inclined to dismiss such rhetoric (meaning references to EMU) as cloudy and unrealistic aspirations which had no prospect of being implemented. We were correct in believing them to be lacking in realism; where we were mistaken was in underestimating the determination of some European politicians to put them into effect.

The outcome was a compromise of sorts. EMU was not accepted as an explicit Treaty objective, but two references were made to it. One was a historical reference in the preamble to the Single European Act, saying: 'Whereas at their conference in Paris from 19 to 21 October 1972 the Heads of State or of Government approved the objective of the progressive realisation of Economic and Monetary Union'. The second reference was in the heading of a new article – Article 102A – to be inserted in the Treaty. The heading was 'Cooperation in Economic and Monetary Policy (Economic and Monetary Union)'. As Thatcher put it in her memoirs when discussing these two references:

> The former had been the official objective, unfortunately, since October 1972: the latter, I hoped, would signal the limits the act placed on it. But this formulation delayed M. Delors's drive to Monetary Union briefly.

What she meant was that she could not help acknowledging the fact that, in accepting EMU as an objective, her predecessors had already yielded on this point. But she tried to make a virtue out of necessity by pretending that Economic and Monetary Union was now given a new, limited, definition: Cooperation in Economic and Monetary Policy, nothing more:

> This enabled me to claim at subsequent forums that EMU now meant economic and monetary cooperation, not moving towards a single currency. There was a studied ambiguity about all this ... I was more or less happy with this, because it meant no more than cooperation. The rest of the European Heads of Government were equally happy, because they interpreted it as progress towards a European Central Bank and a single currency. But at some point, of course, these two interpretations would clash. And when they did I was bound to be fighting on ground not of my choosing.

She blamed this result on the Germans, stating that German Chancellor Kohl had told her 'that the Germans, like us, were totally opposed to any amendment to the monetary provisions of the Treaty of Rome', only to yield under pressure.[8]

In actual fact, the German Government, though objecting to incorporating a monetary dimension in the Treaty for reasons of its own, had a completely different attitude from Britain regarding European integration in general. As early as June 1985, Chancellor Kohl set forth his objectives:

- Enshrinement in Treaty form of the existing political cooperation in the Community, in order to give this 'second pillar of progress towards European unity' a permanent foundation.
- The development of a joint EC foreign and security policy 'worthy of the name'.
- Institutional reforms, in particular a return to the principle of majority voting laid down in the 1957 Treaty of Rome, with enlarged powers for the European Parliament.
- The extension of the existing internal market.[9]

The Germans had their own misgivings about a monetary dimension in the Treaty, but once it was clear that some countries made this a condition for accepting the completion of the internal market, it was obvious to Chancellor Kohl that he had to find a compromise. In his press briefing after the European Council meeting he underlined the importance he attached to political integration in Europe. If this was the aim, then Economic and Monetary Union also had to be accepted. It wasn't possible to pick and chose, and refuse all the rest. But flexibility had its limits where negative consequences had to be expected. Germany's experience meant the independence of the Bundesbank was a necessity.[10] Thus Kohl asked Under–Secretary Hans Tietmeyer to negotiate a wording that did incorporate a monetary dimension in the Treaty but safeguarded the Bundesbank's independence. Like Thatcher, Tietmeyer proceeded to make a virtue out of necessity, but in a far more effective way.

The new Article 102A in the Treaty on monetary issues, mainly drafted by him, mentioned the EMS and the ECU as the French and the Commission had demanded, but only to say that in cooperating, member countries 'shall take account of the experience acquired in cooperation within the framework of the European Monetary System (EMS) and in developing the ECU, and shall respect existing powers in this field.' More important, a second paragraph stipulated: 'Insofar as further development in the field of economic and monetary policy necessitates institutional changes, the provisions of Article 236 shall be applicable.' In other words, in these fields, henceforward new institutions could only be established on the basis of a change in the Treaty, and not on that of Article 235 as Delors had proposed in his draft.

At the Nederlandsche Bank, we were quite satisfied with this outcome. We had not been involved in the negotiations and only indirectly in the preparations, and were far from sure our own government grasped the implications of what was being proposed. Most probably Minister of Foreign Affairs Hans van den Broek did not, when he published an article in a Dutch newspaper in May 1985 advocating to 'codify and insert in the Treaty the European Monetary System that had turned out to be a success.'[11] This was changed somewhat following our explanations, but the Dutch government remained prepared to negotiate on the wording of a monetary paragraph to be inserted in the Treaty, and the Central Bank and even the Ministry of Finance had only limited influence on the government's attitude. Thus when my German counterpart Gleske phoned me on 27 November to express his uneasiness about a Dutch proposal which had apparently been tabled (we had seen a draft but had understood that it would only be used, if at all, as a fall back position in a later stage) I made it clear to him that I shared his misgivings.[12] I certainly preferred the text Tietmeyer later produced.

Until the end of November I had the impression that no monetary paragraph would be agreed upon at all. In a paper for my colleagues in the Bank I wrote:

> In the Monetary Committee on 28 November the Treaty amendment was relatively briefly discussed. This discussion did not indicate any change in positions. Chairman Tietmeyer did not seem to wish to have more than a round of explanations of positions. The issue now is in the hands of the Great Men, he said, meaning the Heads of Government. To prepare it, the Foreign Ministers will enter into a conclave. The image of cardinals apparently appealed to him, for he elaborated on walling up the room and on the hard beds, adding that we had to await whether the smoke would be white or black. He did not give the impression to expect that the fire would be lit with the competences he defended. . . . When I spoke with Tietmeyer for a moment privately he said in answer to my question that he did not expect a monetary change in the Treaty, but perhaps a political statement.[13]

10.4 ASSESSMENT

Events in 1985 and 1986 can, in retrospect, be seen as a milestone on the road to the Maastricht Treaty, perhaps even as a turning point. Agreement on the European Single Act, containing provisions for the completion of the single market that had been started with the Rome Treaty three decades earlier, together with a strengthening of Community decision-making and of the European Parliament, contributed to a new dynamism and a new atmosphere.

No less important was the accession to the presidency of the European Commission by Jacques Delors, an experienced politician who combined a vision of Europe with a feeling for power relations. It was this that made him link – for the Commission and for his country, France – the traditional emphasis on monetary integration with a new drive for capital liberalisation, for which creditor central banks were arguing. No doubt he realised that monetary integration had a better chance if he could commit the Bundesbank at least partially to the integration process, given its political backing in Germany. As Age Bakker put it, 'by embracing the goal of full capital liberalisation, he gambled on setting in motion a dynamic process which would eventually bring German monetary policy into the European orbit.' This policy was made possible by developments in France, which continued after Delors left as Finance Minister, and which reduced France's earlier resistance to capital liberalisation.

> Delors invariably and successfully sensed the lay of the land and adjusted his policies accordingly. From now on the Commission would play a leading part... By aligning himself with a proposal of the hard-currency countries, and therewith discontinuing the perpetual opposition of these countries towards the EMS packages, Delors had made a political and strategic choice, which if successful could bring great reward.[14]

Delors had a case in arguing that capital liberalisation – desired by the creditor countries – increased monetary interdependence, thus constituting an additional argument for monetary integration. He used this argument to push to incorporate into the Treaty an article on monetary issues that was in effect an empowering article for the Council to pursue monetary integration without the need for further Treaty amendments. In doing so he brushed aside the strong concerns of the creditor central banks. In the end, he did obtain the incorporation of a 'monetary dimension' in the Treaty. But the substance of the new Article 102A, making the establishment of new monetary institutions explicitly dependent on further Treaty amendments, was the opposite of what he had proposed.

Events and attitudes in 1985–6 constituted an approach that was to set the pattern for the years to come, leading to the Maastricht Treaty.

– Events showed that Britain with its mainly negative attitude towards integration could not veto everything on its own, and was therefore pushed along one step at the time without having any real influence on developments.
– Events also revealed the important role of Chancellor Kohl, who by 1985 was already explicitly pursuing political integration and who regarded EMU as necessary to attain that ultimate goal, provided certain conditions were met to safeguard monetary stability.

- At the same time a reorientation had started in France which would in the end enable it to accept those conditions.
- Finally, this was a learning period for the new President of the Commission, Jacques Delors, who explored the extent to which he could commit the creditor central banks to the integration process, but also the extent to which he could afford to brush their concerns aside. The experience he gained undoubtedly played an important part when, in 1988 and 1989, Delors was to chair the Committee for the Study of Economic and Monetary Union, the report of which was to constitute the core of the Maastricht Treaty.

11 French–German Tussle: Monetary Union Revived (1987–8)

The climate regarding European integration was now changing. The renewed drive for capital liberalisation, the European Single Act opening the prospect for the completion of the internal market (of which free capital movements were soon to be made an integral part) were both cause and effect of this changing climate. A shift in French domestic policies and priorities was an important part of the changing scene. It made capital liberalisation possible, but also increased French feelings of dependence on German policy decisions, thus rekindling French interest in Monetary Union in which it could hope to influence those policies. For Germany, the change in French policies made the prospect of Monetary Union more attractive. In the same period fundamental political changes took place in Eastern Europe after Mikhail Gorbachov rose to power in the Soviet Union in 1985; for Germany, this opened up the perspective of a more active involvement in developments in Eastern Europe, which was in turn an incentive for more dynamism in Western European integration in order not to disturb the fundamental balance in German foreign policy.

11.1 FRENCH DEPENDENCE ON GERMAN POLICIES

In 1983 France made its decision to remain in the EMS and changed its policy priorities accordingly. This increased its dependence on German monetary policies. Still, this dependence was relative so long as it felt that exchange rates could be adjusted if necessary. It is true that France did not want to be seen devaluing the franc, but it did not necessarily object to changes in the exchange rate relationship between the franc and the German mark, so long as this was not presented as a devaluation of the franc.

From 1987 onwards, however, the French attitude in this respect was changing: it no longer objected to the presentation of a change in the central rate with Germany as a French devaluation, but rather to a change in the central rate itself. By now, price stability had a high priority in France, a result no doubt of the drive for liberalisation and deregulation by the new Chirac government, reflecting similar attitudes abroad. Devaluations of the franc, no matter how they were presented, were bound to increase inflation and were therefore resisted. This further increased France's sense of dependence on Bundesbank policies, stimulating it to find ways to influence those policies.

France explored three ways of influencing German monetary policy:

- By proposing or supporting technical changes in intervention and settlement obligations and credit arrangements in the European Monetary System it wanted the Bundesbank to assume additional obligations resulting in a more expansionary monetary development.
- By proposing the institution of a French–German Financial and Economic Council it hoped to be able to exert political pressure on German monetary policy.
- Failing these efforts, the only possibility that remained was to transfer decision-making from the national to the European level. To this end, it raised the issue of establishing a European Central Bank.

11.2 CHANGES IN TECHNICAL ARRANGEMENTS

Almost from the start of the snake, France tried to obtain modifications in the arrangements for interventions, settlements and credit, with the aim of making the system more 'symmetrical', i.e. to shift the burden of adjustment to the strong currency countries, notably Germany. It failed in its efforts to reform the snake, and twice felt it had to leave it, notwithstanding the importance it attached to European monetary arrangements. When in 1978 the European Monetary System was being negotiated, French desires first seemed to stand a better chance, but in the end the EMS turned out to be hardly different from the snake it replaced, as discussed in chapter 7. Subsequent efforts to obtain what could not be ensured in 1978 by proposals to promote the ECU also failed, as described in Chapter 9. Though France continued to make proposals, sometimes with partial success, as in the Basle–Nyborg arrangements of 1987, the reaction of the public in Germany on that occasion made it clear that the Bundesbank had sufficient backing to be able to resist any further technical changes that would really loosen its grip on the money supply.

Though French efforts to effect changes continued after 1987, it was obvious by then that this approach would not yield the desired shift in the burden of adjustment. If France wished to be able to influence German monetary policies, a more direct, political approach had to be tried.

11.3 FRENCH–GERMAN FINANCIAL AND ECONOMIC COUNCIL

On 22 January 1988 Chancellor Kohl visited Paris to commemorate the 25th anniversary of the French–German Treaty of Friendship. On that occasion he and President Mitterrand signed protocols to that Treaty, establishing a French–German Defence Council and a French–German Financial and Economic Council. Part of the latter's task was to discuss periodically the monetary policies of both countries in the national, European and international context with the aim to coordinate it as far as possible.[1] Both central banks would be represented in the Council.

The institution of a Defence Council was close to Chancellor Kohl's heart, for he regarded it as a nucleus for a closer European defence cooperation in the future. It had been the French government, and reportedly Prime Minister Jacques Chirac in particular, who had insisted on linking monetary cooperation to cooperation in defence.[2] The agreement between the governments of both countries to institute a Financial and Economic Council had been known for some time. But the Bundesbank was only informed on the evening of 20 January that on French insistence this would take place in the form of a protocol to the Treaty of 1963. This set alarm bells ringing in Frankfurt, where it was feared that a body possessing Treaty status could well impinge upon the autonomy of the Bundesbank based on national legislation. These fears were neither allayed by the haste with which the preparations had been conducted in order to enable the protocol to be signed to commemorate the 1963 Treaty, nor by French Prime Minister Chirac's recent criticism of Bundesbank policies.

Chancellor Kohl, who had agreed to the French demands in order to obtain his Defence Council, understandably played down the implications, and government officials argued that nothing more was intended than to formalise consultations that were already taking place. After some political bickering, a solution to the problem was found when the Bundestag adopted a preamble to the law approving the protocol, in which it stated that the Bundesbank's autonomy would not be affected. This seemed to be a fitting contribution indeed to the commemoration of the Treaty of 1963, when – as discussed in Chapter 3 – the Bundestag had also adopted a preamble containing a unilateral statement declaring that the Treaty would not affect German relations with Britain and the United States, much to the frustration of General De Gaulle, who felt that as a result the point of the Treaty was largely lost.

Whether French insistence to institute the Council by protocol to the 1963 Treaty really was based on the motives attributed to it by the Bundesbank cannot be answered with certainty. But there is little doubt that the Council was meant to provide France with another channel to try to influence German monetary policies. Its effectiveness to achieve that aim, however, was doubtful from the start. Thus at the same time that this bilateral instrument was being created, France renewed discussions on a future European Central Bank, the creation of which would imply transferring monetary decision-making from the national to a European level.

11.4 FRENCH PROPOSAL FOR A EUROPEAN CENTRAL BANK

On 8 January 1988 the French Minister of Economics, Finance and Privatisation, Edouard Balladur, addressed a letter to the other Finance Ministers of the EC. In this letter he referred to recent disturbances in the foreign exchange markets as well as the stock exchange, and to resulting doubts in public opinion regarding economic growth. Ministers had a duty to think about ways to avoid the most negative consequences of what he called this global crisis. In doing so, exchange rate stability within Europe should have priority. To this letter, he annexed a memorandum called *La Construction Monétaire Européenne*. The greater part of the memorandum was devoted to technical proposals to diminish the asymmetry of the European Monetary System, but the last part was entitled

'The construction in the longer term of a zone with a single currency'. This part started with a reference to the completion of the internal market in 1992, and stated that logic required that a zone with a single currency should then be created. A number of proposals had been made concerning the creation of a European Central Bank. This would pose questions which the memorandum then enumerated. The paper finished by stating that it was desirable that this theme should be reflected upon in the coming months. This cautious letter to his ministerial colleagues had been preceded – not for the first time – by a more blunt statement for television two days earlier: 'The moment has come to examine the possibility to create a European Central Bank that would control a common currency, the ECU. I intend to approach my colleagues in the coming days to discus it.'[3] In fact, Balladur's initiative followed what could be seen in retrospect as a year of preparation, during which time and again France addressed the question how to lessen the asymmetry of the EMS.

On 12 January 1987 the French franc was once again devalued against the German mark and the guilder, this time by 3 per cent, only nine months after a previous devaluation by 6 per cent in April 1986.[4] Less then a month later Balladur started to call for reforms of the EMS to make it more balanced:

– On 9 February 1987 Balladur announced to his ministerial EC colleagues a French memorandum on monetary issues. This memorandum contained a number of technical proposals aimed at increasing 'symmetry' in the EMS.
– This was announced to the press. (*Financial Times*, 10 and 12 February 1987.) At about the same time, *Le Monde* published an interview with the French Minister in which he also entered into discussions of monetary issues.[5]
– In the *Financial Times* of 17 June 1987 Minister Balladur published an extensive article under the heading 'The EMS: advance or face retreat'. Here, for the first time in public as far as I know, he broached the issue of a future European Central Bank. He did so in the form of questions, as he would in his memorandum in January 1988. Having reminded his readers of the plans dating from 1978 regarding a second phase of the EMS, which was to be completed 'through the creation of a European monetary institution endowed with a degree of supranational authority', he wrote 'I am convinced that these reforms should be

rapidly considered and implemented'. He then continued:

> Will we move toward a common currency through several gradual
> stages, as would seem logical, or rather in one great leap? Will
> the European Fund for Monetary Cooperation turn out to be
> the embryo of a European Central Bank? What powers should
> such a body have? What would its relations be with political
> authority and what would this latter be? These are questions
> for the future. But they cannot serve as an alibi for a passive
> attitude, which in today's troubled world could endanger the
> valuable asset which the EMS represents.

The article ended with a call to reform the EMS, making it more
balanced:

– On 22 October 1987 President Mitterrand made a speech in which
  he called for a common currency and 'a central organism', and
  on the same day at a press conference, in answer to questions,
  he said that there should be a European Central Bank.[6]
– In a speech on 6 December 1987 Minister Balladur called for a
  European Central Bank.
– On 14 January 1988 *Le Figaro* published an interview with
  the Minister under the heading: 'Balladur: toward a European
  currency'.

Thus, almost immediately after what would turn out to be France's
last devaluation in the EMS, the French government started a campaign to build up pressure for reform of the system in order to
make it more symmetrical, first stressing technical reforms as it
had done for many years, then calling for a European Central Bank.
Balladur's letter to the other Finance Ministers in January 1988
was sent only a few weeks before the protocol regarding the French–
German Financial and Economic Council was signed, which was
discussed in the previous paragraph.

11.5 GERMAN REACTIONS

Most German reactions to the French suggestions regarding a
European Central Bank were reticent. As Bundesbank President
Karl Otto Pöhl put it as early as mid-1987:

I . . . continue to advocate that a single European currency issued and controlled by a European Central Bank should be the final objective of monetary integration in Europe. There is no doubt, of course, that this goal cannot be reached tomorrow, but it is part of our longer-term perspective.[7]

This view was shared by Finance Minister Gerhard Stoltenberg.[8]

However, a strikingly different message came from Foreign Minister Hans-Dietrich Genscher. In September 1987 Genscher gave a speech that attracted little attention at the time but which with hindsight is highly remarkable, both for its content and its timing. The times of stagnation in East–West relations are over, he said. We find ourselves at the eve of dynamic developments. The German Federal Republic, anchored in the European Community of democracies and in the western alliance, should profit from the mobility. To this end, the Community should prepare itself for the future (*Dafür müsse die Europäische Gemeinschaft 'zukunftsfähig' gemacht werden.*) The emerging mobility in East–West relations requires at least the same dynamics within the EC. Genscher warned against an imbalance between mobility in East–West relations and stagnation in European unification. A European internal market requires a Monetary Union, and Genscher called for 'courageous steps' in that direction. Europe should not leave East–West relations to the two superpowers but should profit from it. And it should link to this a European identity in security. In French–German relations all decisions should be made in this perspective.[9]

This remarkable speech, which is reminiscent of Willy Brandt's initiative in 1969 regarding Economic and Monetary Union at a time when he was preparing his *Ostpolitik*, was made more than two years before the Berlin Wall came crashing down. When French government officials started to raise the topic of a European Central Bank for further discussion, Genscher – making no effort to hide the difference with his colleagues – went out of his way to support it in public, for instance in a speech for the European Parliament on 20 January 1988, this time citing the financial crisis of October 1987 (Black Monday) as an argument for the necessity for being better armed against currency turbulence.[10]

Genscher's next step was most unusual. On 26 February he published a paper under the title 'Memorandum for the creation of a European monetary space and a European Central Bank'. Given the difference of opinion with the Minister of Finance, he did this in the form of a discussion paper for the Liberal Party, the FDP. While other German voices stressed the longer-term character of the objective of Economic and Monetary Union of which a European Central Bank would be part, Genscher's emphasis was clearly different. He regarded the Central Bank as part of an undefined 'monetary space' (*Währungsraum*) which he linked to the internal market that was to be completed in 1992. Moreover, he wrote that the coming European Council meeting that would take place on 27/28 June in Hanover under the German presidency should give a 'signal for the creation of a European monetary space and a European Central Bank'. It should give a mandate to a group of five to seven 'wise men' to elaborate within a year the principles for a European monetary space, a statute for a European Central Bank and a draft for a transitional period.

Understandably, Finance Minister Stoltenberg did not appreciate this intrusion into his sphere by the Foreign Minister. In his turn he produced a paper which referred to 'various recent proposals based on different objectives and time horizons'.[11] In the paper he quoted the federal government's official position as formulated on 3 February, which said in part: 'The longer-term objective is the European Economic and Monetary Union, in which an independent Central Bank with price stability as its goal can effectively support a common economic and monetary policy.' The paper, stressing the long-term character of EMU, reflected the traditional German position.

Chancellor Kohl's reaction to the suggestions regarding a European Central Bank was cautious and seemingly more in line with those of the Bundesbank and the Finance Minister than with the urgings of the Foreign Minister, stressing its character as a long-term objective.[12] He repeated this position in May, one month before the Hanover European Council: 'As for a European Central Bank, this is something that is perhaps not for tomorrow', and refused to be drawn when asked about proposals at Hanover regarding the creation of a group of 'wise men'.[13] Still, for all his caution, there was an emphasis in his remarks that placed him nearer to the Foreign Minister. This was the link he saw between the future European Central Bank and Political Union. Earlier, in 1985, we saw how he defended the incorporation of a monetary dimension in the Treaty with the argument that whoever wants political integration in Europe also has to accept Economic and Monetary Union. He now repeated the same view in a speech on 15 March 1988:

The German–French agreement has of course been concluded by both sides in a clear European perspective. It should contribute to the realisation of a European Economic and Monetary Union, that remains the objective of the federal government. Part of it is a close integration of the currencies. We shall only achieve the political unification of Europe if we also create a common currency for Europe, with a European Central Bank that bears the responsibility for that currency independent from directives of other institutions, that controls its supply and guarantees its stability. For this, the conditions should be created. The federal government will actively contribute to that development.[14]

11.6 THE LINK WITH SECURITY AND DEFENCE

There is a link between monetary integration and intensified cooperation in security and defence. Elements of this link in French–German relations were discussed earlier. In 1978, when Helmut Schmidt and Valéry Giscard d'Estaing took the initiative to replace the snake by the EMS, they agreed that their intensified cooperation also required initiatives in the sphere of defence. It was the German Chancellor in particular who reacted to the unpredictability of the US Administration's policy under President Carter by advocating closer French–German cooperation (see chapter 7). Giscard, though willing to go along with that, thought it expedient to postpone defence initiatives until after the presidential elections, which he lost.[15] In February 1982, Helmut Schmidt and François Mitterrand announced that they intended to revive the military clauses of the Elysée Treaty.[16]

In the years that followed, cooperation in the field of security and defence was intensified under Helmut Kohl and Mitterrand, and 'By 1986, Franco–German security relations were as good as they had ever been.' After 1987, according to Philip Gordon, these relations took on a new character: 'as Germany sought to take advantage of change in Moscow to pursue disarmament and detente, Franco–German cooperation meant most of all French solidarity with Bonn's new security policy stance'. In this context, it is worth remembering Genscher's speech of September 1987 in which he argued that Germany should not leave the change in East–West relations to the superpowers, but take advantage of it, balancing it with at least an equal dynamism in European integration. In this context, he not only mentioned progress towards Monetary Union, but also cooperation in foreign and security policy. As far as security policy relations with France were concerned, it should be noted that what Genscher sought was not only to balance Germany's new *Ostpolitik*, but also to support it. At this stage, in which German unification did not yet seem to be an early prospect to anyone, France seemed prepared to continue its 'support for Germany's priorities of disarmament and detente . . .' and thus for Germany's new policies towards Gorbachov's Soviet Union.[17] In this respect, Germany had become *demandeur*.[18]

Another contributing factor was the fact that in October 1986, at the summit with Gorbachov in Reykjavik, US President Ronald Reagan had come close to bargaining away US strategic missiles. This 'could not but unite the Europeans, who were vastly disturbed to discover that such revolutionary changes in the Western security system affecting Europe could be proposed and negotiated without prior consultation.' Just as in 1978, American unpredictability in the sphere of security stimulated intensified cooperation between Germany and France. In October 1987, the West European Union – revived some years earlier on French initiative – adopted a platform pledging closer cooperation on security matters, and declaring: 'We are convinced that the construction of an integrated Europe will remain incomplete as long as it does not include security and defence.'[19] All this goes a long way to explain why Chancellor Kohl was so intent on creating a Franco–German Defence and Security Council in January 1988, and why he was flexible when the French government wished to link this to the creation, also by protocol to the Elysée Treaty, of a Franco–German Financial and Economic Council.

11.7 ASSESSMENT

In the years 1987 and 1988 the climate regarding European integration continued to improve. The economic conditions for further steps were being met, and the political motives were becoming clearer. For France, Bundesbank dominance of monetary decision-making had long been a major reason for wishing to proceed with monetary integration. French acceptance of the need for deregulation and the increased importance it attributed to market mechanisms – a global phenomenon in this period – made it accept the need for capital liberalisation. This further increased international monetary interdependence and enhanced French feeling of being dependent on Bundesbank policies. Efforts to influence those policies by proposing arrangements to make the EMS more symmetrical or by political pressure were getting nowhere. The only prospect remaining for France to influence monetary policy was to transfer monetary decision-making in Europe from the national to the european level, in other words, to create Economic and Monetary Union, establishing a European Central Bank. In 1989 President Mitterrand was explicit that this was a main motive. Explaining EMU on French radio he said:[20]

> Today the strongest currency in Europe is West Germany's . . . should we live in a mark zone where only the Germans would express themselves? . . . I would prefer an assembly, a meeting, a permanent conference of the different authorities where France could have its say on all aspects of economic policy.

For Germany, its position in the centre of Europe and its relations with Eastern Europe had long been a major reason for integration in Western Europe and thus to meet French wishes for monetary integration. This had been the case when Willy Brandt, preparing his *Ostpolitik*, had taken the initiative in 1969 for Economic and Monetary Union as an objective. It was again the case when by 1987 East–West relations showed increased flexibility, thereby offering West Germany new opportunities in its relations to the East.

On both occasions German initiatives towards the East required support in the West, and cooperation with France was one of the keys to that support. In addition, whenever doubts arose in Germany about the predictability of US security policy, under Jimmy Carter in 1978 and under Ronald Reagan after Reykjavik in 1986, the German reaction was to seek intensified security cooperation with France.

Thus, when France took the initiative in 1987–8 to revive Monetary Union, this could be regarded as part of a broader pattern of cooperation involving both economic integration (the prospect of completion of the internal market) and intensified European cooperation in the field of security and defence. Chancellor Kohl, personally far more involved in foreign and security policy than in monetary issues, was pursuing European Political Union. He had made it clear in 1985 that he regarded Monetary Union as a step towards that end (see chapter 10). It was against this background that the European Council met in Hanover in June 1988 under his chairmanship.

12 The Delors Report

By the time the European Council under Helmut Kohl's chairmanship met in Hanover on 27 and 28 June 1988, there was no doubt a group would be created to look into Economic and Monetary Union as a result of the expectations that had arisen, largely thanks to Genscher. As is so often the case with political meetings of this sort, the real issues were not discussed: why create such a group, why establish EMU, what would be its implications, and how did it relate to political integration. Instead, the European Council focused on procedure: the mandate and, even more controversial, the composition of the group to be created. The fundamental disagreements on EMU were reflected in disagreements on these procedural issues, in particular on the group's composition. A compromise was reached which, ironically, ensured its success more than anything else.

12.1 COMPOSITION AND MANDATE OF THE DELORS COMMITTEE

Genscher had proposed a group consisting of five to seven 'wise men'. In doing so he no doubt wished to prevent the competent committees in the Community – the Monetary Committee and the Committee of Central Bank Governors – being charged with the task; entrusting it to the 'monetary establishment' was likely to be in his view the best way to ensure that the initiative would be bogged down. For the British Prime Minister Margaret Thatcher, however, this was precisely the reason for opposing a group of outsiders and insisting that the Central Bank Governors be entrusted with the task. In this she mainly got her way, though a few outside personalities were added, probably to stress the difference with the Committee of Governors. Jacques Delors, President of the European Commission, was appointed chairman of the group.

In establishing the group's mandate, the European Council 're-called' that, in adopting the Single Act, the Member States of the Community had confirmed the objective of progressive realisation of Economic and Monetary Union. The Heads of State therefore decided to examine at the European Council meeting in Madrid in June 1989 the means of achieving this Union. To that end they decided to set up a committee, chaired by Delors, with 'the task of studying and proposing concrete stages leading towards this Union'. This mandate implied that the committee was not being asked to give an opinion on the desirability of EMU, but merely to make proposals on its implementation.

British Prime Minister Margaret Thatcher, who found herself in a rather isolated position in Hanover, accepted this mandate as a compromise. In his memoirs her Chancellor of the Exchequer, Nigel Lawson, is highly critical about what he calls her mishandling of Hanover. According to him, she had two objectives at the meeting: 'first and foremost', she wanted to prevent any mention of a European Central Bank in the terms of reference, while

> her secondary objective was to prevent the study group from being a committee of so-called experts. She always distrusted 'experts', whom she felt produced airy-fairy ideas unrelated to political realities; and believed that any post-Hanover study group should be composed of Central Bank Governors, who not only possessed the expertise required but could be relied upon to keep their feet on the ground... The others, when they discovered where she stood at Hanover, must have been amazed at her innocence. At any rate, after sufficiently long argument to enable her to feel that she had scored a signal success, they agreed that the study group should essentially be a Committee of the Community's Central Bank Governors... but that the chairman should be, of all people, Jacques Delors.

Avoiding all mention of a European Central Bank in the terms of reference was meaningless, Lawson rightly thought, since Monetary Union already implied that in everyone's opinion but hers. Nor could she have prevented mention of the latter at Hanover,

> having sold the pass over EMU and the Single European Act in 1985... but she could have avoided the disaster of having Jacques Delors as the committee's chairman, or even as one of its members. Any number of independent experts would have been better than that, and nothing could have been worse than that.[1]

She counted mainly on Bank of England Governor Robin Leigh-Pemberton and 'the sceptical Herr Pöhl (the Bundesbank President) . . . to put a spoke in the wheel of this particular vehicle of European integration.'[2] As she explained in her memoirs, 'Herr Pöhl we considered strongly hostile to any serious loss of monetary autonomy for the Bundesbank and Robin Leigh-Pemberton was in no doubt about the strength of our views.'[3] However, it so happened that the part she intended Pöhl to play was precisely the one he had in mind for her. At the Nederlandsche Bank, we shared Thatcher's misgivings about 'wise men' and preferred the competent committees in the Community to be charged with the studies. When, to our surprise, this was not supported by Pöhl, I asked my German counterpart Gleske for an explanation. He replied that Pöhl did not mind 'wise men' making unrealistic proposals, which would no doubt be rejected by Britain without him having to say no yet again.[4]

Lawson was probably right in thinking that, both from her point of view and his, Thatcher's biggest mistake in Hanover had been to accept Delors as chairman of the group, though not quite for the reasons he gives. In his view, because of Delors' position and prestige, any proposals associated with him were bound to have an impact that other proposals would not, and these would be automatically assured of the European Commission's support. In my view, it was not this that mattered. What really mattered was that Delors was a consummate politician who had a policy vision and the capacity to spot opportunities. Thatcher, focusing on what she wanted to prevent, agreed to a group mainly consisting of central bankers because she calculated that they would never agree on schemes that would bring Monetary Union nearer.[5] Delors, focusing on what he wanted to achieve, saw the opportunities that arose if a group of this composition did agree: not because he happened to be the chairman, but because they happened to be the Central Bank Governors, embodying the Community's monetary establishment. Any scheme regarding EMU which they agreed to was bound to create a political impact.

12.2   THE REQUIREMENT OF UNANIMITY

Delors is likely to have realised from the start that in order to have the impact he desired his committee's report had to be virtually unanimous. In other words, the participating Governors had to agree on the substance of the main issues. These issues, as stated before, were not about whether in their opinion Monetary Union was desirable or likely to be realised in the foreseeable future. Such questions had purportedly been settled by the Heads of Governments themselves in their terms of reference, confirming the progressive realisation of Economic and Monetary Union. The question the Governors really had to agree upon was what EMU would have to be like in order to be acceptable and sustainable. It was to that end that the mandate asked the committee to make proposals.

In the committee, Bundesbank President Pöhl was in a crucial position. This was not because of his scepticism, on which Prime Minister Thatcher counted so much. Unlike British eurosceptics, Pöhl was not opposed to EMU, but as he later wrote, he was sceptical whether governments, parliaments and ultimately the population really accepted its implications. His scepticism was not lessened by the Hanover mandate endorsing EMU, to which – 'surprisingly', as he writes – Prime Minister Thatcher had agreed despite her well-known rejection. He probably realised that she expected him to pull the political chestnuts out of the fire for her, and writes that his first reaction was to decline participation since he expected a conflict of interests, a concern 'that turned out to be only too justified'. He finally accepted, however, because 'only when the President of the Bundesbank participated could the German view be represented with the necessary weight.'[6] Once he did participate his scepticism could only encourage him to spell out the implications of EMU as clearly as possible in the committee's report. For Pöhl, the root of the matter was that Monetary Union was only sustainable, and therefore only acceptable, if monetary policy were entrusted to a European Central Bank as independent from politics and as committed to price stability as the Bundesbank, if there would be parallelism between monetary and economic integration, and if there would be a commitment to that objective from the start, rather than a series of small steps without a clearly agreed objective. Pöhl could not be expected to agree to any report which was unclear on any of these points.

As far as parallelism between monetary and economic integration was concerned, the committee's task was facilitated by the fact that it could build on the Werner Committee's Report on Economic and Monetary Union produced two decades earlier (see chapter 4). Parallelism had been one of its main principles and it was not seriously contested in the Delors Committee. As discussed earlier, the acceptance of the final objective, though giving rise to discussions, really followed from the mandate. Under these circumstances, the most difficult point that had to be agreed upon was the issue of Central Bank independence and the primacy of price stability. Probably few Governors disagreed with this in their heart – in as far as central bankers are supposed to have one – but that is not the same thing as central bankers lacking independence to agree on a report to their governments making this a main issue.

The Central Bank Governors had been appointed members of the Delors Committee in their personal capacity. Yet not all Governors felt they could function in the committee without close consultations with their governments. We know from Nigel Lawson's memoirs that Governor Robin Leigh-Pemberton discussed the line he should follow in the committee both with the Chancellor and with the Prime Minister. There are reasons to believe that Banque de France Governor Jacques de Larosière also consulted his Government.[7]

By the end of the year at the latest Delors must have concluded that in order to get a unanimous report its main feature had to be the independence of a European Central Bank committed to price stability as its primary objective. This follows from a public statement he made at the beginning of January 1989:

> There will not be an Economic and Monetary Union in Europe as it exists at the moment with our partners being what they are unless ... the European system of central banks has an independence comparable to the Bundesbank vis-à-vis the German government.[8]

To obtain agreement on this, it was essential to get French consent. After all, France was the driving force behind Monetary Union. Once France agreed, it would be easier for the governors of other countries to follow suit. For France, this cannot have been an easy decision. An independent Central Bank was at variance with French centralist tradition. It wanted to pursue a European Central Bank so as to be able to influence monetary decision-making. Would not an independent Central Bank with price stability as its primary objective defy the purpose? It is here that Delors' chairmanship of the committee is likely to have made all the difference. Nobody in Paris could have been in a better position to argue the importance of obtaining a unanimous report. His task was probably facilitated by the fact that in May 1988 the first period of *cohabitation* had come to an end. The Chirac government was replaced by that of Rocard, with Pierre Bérégovoy succeeding Balladur as Finance Minister. This reinforced Mitterrand's position, and according to French sources he overruled Bérégovoy's objections.[9]

Two considerations may have encouraged French consent. First, Central Bank independence is not in practice established by a 'declaration of independence' by itself, but by the details of legal provisions. These would be discussed only at a later stage, when the statutes of the European Central Bank were drawn up. At such a time there would be plenty of chances to fight another battle, as indeed France was to do, and even if it was not won, it would result in compromise texts that would have to be interpreted at a still later stage. Second, while the third and final stage of EMU as described in the report clearly reflected the German (and Dutch) view, the second stage was far more ambiguous, since the presidents of the creditor central banks could hardly expect the whole report to present only their view. Governor De Larosière even insisted on incorporating a proposal to establish in the first stage a European Reserve Fund 'that would foreshadow the future European System of Central Banks' and would be allowed to intervene in the exchange market.[10] Though deemed 'not opportune at this stage' by others, the latter did not reject the possibility to establish a European Central Bank of sorts in the second stage on the basis of an amended Treaty. This must have appealed in particular to Finance Minister Bérégovoy, who even in public statements did not hide his scepticism regarding the prospects of a European Central Bank, which he regarded as at best a long term aim, but urged common action in the exchange market in the short run.[11] In view of these considerations, the French authorities may well have concluded that they had more to gain from the momentum a unanimous report from this group was bound to create, than to lose by agreeing to the German view at the third stage.

12.3 THE REPORT'S CONTENTS

The Report on Economic and Monetary Union in the European Community, as the Delors Report was officially called, was published on 17 April 1989. The essence of it is summarised below.

Parallelism

Economic and Monetary Union, according to the report, implied

> the need for a *transfer of decision-making power* from Member
> States to the Community as a whole ... in the fields of mon-
> etary policy and macroeconomic management. A Monetary Union
> would require a single monetary policy and responsibility for the
> formulation of this policy would consequently have to be vested
> in one decision-making body. In the economic field a wide range
> of decisions would remain the preserve of national and regional
> authorities. However ... such decisions would have to be placed
> within an agreed macroeconomic framework and be subject to
> binding procedures and rules. This would permit the determina-
> tion of an overall policy stance for the Community as a whole,
> avoid unsustainable differences between individual member coun-
> tries in public-sector borrowing requirements and place binding
> constraints on the size and the financing of budget deficits.[12]

Economic Union and Monetary Union form *two integral parts
of a single whole* and would therefore have to be implemented in
parallel.[13]

The report rejected the view that Monetary Union without Economic Union might be sufficient, due to market forces, provided
misbehaving authorities were not baled out when in difficulties: 'The
constraints imposed by market forces might either be too slow and
weak or too sudden and disruptive. Hence countries would have to
accept that sharing a common market and a single currency area
imposed policy constraints.'[14]

Central Bank Independence

'The ESCB (European System of Central Banks) Council should
be independent of instructions from national governments and
Community authorities ...' The System would be committed to the
objective of price stability; subject to the foregoing, the System
should support the general economic policy set at the Community
level by the competent bodies.[15]

A Single Process

In order to meet German concerns, the report made it clear that the proposals made for the early stages were meant to be steps towards Monetary Union, and not just made for their own sake:

> The Committee agreed that the *creation of an Economic and Monetary* Union must be viewed as a single process. Although this process is set out in stages which guide the progressive movement to the final objective, the decision to enter upon the first stage should be a decision to embark upon the entire process.[16]
>
> One procedure would be to conclude *a new Treaty for each stage* ... if this procedure were chosen it would be crucial that the first Treaty laid down clearly the principal features of the ultimate objective of Economic and Monetary Union.[17]

Other Points

In addition to these main points, the report contained a number of minor points worth mentioning.

> Community policies in the regional and structural field would be necessary in order to promote an optimum allocation of resources and to spread welfare gains throughout the Community. If sufficient consideration were not given to regional imbalances, the Economic Union would be faced with grave economic and political risks ...
>
> Wage flexibility and labour mobility are necessary to eliminate differences in competitiveness in different regions and countries in the Community... In order to reduce adjustment burdens temporarily, it might be necessary in certain circumstances to provide financing flows through official channels.[18]

Here, very cautiously, the report hints at the problem of adjustment once exchange rate changes are no longer possible, and suggests that official transfers might then become inevitable.

In paragraph 47, the concept of 'a parallel currency strategy', so dear to the hearts of academics in particular, is rejected. Clearly, the Central Bank Governors did not think integrating twelve currencies would become easier by adding a thirteenth.[19]

In paragraph 44 the possibility of various speeds is mentioned: 'Pending the full participation of all member countries – which is of prime importance – influence on the management of each set of arrangements would have to be related to the degree of participation by Member States.'

On only one point was the Committee not unanimous. In paragraph 53 'a number of Committee members' advocated the creation of a European Reserve Fund at an early stage 'that would foreshadow the future European System of Central Banks'. This Fund would manage pooled reserves and intervene on the exchange markets.

In its report, the Committee distinguished three stages. The first stage would begin on 1 July 1990. This was possible since it only contained closer cooperation and no new institutions which, according to Article 102A of the Treaty, would fall under the procedure stipulated in Article 236 and require a new Treaty. It was the only date proposed in the report. The second stage would start once the new Treaty was in force and new institutions could therefore be established, while conditions for EMU were not yet met and national currencies would continue to exist. The third and final stage would be the introduction of EMU.

12.4 ASSESSMENT

The Delors Report had considerable impact on further developments. It helped to create a momentum that made possible the conclusion of the Maastricht Treaty, and only started to dissipate during the ratification process. It is most unlikely that a divided report would have had a similar impact, or for that matter an unanimous one in which differences on the major issues had been papered over. This Delors realised. He must also have realised at an early stage that unanimity would only be possible if an independent European Central Bank, with price stability as its main objective, were at the core of the report. Therefore he accepted this concept and helped to make it acceptable, notably in France.

At the Nederlandsche Bank, after our initial surprise, we gradually realised what Delors' strategy was: at times it almost seemed not really to matter to him what the report said about EMU, notably its final stage, as long as it was unanimous. This placed us in a dilemma that must have been felt even more acutely by Bundesbank

President Pöhl. A unanimous report would create political momentum, and once that effect took hold it was far from certain whether events would follow the path prescribed in the report. Political compromises were likely, and these could well mean concrete steps towards a single currency without more than lip service to the conditions that according to the report had to be fulfilled to make it possible. We at the Nederlandsche Bank remembered only too well from the last Intergovernmental Conference how difficult it had been for us to influence even the attitude of our own government at that stage. Yet such misgivings about what might happen once the report was delivered could not justify a refusal to agree to a report spelling out the implications of EMU in a way that reflected our views.

13 British Opposition

The Delors Report received considerable attention in the international press. For some time it dominated the discussion on European integration, in particular during the run up to the European Council Meeting due to take place in Madrid in June 1989. Feelings in member states were mixed. In France, there was a feeling – shared by Finance Minister Bérégovoy – that the report, with its emphasis on price stability and an independent European Central Bank, reflected the German view too much. In Germany there was also uneasiness – shared by Finance Minister Gerhard Stoltenberg as well as at the Bundesbank – since it was doubted whether member states really agreed on the principles laid down in the report, while the report could nevertheless turn out to be a major step towards EMU. Yet the objective of EMU itself was neither really contested in these countries, nor in most other member states. This was different in the United Kingdom. Here the government was adamantly opposed to Economic and Monetary Union, but it realised that development towards it was gathering momentum. In plotting its course to counter this development, Britain was hampered not only by its isolated position, but also by deep divisions within the Cabinet; from now on Europe was becoming a focus for discord within the ruling Conservative Party which would dominate it in future years.

13.1 BRITISH REACTION TO THE REPORT

The British government's reception of the unanimous Delors Report was hostile. When in his memoirs Nigel Lawson called Delors a disaster as chairman of the committee, this of course reflected how he felt about the committee's report. These feelings are understandable in view of his opposition to EMU and in the light of the role EMU has since played in British politics in general and the Conservative party in particular. Yet if his feelings are understandable, the criticism levelled at the report is less so. According to Lawson's description of the series of meetings at Number 10 with the Governor of the Bank of England, the action they urged on him was

> to assemble the widest possible opposition within the committee both to any early Treaty amendment required to achieve the full EMU objective espoused by Delors, and to anything that smacked of a recommendation to take any particular course of action: the committee's role should be confined to saying that *if* you wanted to achieve x, *then* you would need to do y.[1]

In Margaret Thatcher's words:

> Our line was that the report should be limited to a descriptive not a prescriptive document. But we hoped that paragraphs would be inserted which would make it clear that EMU was in no way necessary to the completion of the Single Market and which would enlarge upon the full implications of EMU for the transfer of power and authority from national institutions to a central bureaucracy.[2]

Both seemed to forget the terms of reference to which the British Prime Minister herself had felt she had to agree. It was the Heads of Government who said EMU was the objective and who had entrusted to the committee 'the task of studying and proposing concrete stages leading towards this Union'.[3] This is precisely what the committee did. And in doing so, it did 'enlarge upon the full implication of EMU'. Oddly, it was this that Nigel Lawson at the time singled out for special criticism. It is odd since it was the Chancellor himself who, a few months before the completion of the report, had spelled out the implications of EMU. In a speech at Chatham House on 25 January 1989 he said:

> Nor would individual countries be able to retain responsibility for fiscal policy. With a single European monetary policy there would need to be central control over the size of the budget deficits and, particularly, over their financing.[4]

But when the Delors Report in effect confirmed this, Lawson turned on it. In June he said:

> The report is totally flawed here ... the common currency does not, in my judgement, require of itself ... the control of the

budgetary and fiscal policies of the varying Member States ... To make a Monetary Union work what you need is basically a simple rule that if any member country gets itself excessively into debt by borrowing too much, then there will be a clear understanding of no bailing out; but there is nothing further you need.[5]

In his memoirs he admits these contradictions, though suggesting that when he called the report 'totally flawed' this only referred to its purportedly saying that there had to be 'a huge transfer of resources from the centre to the periphery'.[6] He solved his inconsistencies by concluding that 'both views on this tricky issue were probably correct: my second thoughts were certainly right in theory, but my first thoughts were probably closer to the mark in practice.'[7] It is more likely that his first thoughts, published before the report was finalised, were meant to scare people off EMU when he still hoped that this might work, while the second thoughts were more in the nature of damage limitation once a single currency seemed to have become a real prospect as a result of the Delors Report's impact. The Prime Minister herself never felt the need for such vagaries, always maintaining that a single currency meant the loss of national sovereignty. She blamed the report, not for saying it too, but for not condemning it. Given the terms of reference to which she herself had agreed, this was not quite fair.

13.2 THATCHER'S OPTIONS

With the approach of the European Council Meeting in Madrid in June, where the Delors Report was to be discussed, the United Kingdom Government had to set out the course it would follow. Given its isolation in its total rejection of EMU, this would not have been easy in the best of circumstances. In essence, Britain had three options:

- It could fully utilise the requirement of consensus, making clear from the outset that it would not allow the Treaty to be amended to incorporate EMU as an objective.
- It could opt for a 'variable geometry' approach, meaning that Treaty references to EMU as an objective could not be binding, leaving Member States free to decide at a later stage whether they would 'opt in'.

– It could try to exploit the existing differences between the other Member States, notably between France and Germany, in order to delay developments and water down commitments.

Nigel Lawson, criticising Thatcher's policies in his memoirs, complains about 'just how counter-productive and damaging to the United Kingdom's interests her tactics were. For her, unanimity meant she had a veto; and if you had a veto you used it. It was as simple as that.'[8] In fact, it was not that simple. The facts are that where EMU was concerned she postponed confrontation as long as she could. In 1985, she accepted the incorporation in the Single European Act, and thus in the Rome Treaty, of references to EMU, ambiguous as the wording was. Lawson regarded this 'a fateful step': 'having sold the pass over EMU and the Single European Act in 1985, the committee set up at Hanover could scarcely have had terms of reference that led to a different destination.'[9] Then, in Hanover in June 1988, she allowed herself to be pushed one step further down the slope, by agreeing to a mandate for the Delors Group that referred to the ambiguous wording in the Single European Act as an unambiguous commitment to EMU. In Madrid, she would once again avoid confrontation. It was only at the very last European Council Meeting she attended, in Rome in October 1990, that she felt it could no longer be delayed.

There were several reasons for this cautious attitude, which was so at odds with her character as well as with the general perception of the facts. First, she was enough of a politician to perceive the limits of a veto if you are really isolated. As she later wrote herself: 'We could, of course, look to the veto, to legal safeguards, and to declared exemptions. In the future, however, these would increasingly be circumvented where they were not overthrown entirely.'[10] Second, external confrontation required internal unity. She was aware of this even when she was at her most strident, at the time she 'wanted her money back':

Unfortunately, there was a hard core of Euro-enthusiasts on the Tory back-benches who instinctively supported the Community in any dispute with Britain. Though a clear minority, they robbed us of the advantage of unity. So as on previous occasions, I decided not to go down the path of withholding contributions.[11]

That was 1984. By 1988, it was no longer a clear minority of back-benchers but her Foreign Secretary and her Chancellor of the Exchequer she had to contend with, and both opposed a head-on confrontation. As Geoffrey Howe would put it later in his resignation speech:

> The risk is not imposition (of a single currency on Britain) but isolation. The real threat is that of leaving ourselves with no say in the monetary arrangements that the rest of Europe chooses for itself, with Britain once again scrambling to join the club later, after the rules have been set and after the power has been distributed by others to our disadvantage. That would be the worst possible outcome.[12]

With a divided Cabinet, she could not afford external confrontation, and when she felt she could no longer postpone it, it spelled the end of her prime ministership. Howe, who did more than anyone to trigger it, wrote in reviewing her memoirs:

> In late October 1990, she allowed what we had avoided at Madrid to occur in Rome – total isolation on EMU. She did it by saying 'never' and refusing to negotiate. I was deeply concerned by the 11–1 outcome. I was shocked by her cavalier announcement to the media afterwards that we would simply veto any EMU Treaty others negotiated.[13]

Since the prospects for the United Kingdom to effectively veto EMU looked poor, some form of 'variable geometry' seemed an obvious option to consider. This, apparently, was not done seriously before the spring of 1990. By then John Major had succeeded Nigel Lawson as Chancellor of the Exchequer. Having been startled by the determination of his EC colleagues to push on with a Treaty for EMU regardless of British opposition, he recommended working for a Treaty that would contain the definition of EMU and its necessary institutions, but leaving member states free to decide when to 'opt in'. The Prime Minister used to say, if others want to have a single currency, let them! But this did not mean that she was prepared to do anything to make it possible: how could she, if what they wanted was all wrong. It merely meant that she was prepared to take the risk that others would resort to a separate Treaty to establish EMU. 'But anyone who does not sound the alarm on seeing great nations in headlong pursuit of disastrous goals is grossly irresponsible – and indeed a bad European.' Thus, she rejected the option recommended by Major, noting in her memoirs that 'it was already clear that he was thinking in terms of compromises which would not be acceptable to me and that intellectually he was drifting with the tide.'[14]

The option that remained was to make use of the differences that existed between the other countries, notably between Germany and France, in order to delay Treaty amendment and water down any commitments regarding EMU. This is what the Prime Minister tried to do: for instance in 1985 she tried to prevent the incorporation of a 'monetary dimension' in the Treaty by joint German–British opposition, and she also hoped that the German and British Central Bank Governors would not agree to a unanimous report by the Delors Committee. It should be noted that in these cases there was no question in her mind of any German–British 'deal' with mutual give and take. She merely expected the two countries to prevent jointly what each of them opposed. Here she miscalculated. Kohl certainly did not oppose EMU, and even Pöhl – despite his misgivings – did not. Thus they were willing to enter into deals with others, provided their concerns were met. Lawson and Howe also wanted to make use of the differences between other countries, but though joining Thatcher in her criticism of the Germans for not playing the part they were expected to play, they felt that the Prime Minister's attitude was not conducive to bring this about. In their view Britain could only play its part if it made an effort to win the confidence of its partners by a more positive tone in general and by joining the ERM in particular. On the latter, the Prime Minister could not disagree more. Exchange rate obligations, advocated by Lawson even apart from tactical considerations, violated her strongly held monetarist views: 'you cannot buck the market, or the market will ultimately buck you!' Lawson's argument that the ERM would provide decision-making with a much needed external discipline merely added insult to injury: she did not need the Bundesbank to impose discipline on British decision-making.[15] Finally, she did not believe – probably correctly – the argument that by entering into the ERM, Britain would be able to diminish pressure for EMU; on the contrary, she felt that the ERM was increasingly regarded as a first step towards EMU.[16]

But here, whatever the merits of the case, she faced a major problem. As she herself admitted in her memoirs, regarding ERM 'I knew that I was in a very small minority in the Cabinet on this matter.'[17] She did not feel that in this major policy issue the majority view should be decisive, but wanted her own view to prevail. This could not fail to affect government decision-making in general, at least where its European policy was concerned. She tended to avoid collective decision-making and deal with the Cabinet ministers concerned, if at all, on a one-to-one basis. When, just before the Madrid European Council, her Foreign Secretary and her Chancellor of the Exchequer insisted on seeing her together, she regarded this as a kind of coup; this was soon to cost the Foreign Secretary his job, and ultimately his resignation from the Cabinet was the trigger for her own demise.

With the Prime Minister outnumbered on the issue of entry into the ERM, Lawson and Howe increased the pressure during the run up to the Madrid European Council. They were instrumental in inviting Dutch Prime Minister Ruud Lubbers, 'the closest thing to an ally Margaret had within the Community'[18], and 'one of the few European statesmen whose company Margaret almost enjoyed',[19] for a kind of seminar at Chequers. Lubbers was accompanied by Foreign Minister Hans van den Broek and Finance Minister Onno Ruding. As the latter later told Dutch Central Bank President Duisenberg, when the report was mentioned during the discussion, Thatcher turned on her Dutch guests and denounced the whole thing as a socialist plot. 'Delors: a socialist! Pöhl: a socialist! And your Central Bank Governor: isn't he a socialist too?' Duisenberg delightedly spread the story, including Michel Camdessus, Managing Director of the IMF. Camdessus said: 'Somehow, I always have some difficulty seeing you as a socialist!' Duisenberg, slightly miffed exclaimed: 'Why, I am not less of a socialist than Karl Otto (Pöhl)!' To which Camdessus replied: 'That is a pretty low standard!'[20] The real purpose of the Chequers seminar, selling the ERM to the Prime Minister, was not successful. As Ruding later told me, when he finally got around to expose his arguments why Britain should join, the lady kept interrupting him, so that finally he gave up.[21]

On the eve of the Madrid Summit where the Delors Report was to be discussed, neither the Foreign Secretary – who was to accompany her – nor the Chancellor of the Exchequer knew what position she would take. They asked to see her jointly twice, to which she agreed with extreme reluctance, and both threatened to resign unless she would enter into a definitive commitment for the United Kingdom to join the ERM in the not-too-distant future. Though seething, and determined never to let this happen again, she realised that she could not afford to let them resign jointly. Thus while not giving them any indication what she intended to do at the meeting, once in Madrid she gave a more definitive commitment on ERM than she had up until then, stopping short of mentioning a date – as they had wished her to do – and emphasising this fact afterwards. At the same time, she surprised the meeting by the moderation with which she expressed her views on the Delors Report, yet again postponing a confrontation.

13.3 ASSESSMENT

The objective of British policy in this period was not merely to avoid any United Kingdom commitment to EMU, but to prevent other EC countries from committing themselves, and therefore to prevent any substantive incorporation of EMU in the Treaty. Since in this respect Britain was isolated, this would have been difficult to achieve in the best of circumstances. As it was deep internal divisions – including the Cabinet, and in particular between the Prime Minister and the two Cabinet Ministers most concerned – made it even more difficult.

Fundamentally, the disagreement concerned the Prime Minister's general attitude towards (continental) Europe, which many of her colleagues did not share. Her heart was set on the special relationship with the United States. There she accepted the give and take a close relationship requires. With Europe she did not. Often, she did not bother to hide her distaste, whether in private – 'they are all a rotten lot' she told Roy Jenkins, then President of the European Commission, referring to her European colleagues[22] – or later in her memoirs, where less flattering references abound. About the Italians, she said 'as always . . . it was difficult throughout to distinguish confusion from guile: but plenty of both was evident.'[23] She spoke of 'Gallic bluff' with reference to the French.[24] And, in more general terms, to 'that un-British combination of high-flown rhetoric and pork-barrel politics which passed for European statesmanship.'[25]

Her emotions probably made it even more difficult for her to take seriously her partners' intention to establish EMU:

We . . . were inclined to dismiss such rhetoric as cloudy and unrealistic aspirations which had no prospect of being implemented. We were correct in believing them to be lacking in realism; where we were mistaken was in underestimating the determination of some European politicians to put them into effect.[26]

Given that determination, it is doubtful – whatever tactical mistakes she may have committed – that she could have stopped them. She might have taken the risk – as she suggests in her memoirs she would have – to force them to establish EMU on the basis of a separate Treaty, counting on the Germans to shrink back from such a step, and more generally bringing 'our Community partners up against the harsh realities which would make them think twice.'[27] But it was not without reason that, while in office, she kept postponing such a confrontation.

Had she tried might the general 'opt in' option, sparing Britain the isolation later embodied in the Maastricht Treaty, have been achievable? Since it would have implied a watering down of the commitment of all member states to the final objective of EMU, it would have violated one of the fundamental recommendations of the Delors Report, stating 'that the creation of an Economic and Monetary Union must be seen as a single process' and that 'the decision to enter upon the first stage should be a decision to embark on the entire process.'[28] For the Bundesbank, this early commitment to EMU was essential to ensure that the prospect of EMU at some future stage was not merely a ploy to erode its autonomy at present. The Nederlandsche Bank firmly supported its view, and I was surprised to read in Lawson's memoirs that during the Chequers Seminar with the Dutch, Prime Minister Lubbers allegedly said that 'The Netherlands preferred ... to proceed step-by-step and gauge exactly what was needed at each stage rather than opt at the outset for amendments to the Treaty of Rome.'[29] One of the main British objections against the Delors Report concerned precisely this single process issue. Trying the 'opt in' option would therefore have had some logic, and had it happened at an early stage, it would probably have caused confusion in the ranks of the other Member States. They might have considered some compromise language if the alternative had been the threat of a British veto to Treaty amendment. But Prime Minister Thatcher was too much of a crusader to consider such tactics. She also feared that if EMU was incorporated in the Treaty, Britain might finally be sucked in, whatever the Treaty language was. Finally, this option, and notably the threat to veto alternatives, also required internal unity to make it credible; one may wonder whether by this stage she would have been able to acquire it. She was unlikely to do what more calculating politicians might have done in similar circumstances: try to link their colleagues (if they could not get rid of them) with their policies and, by involving them in the preparation and by making token concessions, present their policies as common policies. But she went to the other extreme. In order to be heard during the preparation of the European Council Meeting in Madrid, the Foreign Secretary and the Chancellor of the Exchequer almost had to gate-crash. And while she felt she could not avoid taking their views into account, her main worry seemed to be to pretend that she had not done this, emphasising that her will had prevailed. Thus in her relations with her European colleagues Thatcher made them feel that her mind was set on obstruction, while in her relations with her Cabinet colleagues she made them feel they were being ignored.

The option that remained under these circumstances was an uncoordinated rearguard action, with the aim of dividing the other member states but with little to offer to strike deals with any of them. Since the Prime Minister was outnumbered on the issue of British entry into the ERM, this became the only negotiable element in the United Kingdom's European position. It thus acquired a major political significance, rendering a political deal inevitable in the end. In practice this meant that Britain would accept ERM participation, although not its implications. From here, there is an almost direct link to Black Wednesday. For the ERM the consequences were serious. For Britain's ruling Conservative Party, it was even worse.

14 The Madrid Summit (June 1989) and its Follow-up

At the European Council meeting in Madrid in June 1989 two decisions had to be taken. One was to adopt the Delors Report as a basis for further negotiations. In view of its unanimity, this was largely a foregone conclusion, but British opposition caused some difficulty with the wording. It had to be a compromise, stating that '(t)he European Council considered that the report . . . fulfilled the mandate given in Hanover.' The other decision concerned the procedure to be followed and the timing of the negotiations. France, supported by the Commission and by the Mediterranean countries, wished to put the procedure under time pressure: the Intergovernmental Conference, prescribed for Treaty amendments, should start as soon as possible. The German Government, though favourable to Economic and Monetary Union, dragged its feet. The ruling coalition was facing adverse opinion polls and Chancellor Kohl did not wish to thwart his prospects by provoking a public controversy on EMU during the election campaign. He therefore preferred to delay the start of the Intergovernmental Conference. In working for delay, he was supported by the Bundesbank, who did not want the negotiations to take place under time pressure, and by the British, who welcomed any delay. The disagreement was papered over by the formula that the 'conference would meet once the first stage had begun (on 1st July 1990) and would be preceded by full and adequate preparation'.

In the months that followed, dramatic events started to unfold that would soon dominate the German position: the sudden prospect of early German unification, described in the next chapter (15). One week after the fall of the Berlin wall in November 1989, Kohl agreed to start the IGC before the end of 1990. Before then, 'full and adequate preparation' had to be completed. An important stage in this preparation was the meeting of the European Council in Rome on 27 and 28 October 1990. Here the substance of (the third stage of) Economic and Monetary Union was agreed, as well as the date on which the second stage would start: 1 January 1994. It was confirmed that both IGCs (on EMU and on Political Union) would start on 14 December 1990. Britain dissented.

14.1 TIMING AND SUBSTANCE

In the period following the Madrid Summit of June 1989, the following dates were important:

- In September, the informal Ecofin in Antibes charged a High Level Working Group under the presidency of Elisabeth Guigou with the task of compiling a list of questions to be tackled during the IGC.
- The Group presented its report in October.[1] As far as the French were concerned, this was full and adequate preparation for the IGC.
- On 8–9 December, the European Council established that there was a required majority to call the Intergovernmental Conference and that it would start before the end of 1990.
- In April 1990, in a letter to the Heads of Government, Chancellor Kohl and President Mitterrand called for two parallel IGCs: one for EMU and one for Political Union (Dublin I).
- In June, the European Council agreed on the date for the start of both IGCs (Dublin II).
- In October, the European Council formulated the main characteristics of the final phase and fixed the time path to be followed, with Britain dissenting. The start of the second stage was fixed on 1 January 1994, while that of the Intergovernmental Conferences on 14 December 1990 was confirmed (Rome I).

It would be outside the scope of this study to discuss in detail the negotiations leading to the Maastricht Treaty, which in effect started in the Delors Committee and continued even during the European Council Meeting in Maastricht itself in December 1991. The negotiations are analysed from the German perspective by Schönfelder and Thiel, and from the Italian perspective by Bini-Smaghi, Padoa-Schioppa and Papadia.[2] In this chapter I shall focus on the main controversies – procedural, institutional and substantial – that have a bearing on the issue of timing.

As I stated in Chapter 11, the main motive for France to revive EMU – or, to be more precise, the establishment of a European Central Bank – was the desire to transfer monetary policy decisions from the national to the European level, thus hoping to end its dependence on Bundesbank decisions. It followed from this motive that for France – supported in particular by Italy and by the Commission – the establishment of a European Central Bank was not a far-off prospect that would follow a gradual process of integration, but a primary objective to be realised as early as possible. Clearly, in particular after Article 102A had been incorporated into the Treaty as a result of the European Single Act, this could only be achieved by amending the Treaty. France therefore wanted to start the Intergovernmental Conference – necessary for a change in the Treaty – as soon as possible, and establish a European Central Bank as early as feasible after the new Treaty had come into force, without waiting for the central rates to be permanently fixed and the single currency to be introduced. The question of timing and the contents of the transitional – or second – stage were therefore linked.

Italy shared the French position. It was true that this would mean establishing a European Central Bank while monetary decision-making still remained the responsibility of the national authorities. But, as Bini-Smaghi *et al.* were later to argue, this would follow 'the traditional EC approach of giving the planned institution an active task in the pursuit of the agreed goal, adopting the Community method of supranationality and institutional strength as the motor of transition.' It was 'the method by which the Community had been successfully built in the past, that is, by entrusting the powers to implement integration to common institutions rather than to weak mechanisms of voluntary cooperation.'[3]

The German and Dutch monetary authorities strongly opposed establishing a European Central Bank long before it would be entrusted with what was its *raison d'être*, the conduct of monetary policy. On the one hand they wanted to avoid the risk of blurring competences for monetary policy and creating grey areas, thereby restricting the freedom of action of the Bundesbank in particular. On the other hand they feared that an ECB having a rather shadowy position at this stage could not subsequently convert itself into the strong institution they wanted in the final stage. Bini-Smaghi *et al.* had a point when arguing that establishing an ECB before giving it central bank competences would have been in line with EC tradition, but we felt it would be undesirable to follow that tradition where monetary competences were concerned. As I put it at the time:

> There is a certain analogy between an ECB in the second stage and the way in which the European Parliament has been established without real parliamentary powers. A lacklustre performance is the inevitable result, in its turn not necessarily an encouragement to give it more powers.[4]

These, and other, considerations were captured in the phrase that the new institution should not be an 'empty shell'. Bini-Smaghi *et al.* note regretfully that

> the German and Dutch delegates pressed the Monetary Committee . . . into accepting the idea that the institution should not be an 'empty shell' . . . This statement had the innocent appearance of stating the very reasonable principle that there should not be a disproportion between the design of the institution and its functions . . . the view that there should not be an empty shell was subsequently developed to mean that the name 'Central Bank' should be attributed to the monetary institution only after it had been given the full prerogatives of a central bank, that is, on the verge of passage to the third stage, and that no real powers should be given to the institution before that stage.

The Italian presidency attempted to force the issue at the European Council Meeting in Rome in October 1990, exploiting the absence of monetary authorities at such meetings, and succeeded in incorporating into the final statement the phrase: 'At the start of the second phase, the new Community institution will be established.' Earlier, describing Monetary Union in the final phase, the statement referred to the creation of 'a new monetary institution comprising Member States' central banks and a central organ, exercising full responsibility for monetary policy', clearly meaning a European Central Bank. This was therefore a major concession on the part of Chancellor Kohl, made without consulting his own monetary authorities. By not referring to the European Central Bank explicitly, however, the wily Chancellor had left himself a loophole, just in case domestic indignation would turn out to be too strong. The importance of this wording, however, would become clear only at a later stage. At the time, the Italian Foreign

Minister made no effort to hide his jubilation when talking to the
press after the meeting, sitting

> with one of his legs curled beneath him, gesticulating as he spoke,
> repeatedly tapping the shoulder of the journalist beside him: 'It
> is . . . Kohl who has to give the position for Germany . . . No more
> Mr Pöhl, no more Mr Waigel' crowed Mr De Michelis. 'Chan-
> cellor Kohl has spoken and this is the official position.'[5]

14.2 LONG OR SHORT TRANSITIONAL STAGE

An issue already touched upon in the previous paragraph was the
nature and duration of the transitional or second stage. This stage
can be defined as the situation that would arise once the Treaty
had come into force and institutional changes were therefore possible, the obstacle of Article 102A having been removed, but central rates could still be adjusted. As long as the latter was the case,
member states agreed that ultimate responsibility for monetary policy
had to remain with the national authorities. But in the French and
the Italian view this should not prevent a European Central Bank
from gradually increasing its role in monetary policy and interventions in the currency market. Governor De Larosière's proposal to
create a European Reserve Fund even in the first stage, the only
proposal in the Delors Report that was not unanimous, went in
the same direction.

One could envisage two very different transitional stages. One
was a 'technical' second stage of brief duration. This would start
only when the final stage was in sight, and was needed only since
the establishment of a European Central Bank would require some
time. This would have been the German and Dutch preference.
When agreeing to the proposals in the Delors Report for the second stage in which the European System of Central Banks would
be set up, it was a relatively brief second stage that the German
and Dutch central bank presidents had in mind.

At the European Council Meeting in Rome in October 1990 it
was decided that the second stage would start on 1 January 1994.
Since the final stage was unlikely to begin long before the year
2000 this implied a relatively long transitional stage. For the German and Dutch monetary authorities a protracted situation of uncertainty regarding monetary competences that could arise if the

new European institution would be called Central Bank was difficult to accept. From their point of view it helped that the European Council had not explicitly called it that, but had merely referred to 'the new Community institution'. In the end, during the negotiations in the Intergovernmental Conference, member states agreed on a compromise, creating a new institution but calling it the European Monetary Institute.

14.3 ASSESSMENT

De Michelis' gloating, unwise in any circumstances, was thus in addition premature. He had failed to grasp a characteristic of decision-making on European integration. Monetary decisions taken at the highest political level have to be implemented, and therefore to be interpreted and in effect renegotiated, at the monetary level, and they are then determined by the constraints and the forces that prevail there.

There is an interesting parallel between the efforts in 1989 to introduce the European Central Bank at an early stage, and those in the early 1970s to introduce a European Monetary Fund. In both cases Germany had indicated its willingness to give up its dominant monetary position once EMU, with its concomitant safeguards for stability, was established. In each case other countries, having acknowledged this German concession, next tried to obtain it before EMU was established. Each time they were successful in getting a new institution established, but not in the shape that would have restricted the Bundesbank's freedom of action. The Bundesbank had sufficient domestic political clout to prevent this even where the Chancellor would have been ready to yield.

This is not to deny the importance of the Rome Summit of October 1990. The Italian presidency had called an extraordinary European Council Meeting to force the Intergovernmental Conference. In order to do so the basis for the negotiations had to be agreed upon. The final statement contained the essence of Economic and Monetary Union. Regarding the future European Central Bank, the agreed text stated that its prime task would be price stability, and that it would be 'independent of instructions'. Implicitly, France had conceded this point earlier when it allowed the Governor of the Banque de France to agree with the Delors Report, but it was only now that the French Government itself explicitly accepted it (though another round would still have to be fought when the Intergovernmental Conference would negotiate the language of the Treaty). Regarding Economic Union, the text was less precise, referring to 'sound and sustainable financial and budgetary conditions' as well as to the combination of price stability and growth. Though – as will become evident in the following chapters – there still was plenty to interpret, what was now agreed was a sufficient basis to start the Intergovernmental Conference. The date of its start (14 December 1990) as well as that of the second stage (1 January 1994) was now announced.

Prime Minister Thatcher's opportunities for evasive action had come to an end. As I noted in Chapter 13, she had until now avoided formally adopting a dissenting position, preferring to allow herself to be pushed down the path she rejected. Now she felt she was left no choice, and her bitterness towards the Italian presidency that was instrumental in pushing her into this corner can clearly be heard in her memoirs: 'As always with the Italians, it was difficult throughout to distinguish confusion from guile; but plenty of both was evident.' She refers to 'grandiose schemes of Monetary and Political Union with firm timetables but no agreed substance', and concludes: 'Now at Rome the ultimate battle for the future of the Community had been joined. But I would have to return to London to win another battle on which the outcome in Europe would depend – that for the soul of the Parliamentary Conservative Party.'[6]

The drama that now unfolded in British politics may go some way to explain why she had avoided a showdown over Europe for so long. Yet she might still have got away with it had it not been for the stridency with which she turned against European integration when reporting on the Rome Summit in Parliament. Her passionate 'no! no! no!' reverberating in the House of Commons made delighted eurosceptic back-benchers cheer wildly but caused increasing uneasiness with her more thoughtful followers, both outside the Cabinet and within. The show was over for the former Chancellor of the Exchequer as well as the former Foreign Secretary, Geoffrey Howe, who had been made Deputy Prime Minister. He now decided to resign. Two weeks later he rose to deliver his resignation speech to a hushed House of Commons. With Thatcher's other former Chancellor, Nigel Lawson, sitting demonstratively next to him, he held members spellbound for some twenty minutes. By the time he sat down the Prime Minister had been mortally wounded. This speech triggered the leadership contest that she could not win.

15 German Unification (1989–90)

While preparations were proceeding for the Intergovernmental Conference, dramatic events unfolded in East–West relations which would alter completely the European picture that had evolved in the wake of the Second World War. German unification, until now at most a far-off prospect, suddenly loomed large as a real possibility, and then as an event likely to take place within months rather than years. Neither the Germans nor their west European allies were prepared for this turn of events. Chancellor Kohl, feeling he was presented with an opportunity that might fade away as suddenly as it had occurred, unerringly pursued his objective to force the issue, supported by the United States. The European allies, for whom the memory of a large Germany was so much more painful than for most Americans, were thrown into confusion, unable to welcome the prospect, but also unwilling to deny Germans the right of self-determination. President Mitterrand, after some erratic gestures indicating his confusion, concluded that events were beyond his control but that he could try to ensure that they would be linked to the process of unification being prepared in the European Community. Chancellor Kohl, who could not have failed to observe how his European partners were shocked by the prospect of early German unification, concurred, emphasising at every opportunity that German and European unification were two sides of the same coin.

15.1 EXODUS

The chain reaction that would within months obliterate the East German communist regime and then the East German state, began peacefully enough during the summer holidays of 1989. East German citizens, denied the right to visit relatives in neighbouring West Germany but allowed to spend their holiday in supposedly brotherly Hungary, started to avail themselves in increasing numbers of the fact that Hungary had removed the barbed wire and watchtowers and was opening up its frontier with Austria. When Hungarian border guards half-heartedly tried to turn them back, many started to invade the West German Embassy in Budapest, and then also in Prague and elsewhere, soon creating an untenable situation. In the end, East Germany had no choice but to let its people go. The sorry spectacle of mass desertion under the nose of the deeply embarrassed but powerless communist regime was the focus of West German television, closely watched in East Germany. Many of those who did not desert now started to demonstrate against the discredited regime which, demoralised and isolated, was unable to cope with the situation and replaced the aging and ill hard-line communist boss Erich Honecker by the more pliable Egon Krenz. Two weeks later, on 1 November, Krenz saw Gorbachov in Moscow to discuss how to cope with the crisis. During the conversation, according to East German notes, Krenz pointed out

> that the stability of the country was threatened by its lack of foreign exchange. The GDR owed to the West $ 26.5 billion as of the end of 1989 and had a current account deficit for 1989 of $ 12.1 billion. The note taker recorded: 'Astonished, Comrade Gorbachov asked whether these numbers are exact. He had not imagined the situation was so precarious.' . . . East Germany had been living well beyond its means, starting in the early 1970s. If the GDR based its standard of living only on its own output, then the living standard would immediately drop by 30 per cent. . . . Gorbachov advised Krenz to tell the East German people the truth, that they had been living beyond their means.[1]

The Soviets, though willing to help, were themselves in no position to ease the economic problems. West Germany could, but set radical economic and political reforms as a condition.

Until then, even in the GDR few had known how bad the situation really was. Erich Mielke, the Minister of State Security (*Stasi*), did know. Some years earlier he called a collaborator and, not finding him at his desk, later enquired where he had been. Attending a Party lecture, said the collaborator. Did they tell you there that the GDR is bankrupt, the minister wanted to know. No, they did not, was the reply. Well, I'm telling you now![2]

With censorship lifted, the East German public now heard first hand about their former leaders' corruption and their economy's decay. The new leadership meanwhile decided to relax travel arrangements as part of the reforms it realised were inevitable. It announced this intention on 9 November, creating the impression that the frontier was already open, and East Berlin citizens turned out in great numbers at the wall – which until then they had not been allowed even to approach – to see for themselves. The frontier guards, without instructions and completely taken by surprise, let them pass. Thus the wall came tumbling down, and the way it happened robbed the new leadership of any credit for the deed.[3]

Now a new situation arose. According to West German legislation each East German citizen was entitled to West German citizenship and social services. While the East German economy was faltering, paradise beckoned at walking distance. The exodus now assumed staggering proportions, confronting the East German economy with immediate collapse and also creating massive problems for West Germany. By mid-February, the number of those who crossed the frontier since the wall opened up was put at 400 000, with an estimated further two million waiting 'with their bags packed'.[4]

Chancellor Kohl's policy since the eruption of the East German crisis had been to put the perspective of German unity back on the political agenda and to keep it there. In doing so, he had no specific timetable in mind. His time frame shortened as the pace of events quickened. When the exodus continued unabated, an emergency arose. Everyone agreed that the haemorrhage had to be stopped, and that rebuilding the wall was not the way to do it. Since no other practical remedy was offered, this opened the way for a solution that under the circumstances could only be a major step towards unification, making it necessary, rendering its implications acceptable and providing its justification: German Monetary Union.

15.2 GERMAN MONETARY UNION

It seems that the possibility of gradually establishing monetary union between the two Germanys did come up as early as December 1989 in discussions in the West German opposition Socialist Party. In the course of January it was mentioned with increasing frequency in the West German press. Whether those in favour understood the implications is another question. Bundesbank President Pöhl, in an interview with *Die Zeit* on 26 January, explained that talk of monetary union in this connection would be running ahead of events . . . If [the East German] government were to decide tomorrow to introduce the Deutsche mark, . . . then the GDR would no longer have a monetary policy or a currency of its own. The GDR's currency would thenceforth be managed from Frankfurt. Do you believe the GDR's government would accept that?

And when the journalist ventured to suggest that it might have no choice, Pöhl retorted: 'These are quite fanciful ideas.' In the same interview, Pöhl announced that he would visit his East German counterpart on 6 February. It turned out to be a historical date. While Pöhl, speaking to journalists in East Berlin, still adhered to a step by step approach, Kohl on the very same day announced his intention of proposing the introduction of monetary union with the least possible delay. The immediate objective of the proposal, formalised on 13 February, was to induce East Germans to stay home. It was a reply to slogans carried at demonstrations in Leipzig saying 'If the German mark comes we stay, If not, to meet it, we go away'.[5]

Monetary union between two such unequal partners could only mean in effect monetary annexation. The Bundesbank simply took over the East German Central Bank, and with it responsibility for monetary policy. The rate of one to one against which East German marks were to be converted into West German marks, followed by wage increases under the influence of the much higher West German wages, implied that a large part of East German industry would become uncompetitive and have to close down. Unemployment soared. The ensuing costs had to be met from the West German budget.

The public sector, in equilibrium in 1989, in the following years developed a deficit in the order of 5 per cent of the GDP.

The Bundesbank, which was very concerned about the impact of these developments on inflation and on the German mark's standing in the market, felt it could take no risks on the credibility of its policies. The government, while deciding to force the pace of German monetary union and establish the conversion rate on the basis of political considerations, disregarded the Bank's advice but made it clear that the Bundesbank's independence in pursuing a monetary policy aiming at price stability was not affected. The resulting mix of budgetary and monetary policy was to have repercussions in the EMS in 1992 and 1993, and will be discussed in Chapters 19 and 20.

Table 2 Germany[1]: the impact of unification

	1989	1990	1991	1992	1993
Extended public sector[2] deficit	0	–2.9	–4.5	–4.7	–5.2
Current account[2]	4.8	3.3	–1.1	–1.1	–0.9
Consumer price increase	2.8	2.7	3.6	5.1	4.5
Short-term interest rates	7.1	8.5	9.2	9.5	7.3

[1] Up to end-1990 West Germany only, thereafter the whole of Germany
[2] Percentage of GDP.

Source: *OECD Economic Outlook*, June 1996.

15.3 TWO SIDES OF THE SAME COIN

On 22 August 1989 Chancellor Helmut Kohl stated publicly that the German question was back on the political agenda.[6] In the months that followed he did what he could to keep it there, deftly adjusting his position and pronouncements to the gathering pace of events until exactly one year later, on the night of 22–23 August 1990, the East German Parliament voted in favour of entry into the German Federal Republic.

The opening of the Berlin wall on 9 November 1989 caught Kohl in Warsaw, as surprised as everyone else. After sizing up the new situation, he addressed the Bundestag towards the end of the month. Without consulting even his own Foreign Minister, he presented a ten point programme for German unity. Under point five he spoke of the development, after free elections in East Germany, of 'confederate structures' and, eventually, of a federal system for all Germany. After the opening of the wall and the exodus from East Germany had led to the imminent collapse of the East German economy and created an untenable situation, Kohl again made a major move. Without consulting even his own Central Bank President, on 6 February 1990 he announced his proposal for creating German monetary union as soon as possible, implying what amounted to the monetary and financial take-over of East by West Germany.[7]

The Federal Republic's constitution contained two provisions dealing with German unification. On the basis of Article 146, the two Germanys could merge, creating a new, unified state. But there was also the possibility, on the basis of Article 23, of East Germany seeking accession to the Federal Republic so that it would still legally continue to exist. As Kohl told US President George Bush at Camp David on 24–25 February, it was in the beginning of February that he decided to discard his earlier, gradual approach outlined in his ten points programme, and push for accession of East to West Germany. German monetary union, taking effect on 1 July, was to prepare the way. Looking back, Kohl may well have been right when he said to George Bush at Camp David: 'everyone is confused but me.'[8]

The main obstacle to unification, of course, was Soviet opposition. It was less determined and less consistent than it used to be, since Gorbachov had ruled out the use of force, and Soviet domination of Central Europe was crumbling. Furthermore, Soviet leadership was beset by domestic problems. It was preoccupied with *perestroika*, restructuring the economy, and by the Baltics' efforts to secede from the Soviet Union, thus threatening to set into motion a chain reaction. Clearly, internal weaknesses hampered Soviet opposition to German unification. But that did not mean that it could be ignored. For one thing, there was the Soviet military presence in East Germany. And while Gorbachov was hardly in a position to engage in a confrontation with the West, neither could the West afford to have one with him, risking that the Soviet Union – still after all a superpower – would topple Gorbachov and revert to hard-line leadership. Gorbachov himself warned of a military take-over in case of German unification.[9] For West Germany and the United States this risk was no reason to renounce unification, since they felt that Gorbachov's days might be numbered anyway, and wanted to act before the window of opportunity closed. But it was a strong reason to avoid humiliating the Soviet Union. Unification therefore required East–West agreement. For this, western unity was indispensable.

The United States was supportive on condition that a unified Germany would be a NATO member. Kohl fully agreed, though this became a major problem once Gorbachov decided to acquiesce to unification but under the opposite condition.[10] Prime Minister Thatcher was greatly disturbed by the prospect of German unification, and did not hesitate to let Gorbachov know. She also approached President Mitterrand: 'If there was any hope now of stopping or slowing down reunification it would only come from an Anglo-French initiative.'[11]

President Mitterrand shared her misgivings. He resented Kohl's ten points programme, launched without any prior Franco-German consultation, and for some time his actions seemed erratic. He paid a much publicised visit to Gorbachov in Kiev on 6 December, and on 20 December to the East German leadership. But he realised that whatever his feelings about German unification, he could not put at risk French–German cooperation, the cornerstone of French as well as German foreign policy. Therefore, he soon focused on linking German unification to European integration. In order to make sure that integration would not be delayed by events in Germany, but accelerated instead, at the meeting of the European Council in Strasbourg in December, he insisted on a decision that the Intergovernmental Conference would start not later than the end of 1990. Until then Chancellor Kohl had been dragging his feet. He was facing parliamentary elections in December 1990. Prospects for his Christian Democrat party did not look too good until after German unification, and he preferred to avoid provoking a debate on EMU before the elections.[12] But in a letter of 5 December and at Mitterrand's insistence, he now agreed, less than a month after the opening of the wall, as Mitterrand emphasises in his book on French–German relations, though the precise date of the start of the IGC would only be formally agreed at the European Council meetings in Dublin and Rome in June and October 1990 respectively.[13] Kohl in return wanted his colleagues' support for German unification.[14]

The Strasbourg European Council on 8–9 December, Kohl wrote, was the iceiest one he ever attended.[15] He was confronted by colleagues suspicious over his ten points programme and subjected to what he later called an interrogation as if by a tribunal; in her memoirs Margaret Thatcher singles out Dutch Prime Minister Ruud Lubbers for praise for what she calls his courage in opposing Kohl.[16] Kohl's reluctance – for electoral reasons, though he cited legal ones – to publicly recognise the existing Polish–German frontier at this stage further complicated matters. He did not wish to raise doubts about the permanence of the Oder–Neisse frontier. Making it an issue at that particular time, however, as some wanted, might just help the right-wing nationalist 'republicans' to pass the 5 per cent hurdle to entry into Parliament. This could endanger his own party's position, preventing him from completing reunification.[17] In the end, however, the European Council in its statement in effect confirmed the link between German unification and further European integration, though in compromise language due mainly to Thatcher's opposition to any explicit support for unification.

In the months that followed, French–German cooperation, troubled after the presentation of Kohl's ten points programme, was gradually restored. Kohl took every occasion to emphasise that German unification and European integration were two sides of the same coin. Regarding the latter, Kohl wanted to advance beyond EMU and establish political union as well. Mitterrand did not share Kohl's federalist views in this respect. But on 18 April they agreed to address a joint public letter to their colleagues proposing the start, at the end of the year, of two Intergovernmental Conferences, one dealing with EMU and the other with the establishment of a 'European Union'.[18]

15.4　ASSESSMENT

The change that caused the map of Central Europe to be redrawn could not fail to affect the process of European integration, imparting it with a new impetus and providing it with a rationale less clear until then. As early as 1987, changing East–West relations were a major factor for Germany to reintroduce EMU on the political agenda, just as almost twenty years earlier the prospective *Ostpolitik* had been an important reason for introducing it in the first place. By the end of 1989, following the dramatic events culminating in the opening of the wall, German unification had become a serious prospect, and Germany and France agreed that it should take place in the context of European integration, EMU being its most tangible manifestation. This agreement took the specific form of a common position on the start of the Intergovernmental Conference, i.e. the start of the countdown to Maastricht.

For both France and the United Kingdom the sudden emergence of an early prospect of German unification came as a shock. It is instructive to note their different reactions which were reminiscent of the way in which each reacted to the shock of the Suez crisis in 1956 that brought home to them the termination of their status as great powers. France accelerated negotiations on the European Economic Community and started on the road to French–German cooperation that would be characterised, not by the absence of differences, but by a mutual determination to overcome them. Britain loosened its ties with the Continent and became a bystander, looking on from the side-lines at the efforts to reconstruct Europe.

In 1989 the United Kingdom and France again drew very different political conclusions from a development threatening their positions. Prime Minister Thatcher tried to stop or delay German unification. Her view on foreign policy was dominated by suspicion of Germany.[19] Of Willy Brandt's *Ostpolitik* in the 1970s she felt that its 'hidden agenda . . . was German reunification on Eastern terms.'[20] Now again the prospect of unification filled her with foreboding. Since the United States was supporting it, 'the last and best hope seemed the creation of a solid Anglo-French political axis which would ensure that at each stage of reunification – and in future economic and political developments – the Germans did not have things all their own way.' Mitterrand shared her concerns, 'but his public attitude hardly betrayed his private thoughts' and though she did what she could to make him 'overcome this tendency to schizophrenia' she did not succeed.[21]

One can feel her exasperation with those statesmen who said one thing to her and did the other; with Mitterrand in 1989, and with Helmut Kohl in 1985 when she thought she could rely on him to oppose French initiatives to introduce a monetary dimension into the Single European Act, only to see him seek a compromise with the French.[22] To her, this may have confirmed the unreliability of continental politicians. In reality, more than anything else it illustrated the limitations of *ad hoc* coalitions compared with permanent ones. For both France and Germany, French–German cooperation was a cornerstone of their foreign policy, implying that neither would enter into an *ad hoc* coalition against the other on an issue really important to the other. It is true that what she proposed to Mitterrand went beyond an *ad hoc* coalition. It was a *renversement des alliances*, replacing French–German by Anglo-French cooperation. She was aware this would mean that France would have to abandon its policy of anchoring Germany into an integrating Europe. This she presented in her memoirs as a 'return to (the policy) associated with General De Gaulle – the defence of French sovereignty and the striking up of alliances to secure French interests.'[23] Here she seems to forget that it was De Gaulle who, though clinging to national sovereignty as she did, was one of the founding fathers of the French–German alliance, preferring it to an Anglo-French one. What she was seeking was something entirely different: a return to the pre-war *entente* based on containing Germany. Her way of thinking is illustrated by her worries expressed to Mitterrand 'about the Germans' so-called "mission" in Central Europe' and her argument 'that we must not just accept that the Germans had a particular hold over these countries, but rather do everything possible to expand our own links there.'[24]

Mitterrand, though sharing her worries, did not see the solution in turning back the clock. In his version of their conversation on 20 January 1990, published after his death, he said: 'I don't see what force in Europe could prevent (German unification)... Better accept it with eyes wide open, and link German unification to the construction of Europe and to the guarantee of frontiers.' When the Prime Minister passionately warned against the dangers of German domination, and asked Mitterrand to consider a French–German *rapprochement* capable of counterbalancing it, he replied,

> as each time that our conversations touched upon this subject, that to my great regret the alliance between our two countries... did not have content... and that I would not exchange the construction of Europe, of which Federal Germany is one of the pillars, for a French–German *entente* desirable but limited to good intentions.[25]

16 Monetary Union

Monetary Union, as defined in the Werner Report as well as in the Delors Report, means permanently fixed exchange rates and full convertibility without fluctuation margins. In effect this implies a single currency, preferred in both reports in form as well as in substance. It requires a common monetary policy pursued by a European Central Bank. One of the main differences between the two reports is that the Delors Report explicitly stated that the European Central Bank should be committed to price stability and should be independent of political instructions. It meant adopting the Bundesbank model for Europe, even though most member states had different models which they would have preferred to transfer to the European level. Consensus on this point was reached not because it reflected political preferences of all or even most concerned – which it did not – but because no German concurrence could have been obtained otherwise.

For France, in particular, accepting the Bundesbank model was a major concession, deviating as it did from French centralist tradition, and even raising doubts on the purpose of monetary integration, which for France was to ensure more influence on monetary decision-making. Thus having in principle made the concession at the European Council Meeting in Rome in October 1990, it fought a rearguard action when the European Central Bank's statutes were drafted. Though the principle of independence of the ECB and its priority for price stability was clearly established in the Treaty, sufficient ambiguity was incorporated in it to make sure that the issue could be raised again at a later stage.

16.1 CENTRAL BANK INDEPENDENCE

There is a close link between a central bank's independence and the formulation – in law or treaty – of its policies' objective: it would hardly be conceivable to have an independent central bank, and leave its objectives to its discretion. It is therefore not by chance that until recently the Bundesbank and the Nederlandsche Bank were the only central banks in the European Community which had stability of the value of the currency established in law as an explicit objective.

The main argument usually advanced in favour of an independent central bank is that this offers the best prospect for price stability. This is not based on any presumed superior wisdom or competence on the part of central bankers compared to governments. It is rather that governments, even if they have adopted price stability as an objective, necessarily have other objectives as well. Prospects for realising the latter without undue money creation are best, if money creation is the responsibility of the central bank that has price stability as its primary objective.[1]

A more pragmatic argument, following on from the previous one, was advanced by former Chancellor of the Exchequer Nigel Lawson, who argued not only that central bank independence would do something to 'depoliticise interest rate changes' but also that even if a government was fully committed to combat inflation, its policy would never enjoy the same market credibility that an independent central bank has.[2]

Two arguments are often advanced against Central Bank independence, an economic and a political one. The economic argument is in fact directed against priority for the objective of price stability. In this view price stability should be weighed against other policy objectives, and monetary policy should be part of the total arsenal at the disposal of the government. In the early post-war decades this Keynesian view prevailed in most countries, with the notable exception of the Federal Republic. German success compared with the achievements of other countries has contributed to a change. The view gained acceptance that in the longer run price stability and economic growth are not alternatives, but that the former is a condition for the latter.

The political argument is that an independent central bank with an unelected leadership is not consistent with a democratic system. While in the German case this argument can be countered by pointing out that in case of a conflict Parliament can change the law on the Bundesbank with a simple majority, at the European level a change in the Treaty would require too cumbersome a procedure to be a practical possibility. In rebuttal it is argued that the Treaty itself, entered into in a perfectly democratic procedure, has established both the ECB's independence and its objective, as well as its accountability.

More generally, it can be argued that an independent central bank, far from being undemocratic because it is removed from day-to-day politics, can be part of the checks and balances that constitute a constitutional democracy. James Buchanan has pointed out that in what he calls 'constitutional democracy', 'constitutional' is taking precedence over 'democracy' in the sense that constitutional limits, once put in place as a result of democratic procedure, set limits to politics. There are two stages of political decision-making. The first is the design, construction, implementation and maintenance of the basic rules. These define the parameters within which 'ordinary politics' take place. Buchanan regards such constraints on politics, 'politics within rules' as he calls it, a requirement for the effective functioning of market economies. Such constraints should, for example, protect 'economic liberties, without which any market order remains highly vulnerable to piecemeal interferences generated by interest-motivated coalitions.'[3] In the same vein one can argue that the effective functioning of a market economy requires price stability. This can only be maintained if decisions of 'ordinary politics' are taken within a monetary framework that itself is accepted as given.

It was not, however, these considerations that made member states accept the German model for the European Central Bank, but the realisation that otherwise Germany would not be prepared to give up its present dominant position in monetary decision-making.

France, with its centralist tradition, found it particularly difficult initially to accept the German model. Edith Cresson, when French Minister for European Affairs in 1988 expressed her misgivings in her inimitable way. The Bundesbank model, she argued, was imposed by the victor – the United States – on the vanquished, and that could be no reason for Europe to adopt this model.[4] President Mitterrand himself, on one well-publicised occasion when campaigning for a yes-vote in the French referendum on the Maastricht Treaty in 1992, brazenly denied on television that the Treaty contained central bank independence.[5] Later, when installing the policy board of the newly independent Banque de France in January 1994, he was more candid, acknowledging that he regarded central bank independence as a sacrifice to be accepted for the sake of European integration.[6]

Even the Dutch Government did not initially support the Bundesbank model for Europe, preferring the model in the law on the Dutch Central Bank, both because it thought this was superior (as others thought about their model) and because it could be presented as a compromise.[7] By 1987, I myself had come to realise that the Dutch system could not be copied at the European level, since it functioned the way it did owing to specific circumstances that did not prevail in Europe. Not all my colleagues at the Nederlandsche Bank took this view at the time, as was evident at a Board meeting on 31 May 1988. Once they agreed, Dutch Finance Minister Wim Kok next had to be convinced; this was a somewhat delicate operation since, reflecting sentiments in his socialist party, he had declared in Parliament in December 1989 that he would strongly argue in favour of the Dutch model.[8] Finally, in 1991, in an exchange of letters with the Nederlandsche Bank carefully prepared on the basis of mutually agreed drafts, the minister wrote that he agreed with the bank that the democratic rules at the European level could not take the same form they had in the Dutch Central Bank Law as long as the European Central Bank had no political counterpart with full responsibility to the European Parliament.[9]

The Dutch model kept surfacing from other directions as well. Delors, of all people, who had done so much at an earlier stage to enable the consensus on the Bundesbank model to emerge as the basis of his report, gave the impression at a meeting in May 1990 that he would have preferred the Dutch model, which no doubt he would have.[10]

16.2 FRENCH REARGUARD ACTION

As stated earlier, France in effect accepted the Bundesbank model for the European Central Bank when Banque de France Governor Jacques de Larosière received his government's green light to agree with the Delors Report in 1989; it seems that on that occasion President Mitterrand overruled his Finance Minister Bérégovoy's objections (see 12.2). The French Government itself accepted it on the occasion of the European Council Meeting in Rome in October 1990. Though accepting it in principle, this was no reason to refrain from trying to limit its extent.

The main sphere in which France tried to limit the European Central Bank's autonomy was that of external monetary policy. As early as 1988, Pierre Bérégovoy indicated that external and internal Central Bank tasks should be split.[11] During the preparation of the IGC, the French Treasury member of the Monetary Committee returned to this theme. He argued that the competence of the independent ECB should be limited to internal monetary policy, while external monetary policy should be that of governments; in this context he pointed to the parallel with the United States, where decisions to intervene in the foreign exchange market were made by the US Treasury, the Federal Reserve Bank of New York merely carrying them out.

For the German monetary authorities, strongly supported by the Dutch, such a division of competences was not acceptable. If the political authorities were in a position to impose on the European Central Bank the obligation to stabilise the dollar rate, for example, this could completely undercut its domestic monetary policy, and its independence would be on paper only.

The outcome was a compromise, embodied in Article 109 of the Treaty. Concluding exchange rate arrangements and adopting or changing central rates would be the preserve of the Council, though it was obliged to consult with the ECB 'in an endeavour to reach a consensus consistent with the objective of price stability'. In the absence of formal exchange rate arrangements, the Council 'may formulate general orientations for exchange rate policy... These general orientations shall be without prejudice to the primary objective of the ESCB to maintain price stability.'

Who would be the judge as to whether such general orientations would be without prejudice to price stability, and how binding they would be on the ECB, was left open, to be settled in practice. The French view was no doubt reflected in an article that Elisabeth Guigou, one of the French negotiators on the Maastricht Treaty, later wrote, in which she flatly stated: 'And it is the Council of ministers, and not the Central Bank, that will fix the Euro's level against other global currencies.'[12]

In addition, Article 103 of the Treaty enabled the Council, on the basis of conclusions of the European Council, to adopt a recommendation setting out broad guidelines of the economic policies of the member states and of the Community. According to Elisabeth Guigou in the article mentioned above, 'it is the European Council at the level of Heads of State and of Government that will fix each year the economic orientations in the framework of which the Central Bank will conduct monetary policy.'

As will be discussed in the next chapter, in the view of French Finance Minister Bérégovoy the ECB should be balanced by what he referred to as an Economic Government. As Mme Guigou put it, this was 'in order not to leave the steering of the economies to the central banks.' This view did not prevail in the negotiations, but in her view the treaty as it emerged offered a sufficient basis to establish an economic government after all.

16.3   ASSESSMENT

France and Germany together were the driving force behind Monetary Union. Yet for neither of them was it easy to accept Monetary Union as contained in the Treaty.

It was France that attached most importance to money in European cooperation. If it were not for France, Monetary Union would not play the central role in European integration that it does. Nevertheless, for quite some time it was not a single currency that was its objective. France wanted more influence on monetary decision-making, initially to establish a common policy regarding the dollar, later mainly in order to be less dependent on interest rate decisions made in Germany that also affected France. As President Mitterrand once put it:

> Today the strongest currency in Europe is West Germany's . . . should we live in a mark zone where only the Germans would express themselves? I would prefer an assembly, a meeting, a permanent conference of the different authorities where France could have its say on all aspects of economic policy.[13]

It came to the conclusion that this objective required a common currency, but for a long time it was felt in France that this was different from a single currency and merely meant an asset for international transactions, existing parallel to national currencies. Only gradually was the objective accepted of a single currency and a common monetary policy pursued by a European Central Bank reflecting the Bundesbank model.

For Germany, Monetary Union implies surrender of its dominant monetary position. Germany, therefore, is in a position to attach acceptance of the Bundesbank model for the ECB as a condition. Moreover, it has to do this: for the German public, losing the German mark is a sacrifice. If the Bundesbank were not replaced by an institution with comparable commitment to price stability and comparable autonomy, the German public would not accept it.

The agreement was more ambiguous, however, than it appeared at first glance. As is so often the case in the process of European integration, once agreement has been reached, a new round of negotiations starts on how to interpret what it is that has been agreed.

Mme Guigou was not the only one to argue that economic government to balance the Central Bank, though not contained in the treaty, could and should in effect be based on it. President Jacques Chirac went in the same direction:

> Thus, the European Central Bank should be faced with a responsible institution. . . . This responsible Government, this responsible political institution, this should simply be the European Council, of course (those members) who are within the Euro. But all those who are within the Euro should constitute a Government, i.e. a political authority in a position to indicate clearly to the monetary authority what the limits of its actions are, and to call it to account.[14]

Thus, there was and remains a fundamental difference on Monetary Union between its main proponents, France and Germany. This difference was also reflected in the negotiations on Economic Union.

17 Economic Union

While Monetary Union implies a common monetary policy pursued by a European Central Bank, Economic Union as contained in the Maastricht Treaty implies neither a common policy nor a common authority. It merely obliges member states to coordinate their economic policies, as did the Rome Treaty in its original form, and in addition to avoid what are termed excessive budget deficits. This difference between Monetary Union and Economic Union reflects the limits of member states' readiness to give up national sovereignty.

The Werner Report of 1970 and the Delors Report of 1989, both regarded Economic Union as a condition for Monetary Union. In particular, the two reports agreed that Monetary Union would not be sustainable if member states remained free to determine the financing and the size of their public finance deficits. The Werner Report required that the essential elements of national budgets should be determined at Community level. Governments – though not referring to the 'decision centre for economic policy' mentioned in the report – endorsed this, but in fact it was a major obstacle to the establishment of EMU. The Delors Report did not go quite so far; it stated that effective upper limits should be imposed on budget deficits of individual countries, adding that in setting them, the situation of each member country might have to be taken into consideration. But the report left open the institutional implications.

The statement of the European Council in Rome in October 1990 was unspecific, merely stating the requirement of 'sound and sustainable financial and budgetary conditions', adding: 'To this end the Community institutions will be strengthened.' Thus, Member States started the Intergovernmental Conference agreeing implicitly that Monetary Union required acceptance of constraints on national budget policies, but not agreeing what form these should take.

The issue was further complicated by the fact that there was no genuine agreement on the scope of the European Central Bank's independence. As a result, discussions on Economic Union were not limited to questions such as how to constrain and coordinate national budgetary and economic policies and to what extent to centralise them. The discussions also extended – explicitly or implicitly – to the monetary and exchange rate competences governments would have in EMU, and thus to the limits to be put to the ECB's sphere of competence and autonomy.

17.1 WHY BUDGET CONSTRAINTS

The question whether Monetary Union requires constraints to be imposed on national budget policies was controversial both politically and in academic circles. Politically, the issue was particularly sensitive, since budget policies go to the core of national sovereignty. In political as well as academic circles it was argued either that the size of budget deficits does not matter as long as they are not monetised (the view notably of monetarists of the Chicago School) or that market forces will prevent or correct undue deficits, provided the debtor governments are not bailed out by other member states and the Community.

In the Delors Committee, Alexander Lamfalussy submitted a paper arguing the need for constraints on the size of national budget deficits. His conclusion was

> that, in the absence of fiscal coordination, the global fiscal policy of the EMU would be the accidental outcome of decisions taken by Member States. There would simply be no Community-wide macroeconomic fiscal policy. As a result, the only global macroeconomic tool available within EMU would be the common monetary policy implemented by the European central banking system ... this would ... imply the serious danger of an inappropriate fiscal/monetary policy mix and pressures tending to divert monetary policy from the longer-run objective of preserving price stability.

He also argued that large fiscal deficits in one or more member states would push up real interest rates in the EMU as a whole, causing intra–EMU political tensions and pressure on the European Central Bank to relax monetary policy.

Lamfalussy acknowledged that existing federations had no federally-imposed statutory limits on the borrowing capacity of regional entities, but he pointed to the differences with the situation in which EMU would find itself.

- Much of the convergence achieved in federal states is probably the result of tradition and history – factors which in Europe appear to favour divergence.
- In many federations, members themselves have borrowing restrictions included in their legislation.
- The relative size of most federal budgets is much larger than that of the Community budget.

He doubted that market forces would be sufficient to enforce discipline. It was unlikely that the interest premium to be paid by a high deficit country would be very high, since the market would tend not to believe the 'no bail-out' pledge. And in so far as there was a premium, it was doubtful whether it would reduce significantly the deficit country's propensity to borrow.[1]

The Delors Report adopted this view: 'The constraints imposed by market forces might either be too slow and weak or too sudden and disruptive. Hence countries would have to accept that sharing a common market and a single currency area imposed policy constraints.'[2]

17.2 ECONOMIC GOVERNMENT

Is Monetary Union sustainable without transfer of sovereignty in other spheres as well? It will be recalled that this question was controversial from the start of the process of monetary integration. Holtrop, President of the Nederlandsche Bank, in 1963 called money 'an attribute of sovereignty', arguing that it could not be integrated in isolation. This Dutch view was shared by Germany: the two countries represented the 'economist' view against that of the 'monetarists'. It was at the insistence of the former that the Werner Report of 1970 proposed the establishment at Community level of a Decision Centre of Economic Policy. Due to French opposition to what sounded like supranationality, this institution was not mentioned in the Resolution of March 1971, though it endorsed the view that the main aspects of national budgets should be determined at Community level.

At first sight, the positions seemed to be reversed in the 1990s. In a statement by the French Finance Minister Pierre Bérégovoy, published at the start of the Intergovernmental Conference in December 1990, France proposed the establishment of what it called

an 'Economic Government' in parallel to the European Central
Bank:

It is the ambition of the two forthcoming intergovernmental conferences to bring about a pooling of some important elements of
sovereignty by a group of democratic states. It is therefore necessary
that Europe's Economic and Monetary Union should advance in
parallel with the other elements of its Political Union. It is also
necessary to ensure that, in the Economic and Monetary Union,
the 'monetary pole' advances in parallel with the 'economic pole';
the independence of the monetary institution can only be conceived
within the interdependence with a strong 'Economic Government'.
This Economic Government must be fully democratic and its
decisions must be directly binding on the member states, who
will continue to execute the main elements of economic policy.[3]

A few weeks later, Bérégovoy elucidated his views at a meeting of
the Intergovernmental Conference. The European Council should
define the general orientations of policies in EMU (he did not limit
this to *economic* policies), whereas the 'reinforced Ecofin Council'
would be the centre of Economic Government. The Ecofin established the orientations of exchange policies, whereas the European
Central Bank would execute interventions.[4] This clarifies the lack
of enthusiasm on the part of the Germans and the Dutch. While
in their view the decision centre of economic policy as mentioned
in the Werner Report should have been a supranational body comparable to the ECB, in the model envisaged by Bérégovoy both
would be subordinated to the European Council. This was implicit
in his proposals, but was later stated explicitly by Elisabeth Guigou,
who at this time was one of the French negotiators.

For the Bundesbank and the Nederlandsche Bank, an important
consideration for arguing in favour of constraints on national budget
policies was the fear of overburdening monetary policy. A combination of a monetary policy aiming at price stability and too ex-
pansive budget policies will lead to high interest rates. These, as
experience shows, are blamed not on the excessive budget deficits
but on the Central Bank, which will come under heavy political
pressure to relax its policies. Since in the future EMU consensus
on the priority for price stability still has to be established, it would
be difficult for the ECB to withstand such political pressure, however independent it is on paper. The Germans and the Dutch thus

argued for Economic Union because they were concerned for the future ECB's independence in practice. This obviously was not the motivation of the French proposal. Far from ensuring that an independent ECB's monetary policy could realise price stability without undue tensions, it threatened to limit that independence and thus – in the German and Dutch view – endanger price stability. Therefore, Germany and the Netherlands rejected the French proposals to establish an 'Economic Government', even though it had the appearance of going in the direction of Economic Union and even Political Union which they themselves had earlier advocated.

There is a parallel to this reversal of positions. In November 1995, German Finance Minister Theo Waigel proposed the establishment of a stability pact in order to make operational the articles in the Treaty dealing with excessive deficits. His proposal contained the establishment of a stability council by the participating countries. When France later took up this proposal as part of what was, at French insistence, renamed the stability and growth pact, Germany no longer supported it, fearing that the French intention was to use the stability council as a counterweight to the ECB in order to limit its freedom of action.

17.3   EXCESSIVE DEFICITS

Centralisation of budget policies, and therefore a supranational body – comparable to the ECB – determining the size of national budget deficits would have no more chance of realisation in the 1990s than it had in the 1970s. But it now seemed less indispensable for a sustainable Monetary Union than was the case then. The requirement followed from the view that modern economies needed demand management; in a Monetary Union this had to be decided centrally. Subsequent experience with demand management in most countries caused widespread doubts on its desirability and encouraged the view that budgetary policies should have structural rather than cyclical objectives. Structural objectives did not need central decision-making but could be incorporated in the Treaty. It was thus that the concept of 'excessive deficits' emerged.

Initially, there was disagreement whether the Treaty should go beyond general pronouncements that excessive deficits should be avoided. Not surprisingly, the British objected to anything more precise. Perhaps more surprising – in view of the recommendations in the Delors Report – was the fact that the Commission, in its early proposals, did not argue in favour of binding rules either, but rather followed the French line of having the European Council establish general orientations.[5]

Germany and the Netherlands, however, insisted that avoiding excessive deficits should be a Treaty obligation that should be quantified, with sanctions in case of non-compliance. But quantifying them and devising sanctions proved far from easy. Initially, in early 1990, their view was controversial even within their own administrations. The central banks in both countries insisted on binding rules and sanctions, arguing that otherwise excessive deficits were to be expected, overburdening monetary policy.[6] In the Netherlands, our view was also criticised by the Liberal Party, which later was to insist on a very strict interpretation of the criteria regarding budget deficits. At the time it was argued that no such constraints were necessary, since the markets would ensure that excessive deficits were avoided or corrected.[7] The Nederlandsche Bank, in its Annual Report for 1989, called such expectations a triumph of hope over experience, as I had done earlier in the Monetary Committee.

In the course of 1990, during the preparation of the IGC, in discussions that took place mainly in the Monetary Committee, both countries argued in favour of adoption of the so-called golden rule of finance, limiting the size of budget deficits to investment expenditure. This would be less arbitrary than ceilings on overall deficits inevitably were, and it took into account differences between countries' public investment. Though the question of what should be considered investment would no doubt pose practical problems, judgement could be based on international practice. But in the end the golden rule proved unacceptable.

The conclusion to agree on 'reference values' for the ratio to gross domestic product of overall deficits (3 per cent) and government debt (60 per cent) was a compromise. Some members felt that 3 per cent for deficits was too low, in particular if the purpose was merely to signal 'gross errors', or that it should refer to an average rather than to annual figures. Others wished to add some form of non-binding balanced budget norm. The 60 per cent public debt merely reflected the existing overall situation at the time. Members were aware of the link between the two figures – at a nominal growth rate of 5 per cent – but it played no decisive role in establishing the reference values.

The members of the Monetary Committee were aware of the

rather arbitrary nature of these figures. They realised that the judgement whether budget deficits were excessive could not be mechanical, and this awareness is reflected in the procedure incorporated in the Treaty. At the same time, the Germans and Dutch in particular felt that the alternative would have been to leave this judgement entirely to the discretion of the Council. This would be an insufficient basis for Monetary Union, given the tendency in the Council – so often observed in the past – to avoid political confrontation.

The Treaty prescribes the procedure to be followed in order to determine whether a country has an excessive deficit, in which both the Commission and the Council play a role. There is a possibility of imposing sanctions if it is judged that the obligation to avoid or correct excessive deficits is not met. But it was only at a later stage, when the stability pact proposed by German Finance Minister Theo Waigel in November 1995 was adopted in 1996–7, that this was made operational. How it will function in practice is likely to depend on how sustainably participants control their public finances. Should that control be precarious, then an increase above the ceiling of 3 per cent is likely as soon as an adverse cyclical situation presents itself. Should this happen to several countries at once, it would be unlikely that sanctions would really be imposed, and the pact would soon lose its meaning. Thus, there is a close link with the way in which the obligations are judged at the time of entry.

17.4   CONVERGENCE CRITERIA AND THE THIRD STAGE

The obligation to avoid excessive deficits, and the possibility of imposing sanctions on member states that do not respect this obligation, are limited to the third stage. In the second stage, according to Article 109E, member states merely 'shall endeavour to avoid excessive Government deficits'. No sanctions can be imposed if they do not succeed, but it could be argued that in reality they could be faced with the only sanction that might really be effective: no access to the third stage. If, notwithstanding this threat, member states did not establish sustainable control over their public finances, and merely appeared to qualify for participation due to measures that would only have a temporary effect, there would be little reason to assume that they would do so at a later stage.

Though admission to the third stage would inevitably depend on political judgement, it was felt – by the Germans and the Dutch in particular – that it should not be completely discretionary. The convergence criteria should play an important role in providing a quantitative basis for the judgement, and particular significance was attached to the avoidance of excessive deficits. In subsequent discussions attention tended to focus on the deficit ratio to GDP, which is indeed crucial, but the debt criterion should not be ignored if only because a large debt tends to increase governments' insistence on low interest rates even if price stability requires increased rates. As the Nederlandsche Bank argued in its 1993 report, according to the Treaty a deficit is excessive if it exceeds 3 per cent of GDP, but also if the public debt ratio exceeds 60 per cent and the deficit does not contribute to its significant reduction. This implies that the higher the debt ratio, the stricter the requirement the deficit must meet.[8] In this respect it should be recalled that the flexibility clause in the Treaty regarding public debt accepts a ratio exceeding the reference value of 60 per cent if 'the ratio is sufficiently diminishing and approaching the reference value at a satisfactory pace'. The second part, referring to the level, is often ignored.

The Treaty repeatedly refers to the requirement of sustainability. In Article 109J, it requires 'sustainable convergence' when referring to all the criteria. When mentioning the excessive deficit criterion it refers to 'the sustainability of the Government financial position'. Finally, Article 104C dealing with excessive deficits specifies that if a member state does not fulfil the requirements regarding the deficit and/or debt, judgement whether its deficit is excessive should take into account all relevant factors, 'including the medium-term economic and budgetary position of the member state.'

At the European Council Meeting in Maastricht, it was decided to add to the conditions for participation which had to be fulfilled two dates for the start of the third stage. It was to start in 1997 if a majority qualified. If by the end of 1997 the date for the beginning of the third stage had not been set, the third stage was to start on 1 January 1999. By adding this date to the criteria at the last minute and at the highest level, the Heads of State or Government clearly wished to impose time pressure on convergence. Without it, it is likely that convergence would have progressed less than it did. But in doing so they also introduced a potential inconsistency into the Treaty. Whether they realised this risk at the time is uncertain. The chairman of the meeting, Dutch Prime Minister Lubbers, did not even remember this major change in the Treaty a few years later, and flatly denied it.[9] Politicians at summit meeting have other priorities – such as the success of the meeting, especially if they chair it – than to worry about the possibility that some years later their decisions may turn out to contain inconsistencies. The Bundesbank, on its part, was alarmed when it became known that a date had been mentioned. A statement of 7 February 1992 concluded: 'The fulfilment of the entry criteria or the convergence conditions must not be impaired by any dates set.'

The problem is that once a date for the start of the third stage is set in addition to economic requirements, the date is likely to prevail. Without a date, however, the third stage may never start. Countries wishing to participate but not fulfilling the criteria will try to prevent it if their consent is required or if they can muster a blocking minority, unless they are also admitted; if they are, this will threaten EMU's sustainability. In an effort to find a way out of this dilemma, the Dutch presidency made a proposal at the end of August 1991, in essence allowing six member states to move ahead to the third stage if they fulfilled the criteria. This, it felt, reflected the principle agreed earlier that there should be no veto, no compulsion and no arbitrary exclusion. Not surprisingly, there was violent opposition, coming from Italy in particular.[10] Delors, too, objected against a multi-speed approach at this stage. Though there was also support – mainly, but not exclusively, from Germany – Dutch Finance Minister Kok immediately dropped the proposal, stating that it had 'no political status'.[11] This opened the way to the provisions as finally agreed in Maastricht, with their potential inconsistency.

17.5 ASSESSMENT

Economic and Monetary Union as conceived in the Treaty is threatened by some major potential weaknesses. There is an imbalance between Monetary Union and Economic Union. Monetary Union means a single currency and a common monetary policy pursued by the European Central Bank. Economic Union implies that member states have accepted the obligation to do in the future what they should have done all along but failed to do: to coordinate their economic policies and avoid excessive budget deficits. Should they fail to comply with these obligations, pressure on the ECB to relax its monetary policy could become severe, causing tensions between ECB and governments as well as between governments themselves.

It is true that the Treaty introduces the possibility of imposing sanctions on countries failing to respect their commitments. This has been made operational by the adoption of the Stability and Growth Pact. Yet prospects for enforcement are uncertain. It is far from certain that the draconian fines envisaged in the Pact will be imposed in practice, and this is less likely, the larger the number of participating countries having excessive deficits. The Pact can only be respected, if countries reduce their public sector deficits sufficiently below 3 per cent GDP on average to have a safety margin allowing automatic stabilisers to function during cyclical downturns.[12] In view of the difficulty of major countries, among them Germany and France, to reduce the deficit even to 3 per cent, this seems far from certain. Even more uncertain are the prospects for public finances in Italy with its structural problems and considerable and until now hardly diminishing public debt. If the Stability and Growth Pact lost its credibility, the imbalance between Monetary Union and Economic Union would become evident. The ensuing tensions would also expose the differences between member states regarding the extent of the independence of the European Central Bank.

In the final analysis this would raise the question whether Monetary Union can function in practice without intensified integration in other respects, including political integration. The Bundesbank, in a statement by the Central Bank Council published in September 1990, argued that Monetary Union is 'an irrevocable joint and several Community which, in the light of past experience, requires a more far-reaching association, in the form of a comprehensive Political Union, if it is to prove durable.' Chancellor Kohl stated in 1985 that he regarded acceptance of Monetary Union as necessary for the realisation of the ultimate objective of Political Union (see Chapter 10, paragraph 3). He did not succeed in his efforts to link EMU and EPU in Maastricht, but argued a few weeks later that due to what had been agreed there, Political Union would develop a dynamism of its own that no one would be able to resist in the long run.[13] Finance Minister Theo Waigel wrote exactly one year later, that since parallelism between EMU and EPU was not ensured in Maastricht, the Treaty was only acceptable to the German Government due to what he called a 'revision clause', a new Intergovernmental Conference 'providing for a fixed date for the further construction of the European house'.[14]

As we shall see in the next chapters, the dynamism on which the Chancellor counted started to dissipate during the painful process of ratification that followed, while repeated turmoil in the currency market severely tested the credibility of EMU as an objective. The 'revision clause' to which Waigel referred produced the Treaty of Amsterdam in 1997, which hardly brought Political Union any nearer. As the date set for the start of EMU – 1 January 1999 – was approaching, EPU seemed as elusive as ever, remaining on the horizon, perhaps in sight but never within reach.

18 Ratification (1992–3)

In The Hague in December 1969, the Heads of State or Government decided to establish Economic and Monetary Union in stages within ten years. Almost exactly twenty-two years later, on 10 and 11 December 1991, once again in the Netherlands, they agreed to amend the Rome Treaty to incorporate Economic and Monetary Union. On 7 February 1992, the Treaty was signed in Maastricht. Not a moment too soon: the political momentum that had been building up since the mid-eighties and that had been given such a boost by the unanimous Delors Report of 1989, was starting to dissipate. Several factors interrelated caused this reversal. The politicians, carried on by the political momentum, failed to carry their constituents along with them. The public sensed that EMU meant far-reaching changes but failed to understand its reasons or its consequences. At the same time the cyclical upswing, crucial for maintaining a political momentum of this kind, gave way to a downturn: real growth in the EC went down from 3 per cent in 1990 to 1 per cent in 1992, and in 1993 disappeared altogether. The same German unification that had first stimulated the upswing by creating additional demand, now, by pushing up interest rates, became a drag on growth and on the integration process. Apart from its usual negative effect on the general mood, the downturn made it difficult to raise interest rates where necessary to defend the exchange rate. The credibility of EMU started to erode when, partly following the difficulties that the ratification encountered, partly caused by the failure to raise interest rates in time, the exchange rate mechanism ran into serious trouble.

18.1 DANISH DISASTER

Denmark was one of the countries where the ratification of the Maastricht Treaty required a referendum (unless the majority in Parliament had been so large as to make it almost unanimous). When the Government set the date for 2 June 1992, making Denmark the first EC country to decide on ratification, it clearly had no inkling of the disaster that was waiting, otherwise it would no doubt have postponed ratification in the hope that approval in other countries would influence Danish voters favourably. Encouraged by opinion polls taken after the signing of the Treaty, the government had no reason to expect difficulties. A protocol that was part of the Treaty stipulated that Denmark would only participate in the third stage of EMU if it would take a separate decision to do so; that future decision would require a separate referendum. So why would people vote no? Yet that is what they did.

The rejection, with a slight majority, came as a huge shock. It stimulated scepticism elsewhere which until then had been dormant. For some time it was difficult to see a way out. It was hard to imagine that one small country could prevent the Treaty from coming into force in the end, yet such were the rules. For the time being, the other countries proceeded with their own ratification, shelving the Danish problem until later. Renegotiating the Treaty was out of the question, apart from the fact that it was not clear what would have to be changed to make it acceptable to the Danish public. In the end, this latter question was solved when the European Council in Edinburgh in December 1992 took a decision. According to this decision, Denmark declared that

– it would not participate in the third stage of EMU, and
– it would not participate in the common defence policy.

On this basis, a new referendum was called in May 1993, and the Danish voters, having made their point, now voted in favour with a modest majority.

The reason for the no vote in the first referendum is a matter of speculation. There is a traditional reluctance in Denmark concerning European integration. According to opinion polls held after the referendum, the negative votes were mainly motivated by objection to loss of sovereignty, while insufficient information was also given as a motive.[1] Clearly, the government failed to explain both the content of the Treaty and its motives to support it. It was said at the time that the 500 000 copies it had printed – a large number, given a population of 5 million – only served to convince voters they were being asked to enter into obligations of an impenetrable character.

18.2 FRENCH MISCALCULATION

More important than the reasons for the Danish voters' action was its result. The day after the Danish rejection, French President Mitterrand announced he would also call a referendum. In the French case, this was not obligatory: ratification by Parliament was sufficient and was assured, as Parliament had also agreed to approve the constitutional amendment which the Constitutional Court had deemed necessary. Why Mitterrand took this risk is a matter of conjecture. The simplest answer is that he did not think it was a risk: according to opinion polls held on 19 and 20 June, 51 per cent were in favour and only 18 per cent opposed.[2] Later the President was to explain that he thought an important decision like this should be submitted to a popular vote. Lofty as this sentiment was, few believed that the man often referred to as 'the Florentine' because of his alleged deviousness did not have other, more complex motives. A desire to repair something of the damage wrought by the Danish rejection by following it up with an overwhelming yes in France may have been one motive. But it is likely that there were also considerations of a domestic nature. His domestic fortunes were at a low ebb and endorsement of his European policies would have been a welcome boost. Moreover, the referendum could be an embarrassment for the opposition on the right, which was deeply divided over the issue. As things turned out, no one was more embarrassed than the President himself when he scraped home in the vote with the narrowest majority and only thanks to the support of leaders of the opposition.

In France, as in Denmark, there was a shift in public opinion against the Treaty in the months between the announcement of the referendum and its actual date. The motivation was of both a political and an economic nature. In the Gaullist tradition, there were objections to the loss of sovereignty, and in some quarters there was fear of German domination. There was also worry that EMU would result in high unemployment, fuelled by the cyclical downswing that was felt during this period. Opposition to Mitterrand also played a role.

18.3   BRITISH AGONY

Britain was the only member country where the obstacle to ratification manifested itself in Parliament. That this did not happen elsewhere is due to the circumstance that governments, though having lost touch with voters on the issue, did remain in close touch with their parliaments during the negotiations. As far as Britain was concerned, the Government had been aware all along that they would not be able to obtain endorsement at home for any substantial commitment they were asked to enter into. The British negotiators therefore had been in the unenviable position of trying to remain involved in the discussions without being able to commit themselves to anything. In this, thanks largely to the high professional quality of the officials concerned, they succeeded as well as circumstances permitted.[3]

In Maastricht, Prime Minister John Major agreed to the Treaty on condition that Britain was free to decide at a later stage whether or not to join the third stage of EMU, and on condition that the Social Chapter – which Britain rejected – would not be part of the Treaty but an agreement of the other eleven. No doubt the British Government had carefully weighed the inconvenience of this solution against the alternative, refusing to agree, with the risk that the other countries would agree on a separate Treaty. Prime Minister Major's triumphalism after Maastricht – 'game, set and match!' – soon gave way to despondency when he had to obtain ratification in the House of Commons. The Danish vote had greatly encouraged the Tory rebels, and the Government decided to postpone ratification until the autumn. Once the debate started, the Labour and Liberal opposition – unlike the opposition in France – gave priority to party politics over other considerations, using Britain's rejection of the Social Chapter as an excuse to do so, and the Government had to make ratification an issue of confidence, implying the threat of an election which would have been disastrous for the Conservative Party, in order to complete the process. This did not, however, end the British agony over Europe.

18.4   GERMAN LAST COMER

In Germany, as elsewhere, there was a shift in public opinion against the Maastricht Treaty. Its start more or less coincided with the

European Council Meeting in Maastricht in December 1991. Only then did it seem to sink in that Monetary Union meant giving up the German mark. Chancellor Kohl hoped to defuse opposition by securing the establishment of the European Central Bank in Frankfurt. Yet he underestimated the strength of people's feelings; otherwise it is unlikely he would have agreed to the text of Article 3a referring to 'the irrevocable fixing of exchange rates leading to the introduction of a single currency, the ecu.' Later, ecu was changed in the German text into ECU, indicating that it still stood for European Currency Unit, as in Bremen in 1978, and German officials emphasised that the name of the future European currency still had to be agreed upon, and certainly would not be ecu.

By the time the German Parliament had to debate the Treaty, it was too committed to be swayed by changing sentiments in German public opinion. It did, however, secure that the German Government would call for a parliamentary debate before taking a final position on the introduction of stage 3 of EMU. The Parliament also made it clear that it would on that occasion insist on a strict interpretation of the criteria embodied in Article 109J.[4]

This seemed, in essence, to complete the ratification process in Germany. But that was not to be. The growing anti-Maastricht sentiment was reflected in a number of appeals to the Federal Constitutional Court alleging that the Treaty violated the German constitution. It was only after the Court ruled that this was not the case on 12 October 1993, that Germany could deposit the instruments of ratification, being the last member to do so, and thus enabling the Treaty to come into force on 1 November 1993.

The ruling is interesting in several respects. From a political perspective, the following points are of interest. The Court stressed that according to the Treaty, Monetary Union is conceived as a stability-oriented Community, which as a matter of priority must guarantee price stability. The Court regarded this as the basis and substance of the German Law on Accession. Should the Monetary Union not be able to develop continuous stability in the sense of the agreed mandate for stabilisation upon entrance into the third stage, it would depart from the concept of the Treaty. Without explicitly giving its own view, the Court stated that

there may be plausible reasons for holding that the Currency Union could only be meaningfully implemented as a matter of practical politics if it were simultaneously supplemented by an

Economic Union, which would go beyond a coordination of the economic policies of the member states and the Community... it is at present an open question whether the Currency Union will have such an Economic Union as a consequence, or whether the lack of will of the member states for a communalised economic policy and the 'dominant budget' associated therewith... will result in the future abandonment of the Currency Union and a corresponding Treaty amendment.

The ruling went on to state, that 'important arguments' had been made that currency union can ultimately only be realised in common with a political union. 'If it emerges that the desired Monetary Union cannot be achieved without a (not yet desired) Political Union, a new political decision is needed on how to proceed further.'

Thus, in the view of the Court, whether a Monetary Union required a genuine Economic Union (going beyond what is now contained in the Treaty) and a Political Union, was open. The priority for price stability, however, was not open: this was the 'basis and substance' of German participation in Monetary Union. If it turned out that this priority could not be implemented without a genuine Economic Union and without Political Union, then member states were not free to continue regardless. They would then face the choice either to advance or to retreat, abandoning the Currency Union. Each choice would require a new Treaty, and all member states would therefore have to agree. But

the Treaty sets up long-term targets which impose the objective of stability as the standard for Monetary Union, which seek to achieve that objective through institutional arrangements, and which finally – as the last resort – do not prevent withdrawal from the Community if the stability-oriented nature of the Community breaks down.[5]

18.5 ASSESSMENT

Thus, ratification turned out to be a painful and protracted process, causing considerable embarrassment to many governments. Strong opposition manifested itself not only in countries where the governments had been more or less pushed along, like Britain and

Denmark, but also in those where the governments had taken the lead, France and Germany.

What went wrong? With retrospect it is clear that politicians lost touch with public opinion. Governments took care to consult with parliaments, and parliaments in all countries with the exception of Britain were indeed committed by the time they were asked to ratify the Treaty. But both governments and parliaments, were out of touch with the electorate. It is remarkable that during the period of ratification, with all the publicity the Treaty received, one hardly ever heard or read a clear explanation coming from the political authorities as to what it implied and why it was necessary. It was as if they themselves were unclear about it and lacked an overall view.

Sometimes I got the impression this was indeed the case. In May 1990, I attended a meeting in The Hague of the members of the Dutch Cabinet most involved in European issues. The meeting had been called to prepare the Dutch position at the coming Intergovernmental Conference. The Netherlands had for many years been an ardent advocate of European integration in general and of EMU in particular. That was also the position of the Cabinet of the day. On this occasion, however, the question was not whether they favoured it in general, but how to implement it. Listening to the discussion I could not help getting the impression that ministers were looking at the implications of EMU seriously for the first time, and did not at all like what they saw. Prime Minister Lubbers summed up the general feeling around the table when he repeatedly wondered whether the political authorities realised what they were doing! Finance Minister Kok had to remind his colleagues that the process was not starting now but had been going on for quite some time.[6]

Whether or not Chancellor Kohl and President Mitterrand had a clearer view of EMU's implications, I do not know. Since they were the driving force behind the process, they had no doubt a clearer view of the political reasons why to pursue it. Full-blooded politicians, however, have a tendency to keep their cards close to their chest. Knowing that explanations are always controversial, they often prefer political momentum instead of explanations in order to reach their objective. The extent of popular resistance in their own countries took them completely by surprise.

The uncertainty created at the start of the ratification process strongly contributed to the turbulence that soon shook the currency market.

19 Black September (1992)

The agony of ratification had important consequences. Under the influence of the political momentum towards integration markets reflected a fairly general assumption that establishment of Economic and Monetary Union at an early date was almost certain. This prospect created the illusion that a kind of quasi monetary union was already in place, with realignments of central rates no longer likely. After all, none had taken place since the Basle–Nyborg Agreement of 1987. This certainty disappeared after the first Danish referendum. It was now realised that while no realignments had taken place for five years, inflation differentials in member countries had remained considerable, and competitive positions of high inflation countries had worsened as a result. The Italian lira in particular was clearly overvalued. So, if to a lesser extent, it was felt, was the pound. These and other currencies now came under pressure. The rules of behaviour agreed in Basle–Nyborg would have required the monetary authorities concerned, if they felt exchange rates were correct, to raise interest rates in their defence. But the worsening conjunctural situation made them reluctant to do so. The more so since they felt that the German Bundesbank, reacting to the increasing budget deficits resulting from German unification, was keeping interest rates too high and was the one that should counteract currency pressure by lowering them. The authorities did little to keep their disagreements on interest rates to themselves. Market participants could only conclude that if the authorities disagreed among themselves exchange rate changes were likely.

19.1 THE LIRA'S DEVALUATION

Due to high inflation in Italy relative to the partner countries, the Italian competitive position measured in unit labour costs deteriorated from 1987 to 1991 by 10 per cent.[1] The lira was clearly overvalued. Yet the authorities refrained from devaluation. At first an important consideration seemed to have been that lacking an effective government no accompanying measures could have been taken, and devaluation would therefore not have helped for long. Once an effective government was in place, the real appreciation of the lira became an essential part of its policy to bring Italian inflation down, and to spur firms and unions to conclude agreements that contained costs. However, '(t)he practicability of this exchange rate policy was questioned by the failure to control the domestic causes of inflation and, once capital movements had been completely liberalised, by the Government's loss of credibility owing to failure to restore sound public finances.'[2]

According to Carlo Santini of the Italian Central Bank, 'the Bank of Italy made full use of the instruments provided for in the Basle–Nyborg Agreement, namely interest rate variations, exchange market interventions and movements of the lira within the fluctuation band'.[3] I am not so sure, apart from the fact that the Basle–Nyborg Agreement assumed central rates reflecting competitive positions, which was not the case. I remember a discussion in the Committee of Governors where Governor Ciampi was asked why the authorities did not make fuller use of the fluctuation band but allowed the lira to remain persistently at the bottom. He replied that they did not want the competitive position to deteriorate still further. For me this was an indication that the authorities felt they could no longer afford to give priority to crisis prevention. Nor were they in a position to act decisively once a crisis did occur. For that would require a steep rise in interest rates, and, as Santini puts it: 'Such a decision is always difficult and, in Italy, it was impracticable, since it would have threatened to destabilise the Government securities market in a context characterised by a large public debt with relatively short maturity.'[4] In the beginning of July Dutch Central Bank President Duisenberg warned Finance Minister Kok that a realignment initiated by Italy was possible.[5]

This happened two months later. The German monetary authorities felt that the support they had to give to the lira was endangering their own monetary policy, and convinced Italy to ask for an exchange rate adjustment during the weekend of 12–13 September. In telephone consultations it was decided to devalue the lira against all other EMS currencies by 7 per cent, disguised for reasons of prestige as a devaluation of the lira by 3.5 per cent and a revaluation of the other currencies by 3.5 per cent. Later the chairman of the Monetary Committee, Jean-Claude Trichet, was publicly criticised for not calling a meeting in Brussels where the adjustment of other currencies could have been discussed. I have no personal knowledge whether a meeting was requested; when Trichet called me on the telephone towards midnight on Saturday 12 September he asked me whether I could attend a meeting if it were on Sunday, and my answer was affirmative, but next day I was informed that the procedure would be 'by fax and telephone'.[6] I assumed that the British authorities had made it clear they would not contemplate a devaluation of sterling, as was indeed the case. Under those circumstances I imagined that Trichet saw little point in having a meeting, feeling that calling one would merely serve to dramatise the Italian devaluation and foster expectations of further adjustments. As it happened, the lack of a meeting did not prevent attention now being focused on the other currency under pressure: the pound sterling.

19.2   FIRST STEPS TO BLACK WEDNESDAY

Black Wednesday was pre-programmed. It was, more than by anything else, caused by the UK Government's decision to enter into the ERM without accepting its implications. By 1990 Prime Minister Thatcher, outnumbered in her Cabinet on the issue, felt she had no choice but to acquiesce to entry. But, as she made clear in her memoirs: 'I was not prepared to keep to any particular parity at the expense of domestic monetary conditions.' If there would be pressure on the pound, the exchange rate would have to give way: 'In fact, a rate that is right today can be wrong tomorrow and vice versa.'[7] Moreover, she intended to lower interest rates, 'and continuing to cut them even if that would entail a changed parity in the ERM.'[8] In other words, she could not stop the pound entering into the ERM, but she intended to let the pound float within the ERM! She made this attitude clear by the way in which British entry was handled, as we shall see. Her Chancellor of the Exchequer John Major, soon to be her successor, would follow her in one respect, but not in another. Unlike her intentions, he would cling tenaciously to the once chosen central rate. Like her, he would not do so at the expense of domestic monetary conditions, and would continue to cut interest rates.

Personally I cannot say that the British government's policy came as a surprise to me. The controversy in Britain over whether or not to enter into the ERM, the evidence that even the proponents of participation had views very different from the rules of conduct agreed upon in Basle–Nyborg, made it clear to me that early British participation could only bring grave risks to the system as a whole. I therefore found it difficult to understand why the other countries kept pressuring the United Kingdom to join, especially if that pressure came not from politicians – who probably did not realise the consequences if they got their way – but from central bankers, as was the case occasionally from Bundesbank President Pöhl.[9] During a visit to Amsterdam in August 1987 he supplied an answer, telling me that he was in favour, 'just as you are yourself', of taking a positive attitude instead of being on the defensive and always saying no. He used the German expression *Flucht nach Vorne* (literally, escape forward), adding in his flippant way that he would not be arguing in favour of British entry if he thought they would listen![10]

As a central banker I had to be cautious, of course, in airing my misgivings in public. Yet I did so in a speech for the European Finance Symposium in November 1988 in Antwerp. Having enumerated the advantages of British participation, I said:

> But they can only be expected if Britain would be willing and feel able to respect the rules of the game. The rules of the game imply that if there seems to be a conflict between internal and external objectives, a participant should be prepared – at least in the short run – to give priority to the exchange rate objective.

I pointed out that the markets would inevitably test the authorities' determination, and continued:

> Credibility always has to be earned, and participation therefore – as the British Prime Minister rightly pointed out – is not a soft option. Such testing implies costs both for Britain and for the other participants. To some extent these costs are inevitable and should be accepted if we want British participation. But they will be higher the more markets doubt – with or without reason – the authorities' determination to maintain the exchange rate and accept the implications for their policy mix. It might be added that Britain has not participated in any exchange rate arrangement since 1973 and may to some extent have lost the habit. These reflections are by no means arguments against full participation. Rather they are arguments in favour when the time – and the mood in high places – is right.[11]

On the Continent this was a lone voice, and I must confess to a certain grim satisfaction – in as far as being able to say 'I told you so' can ever give satisfaction – when Peter Norman and Lionel Barber quoted from it in their postmortem of Black Wednesday in the *Financial Times* of 12 December 1992.

On 6 October 1990, British entry into the exchange rate mechanism with fluctuation bands of 6 per cent was announced. The Brussels communiqué stated that the decision had been made 'by mutual agreement, in a common procedure involving the Commission and after consultation with the Monetary Committee, on the terms on which the pound will participate from October 8, 1990. The Ministers, the Governors and the Commission warmly welcome the participation of sterling.' The truth is that the exchange rate was unilaterally decided by the British government; when the partner countries wanted to discuss it in the Monetary Committee, they were told that it had already been announced. The truth promptly found its way to the press, and was a taste of what was in store.[12] As to the timing, the announcement took place just after the opposition Labour Party had finished its conference, and on the eve of the conference of the Conservative Party, but according to Chancellor of the Exchequer John Major, the timing was not politically motivated. The announcement of a one percentage point cut in bank base rates coincided with the announcement of ERM participation: the government's implied message seemed to be that participation spelled lower, not higher, interest rates.[13]

This first cut was followed by eight others, cutting interest rates in total by five percentage points.[14] By doing so, even while resisting persistent political pressure for further cuts, the government created the impression that cutting interest rates had a higher priority than maintaining the exchange rate, and that interest rates would not be raised to defend the exchange rate. Margaret Thatcher later in effect confirmed this in her memoirs, when writing about the timing of the first cut: 'I for my part was determined to demonstrate that we would be looking more to monetary conditions than to the exchange rate in setting interest rates.'[15] When Margaret Thatcher was succeeded as Prime Minister by John Major, who soon had to call elections, raising interest rates became nearly impossible, and would not have strengthened the pound anyway since it would, in the view of most market participants, have further diminished the Conservative Party's chances of winning the election. In this period sterling was therefore practically defenceless, and I am still amazed that no speculative attack occurred. With the elections out of the way and this critical period over, I congratulated my British colleagues on their incredible luck, but they seemed genuinely puzzled: luck had nothing to do with it! The political authorities seemed to live in an even more blissful world, John Major reportedly dreaming aloud of sterling replacing the German mark as the anchor currency. As things turned out, this was wide of the mark.[16]

In the course of July and August, a public debate raged in Britain on the advantages and disadvantages of staying in the ERM and maintaining the central rate. The debate was intensified by rising interest rates in Germany – the Bundesbank increased the discount rate by three quarter percentage points on 16 July – and by the resulting further decline of the dollar. All this led to an increasing downward pressure on the pound in the course of August. The government, though verbally defending the ERM and the exchange rate, declined to react to the market pressure by increasing interest rates. In the face of growing opposition to the ERM, in particular within the ruling Conservative Party, this was understandable politically: one could even argue, as Bank of England Governor Robin Leigh-Pemberton was to do, that increasing interest rates would only intensify the debate on the ERM and therefore would not support the pound.[17] But this meant that the British authorities – like the Italian ones – were not in a position to pursue policies to prevent a currency crisis. This, of course, was noticed in the markets.[18] Astute market participants concluded that taking positions against sterling carried little risk and might yield huge gain.

19.3 CRISIS

With two currencies under increasing pressure and with the authorities of those countries unable to increase interest rates while the German authorities felt not in a position to lower theirs, an informal meeting of Finance Ministers and Central Bank Governors was due to take place in Bath on 4–6 September.

The Bath Meeting was a disaster, or at least a prelude to disaster. The chairman, British Chancellor Norman Lamont, made German interest rates the focus of the meeting, raising the issue time and again and reporting his feats to the waiting press. Bundesbank

President Helmut Schlesinger was restrained by his minister, Theo Waigel, from walking out of the meeting, but little doubt remained outside the meeting room that the monetary authorities within the ERM disagreed with each other. The statement issued after the meeting, confirming 'the 28 August agreement not to proceed to a realignment in the European Monetary System', did little to change that. From Bath the Governors flew to Basle in the Dutch government plane. I joined them in Amsterdam and speaking to Bundesbank President Helmut Schlesinger during the flight and later at the meeting I could hear for myself how upset he was.

At this time, with deteriorating public finances and increasing inflation, the beleaguered Bundesbank felt that it was its past performance in combating inflation that still inspired confidence at present. Any appearance of giving in to political pressure would endanger that confidence. The German press, Schlesinger told his EC colleagues in Basle, had the impression that the Bundesbank was yielding to pressure. Matters were not helped by President Mitterrand's recent statement on television during his campaign for the French referendum that the future ECB would not be independent. This was also widely publicised in the German press. Clearly, Lamont's public pressure could make it only more difficult for the Bundesbank to lower interest rates, and Schlesinger made it clear that he saw no scope for any reduction in the near future.[19]

For the British, time was up. On the morning of Wednesday 16 September I learned that – the guilder being situated slightly above the German mark – we were heavily intervening in the market, buying sterling. The British had now at long last increased interest rates by two percentage points. When this did not help it was followed by another rise of three per cent later in the day. But by now it was not crisis prevention but crisis management. That – if at all possible with an overvalued currency – would have required far more drastic measures still. Given the fact that the British authorities had always presented interest rate increases as a kind of last resort, it might well be that now that it had taken place it was taken by many as evidence that the situation was beyond redemption. Almost a year later I heard an illustrative detail. That was at another realignment meeting, on 1 August 1993. During one of the interminable recesses I was seeking solace at the bar and there met the new British Chancellor, Kenneth Clarke, who could afford to be relaxed since by then the pound was floating. He told me that, as Home Secretary, he had attended a ministerial meeting deciding on the interest rate increase. (Prime Minister John Major, unlike his predecessor, took care to involve his senior Cabinet colleagues in the decision-making.) When the meeting was finished and he returned to the Home Office in his official car, his driver switched off the radio and announced: 'They say it did not work!'[20]

In view of this lack of success the UK government realised that, since it continued to rule out a devaluation in the ERM, it had no choice but to let the pound float. The British authorities, however, felt obliged to continue interventions until the market closed: the longest day in his life, Nigel Wicks – second Permanent Secretary of the Treasury – would call that day. Only then did they announce that the pound would float. Late that evening the Monetary Committee met at last in Brussels under intense media attention. The all-night session, starting towards midnight, began with the British telling their tale of woe. But for the others, sterling was no longer the issue. They could do as little about its departure as they could two years earlier about its entry. For them, the issue was how to prevent the exchange rate mechanism from collapsing under the shock to its credibility following the ignominious end of sterling's two years' participation. Some proposed to close the market for the rest of the week. 'Closing the market' in fact did not mean that there would be no trading in currencies, but that central banks would abstain from interventions. It therefore amounted to a suspension of the ERM. For the British (and the Italians) this would have the attraction that their currencies would not be the only ones to float, and they would not be seen as the ones to blame. Most members, however, did not feel that suspending the ERM was the way to preserve it. Others advocated a general realignment of central rates, with the attraction for Spain that it would not be the only one to devalue its central rate against the German mark. In the end, it was agreed to announce that Ministers and Governors 'took note' of the United Kingdom's decision to suspend sterling's participation, that following this decision the Italian authorities would 'abstain temporarily from intervention' and that the Spanish peseta was to be devalued by 5 per cent. It was stated that '[t]hey all stress their unanimous commitment to the European Monetary System as a key factor of economic stability and prosperity in Europe' while those who stayed in urged those who left to return 'as soon as possible'.[21]

As I approached Amsterdam in the early morning after the all-night session in Brussels and my car mingled in the rush hour traffic entering the city, prospects for the days ahead looked bleak. There were still two working days before The Weekend: the French referendum on Maastricht. According to the latest polls, it would be touch and go. For the French franc, this uncertainty did not bode well, and chances were that the full fury of speculation would now turn against it. If the authorities reacted by raising interest rates, this might well be the straw that would break the camel's back, turning a small yes-vote into a no. The French monetary authorities therefore were as helpless during the next two days as their British counterparts had been in the run-up to the election. But could they be equally lucky, now that the spell had been broken and the pound had been humiliatingly chased out of the ERM?

Amazingly, pressure on the franc during the two days of near impotence preceding the referendum was moderate. At an emergency meeting of the Monetary Committee in the IMF building in Washington DC on Sunday, the members were informed by Jean-Claude Trichet that exit polls indicated a small yes-vote: a *'petit oui'*. Only now, when the market realised how precarious French public support for EMU was, did the full force of the speculative storm hit the franc. The French authorities, after an unfortunate initial hesitation, at last raised interest rates. The Bundesbank supported the franc at levels they would never have been prepared to put at its disposal in advance, in the form of 'mechanisms' the French, the Italians and the Commission had so often demanded in the past. French Finance Minister Sapin put German support at French franc 160 billion.[22] The Dutch also helped. Narrowly, the attack was endured. The ERM, though badly damaged, survived.

19.4 AFTERMATH

For the British government, and for the ruling Conservative Party, Black Wednesday turned out to be a traumatic experience comparable to what Harold Wilson's Labour government experienced following the pound's devaluation in November 1967. In both cases, the event was seen as a major defeat over an issue that deeply split the governing party. What would make Black Wednesday worse was the fact that Europe remained prominently on the political agenda.

Governor Leigh-Pemberton, looking back at the crisis, stated in October 1992: 'It is my view that the decision to join the ERM in

October 1990 was right in the circumstances; that having joined, we were right to endeavour to stick with it; and that, in the circumstances which evolved, we were also right to withdraw.'[23] As to the level of the exchange rate he said

> such evidence as has been advanced in support of the assertion that sterling entered the ERM at too high an exchange rate is far from conclusive.[24] ... Our problem arose because the degree of divergence between the domestic policy needs of Germany on the one hand and those of much of the rest of Europe on the other became wholly abnormal, and it was this quite abnormal tension that tested the margin of tolerance built into the ERM to destruction. This imbalance in the mix of German fiscal and monetary policy was transmitted, through the mechanism of the ERM, to policies being applied elsewhere in the Community and was by no means unique to the UK. ... But it was this quite exceptional tension between domestic policy requirements in Germany and the UK, that was the root cause of the pressures that ultimately forced our withdrawal. I freely admit that, although we recognised the possibility of strains of this sort, we did not foresee the degree to which they would develop when the decision was taken to enter the ERM two years ago. I can only say that in this we were in good company![25]

Not surprisingly, Chancellor of the Exchequer Norman Lamont concurred. Relieved of the immediate pressure (but not yet of his job), he told the press that he was singing in his bath again. Asked what he was singing, he said: *Je ne regrette rien*! This was to become his theme. There was nothing for which he or the Government could be blamed. Consequently the blame rested on others, not least the Germans, and in particular Bundesbank President Helmut Schlesinger, who had triggered the crisis with an indiscretion to a journalist, and who was believed to have granted to the French the support he had withheld from the British. The Chancellor made no secret of his views and feelings, and in so doing was less than diplomatic. As *The Times* commented: 'An Ambassador once defined successful diplomacy as an ability to tell a man to go to hell while making him look forward to the journey. Norman Lamont appears to think that the Chancellor of the Exchequer does not need to be a diplomat'[26] The Bundesbank President, perhaps too thin-skinned for the occasion, reacted in a rather unusual form, with a statement containing a point-by-point rebuttal of the criticism. According to Philip Stephens, the paper was intended as a private briefing-note, but instead it was passed by the German Embassy in London to the *Financial Times*.[27] This in turn provoked a statement by the UK Treasury the same afternoon, stating that Schlesinger's rebuttal 'missed the point'. Both statements were published in the *Financial Times* of 1 October 1992. It took some time for the 'War of Words'[28] to subside.

19.5   THE LESSONS OF SEPTEMBER 1992

Confidence in ERM-type arrangements of stable but adjustable exchange rates was badly shaken as a result of Black Wednesday. Much time was spent drawing lessons from what happened. In the months that followed the crisis, both the Monetary Committee and the Committee of EC Governors prepared reports at the request of the Finance Ministers which were published after the meeting of Finance Ministers and Central Bank Governors on 22 May 1993 in Kolding, Denmark.[29] In the discussions in the Committees, the old controversy re-emerged as to how 'symmetrical' the system should be, i.e. how the burden of adjustment should be shared by deficit and surplus countries, or rather countries experiencing outflows and inflows (since Germany, the main inflow country, by this time had seen its current account surplus in the order of 4–5 per cent of GDP turn into a deficit of one per cent of GDP as a result of unification). For obvious reasons, care was taken not to make the disagreements explicit in the reports. Both reports alluded to the insufficient economic convergence and its effect on competitive positions, to increased capital movements, and to the change in perception regarding the prospects of EMU in the summer of 1992. And both emphasised the continued importance of the rules of conduct agreed in Basle–Nyborg, without stating explicitly that these had not been applied, or not sufficiently applied, in the past. The differences remained unsolved.

19.6   ASSESSMENT

Exchange rates have to reflect competitive positions. If they do not, they have to be adjusted. If they do, they have to be defended.

With increasing capital mobility, the defence of exchange rates has to take the form of crisis prevention rather than crisis management. Crisis management has become costly and difficult, and even successful crisis management means poor crisis prevention. These rules, the core of the Basle–Nyborg Agreement, the basis for an exchange rate arrangement like the EMS, were ignored during the developments that led to Black September.

The basic reason was a lack of agreement on the sharing of the burden of adjustment. Some countries felt that countries experiencing outflows and inflows should contribute in equal measure to stop capital flows threatening the system. Germany, supported by the Netherlands, rejected such a 'symmetrical' system. In their view only countries experiencing outflows could take effective measures to stop these flows. More fundamentally, they felt that from the role of the German mark as an anchor currency – an expression first used in an official document in paragraph 6 of the Delors Report – there followed a division of labour, according to which German monetary policy had domestic price stability as its primary objective, while the other countries would stabilise their exchange rate with the German mark and thus import price stability. This disagreement was never really solved.

The United Kingdom, in particular, rejected such implications of the ERM. In this respect one should bear in mind that it had not participated in an exchange rate arrangement since the demise of the Bretton Woods system, until its entry into the ERM in 1990: adjusting to the constraints of an exchange rate arrangement would take time in the best of circumstances. Nor did it participate in the ERM at the time the rules of conduct of Basle–Nyborg were discussed, and though present, it was felt at the time that these rules did not concern the United Kingdom. Even more important, participation in the ERM was controversial in Britain from the start, both with the Government and within the ruling Conservative Party.

For all these reasons, Britain did not feel the need to agree with the other countries on the exchange rate at which it entered. Nor was it prepared to accept external constraints on its domestic monetary policy, i.e. to raise interest rates for the sole reason of defending the exchange rate. The argument that short-term interest rates have a larger impact on the UK economy than elsewhere is correct. Most probably the statement that interest rate increases would make the ERM even more controversial and would therefore on balance not strengthen the pound was also correct. But these were arguments against British participation in the ERM, rather than against using interest rates to defend the pound once Britain had entered.

No doubt there were other, complicating factors. In particular, there was an inappropriate policy mix in Germany following unification, which resulted in higher German interest rates than might have been necessary if the Federal Government had kept the budget deficit better under control. This presented the other countries participating in the ERM with the choice of either maintaining the central rate with the German mark and accepting the consequences for interest rates, or rejecting higher interest rates, in which case the central rate with the German mark was untenable. Refusing to choose between these alternatives meant that the authorities refrained from a policy aimed at crisis prevention.

Governor Leigh-Pemberton was correct in arguing that this situation could not have been foreseen at the time of British entry. There is, however, an implied suggestion that, had this not happened, the ERM could have been managed by mainly relying on 'sterilised' interventions, retaining in essence national autonomy for domestic monetary policy while participating in the ERM. This is not borne out by the experience that led to the rules of Basle–Nyborg.

20 The Collapse of the Old EMS (1993)

As a result of Black Wednesday those who had trusted the authorities' reassurances suffered huge losses; those who had not, made considerable gains. This could not fail to affect the authorities' credibility, both in managing the ERM and in realising their intention of establishing EMU in accordance with the Maastricht Treaty, which continued its tortuous path of ratification in one country after another. The ERM had survived. But its management was bound to become far more difficult. Its prospects looked more uncertain than at any time since March 1983, when Mitterrand had made his choice for Europe, and seemed to depend on the extent to which member states continuing to participate could agree on the lessons to be drawn from the crisis. These lessons concerned above all the authorities' ability to prevent speculation. Since none of the currencies remaining in the system was clearly misaligned, this had to be done in two ways. Interest rates had to be used to defend a currency, not as a last resort but at an early stage. And the possibility of losses had to be added to prospects of profits, making speculation involve a two-way risk.

20.1 LOST OPPORTUNITIES

Basically, France shared Britain's objections at having to increase interest rates to defend its currency, feeling it was the Germans who should lower theirs. But the French were more pragmatic than the British. This was due partly to their much longer experience in the EMS, but mainly to their traditional preference for stable exchange rates and to the fact that Europe was not so controversial an issue in France as it was in Britain. At the same time France continually tried to make Germany assume a larger share in the burden of adjustment. In doing so, it was taking risks of which it did not always seem to be aware.

At the time of the September 1992 crisis there was a fairly general view that the French franc, unlike the pound, was not overvalued. And since its last devaluation in 1987, France had succeeded in building up a certain credibility for its policy of keeping the central rate with the German mark unchanged. So why then did the speculative attack against the franc occur? A major reason was that in the period preceding the September crisis, in 1991 and 1992, the French government had put that recently-acquired credibility at risk by its impatience to cut interest rates. In the first half of 1991 the franc had to be supported by interventions; there was an impression, reflected in the French press, that the authorities were less than candid as to the amounts to which support had been necessary.[1] Then, on 18 October, Finance Minister Pierre Bérégovoy announced a cut in interest rates, and the franc promptly weakened again. The Minister commented that this was 'acceptable' because the currency was still trading within the EMS limits, though he added: 'The franc is getting close to its floor; I would prefer that it rises to its ceiling.'[2] It was not until 18 November that the authorities, having realised that talking up the franc without action was not possible, raised interest rates, conceding that lowering it when the franc was already relatively weak had been a mistake. And they reluctantly followed a German interest rate increase in December, though Bérégovoy publicly criticised what he called German 'egoism'.[3]

In the following months, both Bérégovoy and his successor as Finance Minister, Michel Sapin, repeatedly made public demands for interest rate cuts. In June–July Sapin unsuccessfully tried to engineer a coordinated cut. The Nederlandsche Bank made it clear to the Dutch government that it was not going to participate in anything that would smack of ganging up against the Bundesbank, nor would it be prepared to participate in politicised ad hoc meetings on interest rates.[4] Fortunately, Sapin did not give publicity to these efforts. What had been said in public, however, was enough to cause doubts in the market whether the French authorities who were evidently so keen to cut interest rates would be able and willing to defend the franc by raising them once the franc came under pressure. Later he was to blame the resulting turmoil on speculators, remarking that during the French revolution such *agioteurs* were put under the guillotine, and giving the impression, that he would not mind having at his disposal this tool of exchange rate management.[5]

As mentioned in the previous chapter (19.3), France escaped a full-scale speculative attack during the two days following Black Wednesday, during which time the franc was at its most vulnerable because interest rate increases were out of the question owing to the referendum the following weekend. When the storm erupted after the *petit oui*, a combination of drastic action and German help enabled France to narrowly repulse the attack.

Shortly after the crisis the French Ambassador paid one of his visits to the Nederlandsche Bank. In separate conversations both President Duisenberg and I expressed some doubts regarding the impatience with which we felt the Banque de France was then reconstituting its depleted reserves at a relatively low exchange rate, in stead of first allowing the rate to rise further. On 23 October the Monetary Committee met in former East Berlin. Before the meeting, the chairman, Jean-Claude Trichet – at that time still Director of the Trésor – who evidently had read the Ambassador's report, approached me expressing interest in our view. Thus encouraged I raised the issue in the meeting. Not wishing to criticise the Banque de France directly, I referred to our own experiences in the sixties and the arguments within the Nederlandsche Bank. These followed bouts of speculation against the guilder, and occurred between our market people who wished to supply liquidity to the starved money markets by buying back foreign exchange as soon as the speculation was over, and others, including myself, who wanted the exchange rate to rise further first, in order to give the markets the experience that speculation against the guilder was risky and costly. Before I had finished, however, my Banque de France counterpart, sensing implied criticism, was asking for the floor, but Trichet – who had been listening attentively – remarked that he understood I was merely referring to our own Dutch experience.[6] In later conversations he more than once referred to this occasion, and when the Monetary Committee was composing its report on the lessons to be learned from the crisis he supported my proposal to emphasise the importance of introducing a two-way risk. My new counterpart at the Banque de France, Vice-Governor Hervé Hannoun, shared this view. Had it been applied in 1992, it might have been remembered and could have made a difference in 1993.

20.2   PRELUDE TO DERAILMENT

In retrospect it seems odd that the months preceding the end of the old-style EMS seemed more difficult for Germany than for France. The costs of German unification for the German budget, a deficit rising to more than 5 per cent of GDP in 1993, and the effects for German wages and prices were sinking in. As a result, newspaper headings like 'Dethronement of the German mark' were common.[7] Other countries, and in particular the new French government under Edouard Balladur, made use of this new phenomenon of German weakness by lowering interest rates as soon and as much as they could.

Sometimes it seems as if governments find coping with windfalls even more difficult than coping with adversity. By the second half of June France had cut interest rates for the ninth time in two months, bringing them below German rates. This was considered a great triumph, and musings about the end of the German mark's anchor role reached the press with increasing frequency. At the same time, French government officials felt that the Bundesbank should do more to contribute to lower interest rates in Europe, and they did not keep this feeling to themselves. In this respect, the new Finance Minister Edmond Alphandéry copied the actions of his predecessor Sapin a year earlier. But while Sapin had taken the precaution not to publicise his efforts (fated to be unsuccessful) to organise a coordinated cut, the new Minister felt no need of such discretion. On 15 June he stated in public that Bundesbank cuts until then had been completely insufficient, and that Germany still had its foot on the brake.[8] And a week later, just before German Finance Minister Theo Waigel and Bundesbank President Schlesinger were due to visit Paris for a routine meeting of the French–German Economic and Financial Council, he announced in a radio interview that they were coming for talks on coordinated interest rate cuts in Europe. Alphandéry added that it was he who had taken the initiative, that the Germans should speed up their interest rate cuts and that now, with the franc so strong against the German mark, France 'will be able to speak as equals with the Germans. That wasn't the case a few months ago.'[9] It so happened that the Bundesbank was actually considering a cut, to be decided upon on 1 July. But given all the talk about the weakness of the German mark and the end of its anchor function, it was felt that a cut in the rate would endanger the Central Bank's credibility if it was seen to take place as a result of strong political pressure. To prevent that, the German Finance Minister decided to postpone his, and Schlesinger's, visit to Paris. The announcement of this the same day was of course seen as a response to Alphandéry's statement, and made headlines in the international press.

A few days later, on 29 June, the Monetary Committee had a routine meeting in Brussels. I joined Tietmeyer in his car to go to our usual lunch with a few Central Bank colleagues, and he read out to me with some glee the headlines in the French press as reported to him by the Bundesbank's Paris representative, most of them critical of their own Finance Minister. Later, on the way back, I asked whether the incident would not make the Central Bank Council's decision on an interest rate cut – to which he had alluded during lunch, without indicating what he expected to be the outcome and what his own position would be – more difficult. 'Had we gone to Paris, then no doubt it would' he replied, adding that this had been an important consideration for him to advise the postponement.[10] On 1 July the Bundesbank duly announced the interest rate cut, but whatever positive effect this might have had in the market was, of course, offset by the perceived row between the French and German authorities. Other central banks followed the German cut, including the French Central Bank which had announced its latest cut merely two weeks earlier, keeping market rates below the German level. But the picture was now rapidly changing. Agreement on budget cuts was reached in Germany and as a result the German mark started to strengthen. Reports about the German economy became more upbeat, while those about the French economy became more gloomy. On 9 July French market interest rates were once again higher than German rates. Talk about replacing the German mark as an anchor currency abruptly ceased.[11] By mid-July the French franc was under considerable pressure. The Danish crown also had to be supported, and even the Belgian franc started to weaken.

Two uneasy weeks followed. The press saw the forced pace of the French interest rate cuts in the preceding months as a major factor in weakening the franc. At the same time, while French Ministers emphasised in public statements that a change in the central rate with the German mark was out of the question, it was politically very difficult for them to support such statements by what the recent reports of the two committees had called 'timely action' in official interest rates: too much prestige had been invested in the preceding cuts. Thus the interest rate instrument appeared to be largely frozen where it could have been most effective, on the outflow side. As it turned out, this was also the case on the inflow side.

20.3 THE JULY CRISIS

On Thursday 29 July the last meeting of the Central Bank Council of the Bundesbank before the holiday season was to take place, and there was a general expectation in the press that a further interest rate cut would be decided in order to ease tensions in the EMS. The announcement of a technical cut in the rate of short-term credit (*Pensionsgeschäfte*) on Wednesday was taken as confirming this expectation, and tensions abated somewhat as a result. Then, on Thursday, shortly after lunch-time, an announcement was made that the Bundesbank had lowered its Lombard rate, which was ineffective at the time, but had kept its discount rate unchanged. The next meeting would not take place until one month later. Almost immediately heavy selling of French francs and Danish crowns started, and most other currencies also had to be supported against the German mark and the guilder. This continued all afternoon. Support for the French franc alone exceeded the equivalent of $ 10 billion. With everyone expecting a realignment over the weekend it seemed inconceivable that markets would open on the next day, Friday, as if nothing had happened.

Yet that is precisely what happened. I remember that Friday as the eeriest day I ever spent in my office. We knew there was a deadlock in French–German talks about what had to be done and that a high-level German delegation was secretly visiting Paris in the morning to sort things out. Prime Minister Balladur had sent a fax to the other prime ministers on Thursday evening, putting the blame for the crisis on the Bundesbank. France totally ruled out a devaluation of the franc and considered, more generally, that existing central rates were adequate. It was prepared to resume the normal functioning of the exchange rate mechanism together with those partners that wished to do so, he wrote. Though not spelling it out, this meant that the Germans should continue to support the franc, or else leave the system. Until this time the French authorities had prevented the franc from dropping to the floor by intervening intramarginally. On Friday morning at around 11, they ceased to do so, informing the other central banks a few minutes earlier.

When I received this news by telephone I turned to the screen on my desk and watched the rate descending to the floor. Here the Bundesbank as well as the Banque de France were obliged to support it, the German mark joining the guilder which had until that moment technically been the strongest currency. Huge interventions continued all day. We were waiting for a phone call from Paris where Franco-German secret talks were going on, but none came. Later we learned that the Germans had suggested the Banque de France cease interventions, but the French authorities refused to do so. If the Germans objected to further supporting the franc, it was the German mark that should float, not the franc, in accordance with Balladur's letter. In comments on British television this scenario was aptly called 'the sun leaving the solar system'. The concept was not entirely new. Former British Cabinet Minister Nicholas Ridley had suggested it a year earlier, when the pound was under pressure.[12] It seems the French also briefly toyed with the idea when the franc was under pressure in September 1992.[13] Now the new French government pursued it as the solution to the crisis. Why this could not work became evident once the Monetary Committee met in Brussels on 31 July to prepare the meeting of Ministers and Governors the next day. For the Netherlands, cutting the link between the German mark and the guilder was no option: if Germany left the EMS, so would the Netherlands. In that case, Belgium and Luxemburg made it clear they would not stay either. Remaining in such a depleted system would be of little interest for most others. Too many planets would follow the sun.

The meeting of Finance Ministers and Central Bank Presidents that started in Brussels on the afternoon of Sunday 1 August was not a realignment meeting but an effort to salvage the Exchange Rate Mechanism. The French government's concept of doing so by in effect asking Germany to leave the system came to naught, because once the Dutch followed the Germans too many others would leave. The German proposal to salvage it by widening fluctuation margins to 6 per cent was rejected by France, fearing that the new floor would soon be reached and problems would then start again. Other ideas, some of them quite bizarre, were put forward and rejected. While this was going on, Jacques Delors, who had stayed at home due to back trouble, was causing headaches for participants by trying to conduct parallel negotiations with Heads of Governments over the telephone. Almost until the last minute the only possible outcome seemed to be a suspension of intervention obligations. Only towards the end of the meeting, well past midnight, was it agreed to widen fluctuation bands to 15 per cent at either side of the central rate. The band between the German mark and the guilder remained 2.25 per cent on the basis of a bilateral arrangement of the two countries.

20.4   THE CRISES IN RETROSPECT

A combination of factors contributed to the July crisis which resulted in the end of the old EMS.

- After the speculative attack on the French franc in September 1992 had been repulsed, the authorities failed to fully seize the opportunity to make it clear to the market that speculation can be risky. A clear demonstration then of this two-sided risk might have made a difference in July 1993.
- The temporary weakness of the German mark during the months preceding the July crisis offered too strong a temptation to governments in other countries to lower interest rates too far too fast.[14]
- The French government already in office in September 1992 might have learned its lessons by watching Norman Lamont. The new government, less aware of history, was condemned to repeat it. Not able to resist the temptation provided by the German mark's temporary weakness, it debated interest rates with Germany in public, and it invested so much prestige in its interest rate cuts that it felt it could not afford to increase rates soon afterwards, making this tool of defence inoperational.
- The French government in this period seemed to exaggerate the economic impact of short-term interest rates relative to that of long-term rates and exchange rates. Real interest rates at the time stood at around 5 per cent, a level that in 1988 and 1989 had allowed an economic growth in the order of 4 per cent, as the monthly bulletin of the Banque de France of July 1993 pointed out.

Rather than being a considered position, the French proposal that Germany leave the EMS temporarily while the Germans sorted out the problems created by unification (confirmed by Prime Minister Balladur at his press conference on 2 August 1993) may well have been the Government's reaction to an emergency its short-sighted policy had helped to create. It is doubtful that the more experienced permanent functionaries would have advised it, just as they cannot have been happy with the preceding pace of interest rate reductions creating doubt over the Government's priority for maintaining the central rate. An unusual article in *Le Monde* of 10 August 1993 by Jean-Claude Lefranc, a pseudonym for a group of disgruntled high functionaries, under the heading 'If only Pierre Bérégovoy had been there', reflected their misgivings.

It was unfortunate that France had an inexperienced Finance Minister during this delicate period. Inexperienced Finance Ministers are a 'systemic risk'. It is a risk of which central bankers are only too aware. In February 1990, the new Dutch Finance Minister Wim Kok said in reply to questions from journalists that if the German mark came under pressure as a result of unification, the guilder need not necessarily follow. This made headlines about de-linking the guilder from the German mark.[15] The Nederlandsche Bank, needless to say, was not amused. In the long run, when the temporary weakness of the German mark would be long forgotten, this statement might be remembered, suggesting that the guilder would not follow the German mark upward either. In the short run, it was embarrassing vis-à-vis the German partners. Bundesbank President Pöhl lost no time in telephoning his Dutch counterpart. The conversation went like this:

Pöhl: What on earth is the matter in Holland?

Duisenberg: We have a new Minister.

Pöhl: Oh! I see![16]

At a later stage, there was some discussion whether with hindsight the proper response to the 'external shock' caused by German unification would not have been a German mark revaluation, compensating upward pressure on costs and prices in Germany and enabling the Bundesbank to pursue less strict monetary policies. In Germany itself, there would probably have been considerable resistance against such a policy. Even as it was, Germany's competitive position measured in unit labour costs worsened from 1989 to 1993 by 15 per cent.[17] For the Netherlands, after its experience with the 1983 devaluation, it would have been out of the question to accept a change in the central rate between guilder and German mark. And for France, too, maintenance of the central rate with the German mark had become a cornerstone of its policies.

20.5   ASSESSMENT

Fundamentally, the old ERM became unsustainable for France in July 1993 for the same reason that made the United Kingdom leave the ERM in September 1992. Neither country could accept the implications of the German mark as an anchor currency, meaning that Germany pursued whatever monetary policy was needed to safeguard domestic price stability while the other participants used their monetary policy primarily to keep their exchange rate with the German mark unchanged. It is true that the French were more pragmatic than the British, due to their traditional preference for stable exchange rates, the fact that Europe was not so controversial in France as it was in Britain, as well as France's longer experience in the ERM. But even so the French harboured basic objections against a German-dominated exchange rate mechanism.

The French demand to share in monetary decision-making was a major and consistent feature of French European policy from the 1960s. Awareness that it could not be realised within the EMS, or in any exchange rate arrangement, made it pursue Monetary Union, where decision-making would be transferred from the national to the European level. But this did not prevent France from continuing its efforts to increase its influence on decision-making in the ERM, risking time and again the credibility it had achieved for its exchange rate policy. This made the EMS in its old form inherently unstable. A number of special factors prevailing in 1991–3 contributed to making it unsustainable.

The end of the old EMS did not mean the end of relative exchange rate stability. It would have meant this had exchange rates been allowed to fluctuate within the new fluctuation band of 15 per cent on either side of the central rate, but this was not the case. However, keeping exchange rates stable was no longer an obligation. It depended on voluntary action, meaning in practice that the burden rested on the country whose currency had to be supported. Though the new system might be better suited to discourage speculation, it was even more asymmetrical than the one it replaced, and therefore in the long run just as objectionable to the French.

Therefore, though the old EMS' collapse had the immediate effect of diminishing the authorities' credibility and therefore also affecting the prospects of EMU, the alternatives to EMU did not become more palatable. Since floating exchange rates are not practicable in the longer run for the strongly interdependent continental economies of the European Union, the alternative to EMU is some form of German mark bloc, where the other countries in effect follow German monetary decisions based not only on German priorities but also on the situation prevailing in one country: Germany. For a country like the Netherlands this is acceptable. For France it is not, even though French officials tended to look with some envy at the combination of a stable exchange rate and low interest rates the Dutch policies produced in the early 1990s, and repeatedly asked how we did it.

21 The Guilder: A Case Study of a Hard Currency Policy

After August 1993, when the EMS in its original form ceased to exist, there was a widespread tendency to argue that in a world with unlimited capital mobility exchange rate stability was no longer feasible. I heard this comment made at the IMF and elsewhere, usually followed by the afterthought that, of course, this did not apply to the guilder in relation to the German mark. The question is, why not? One answer is that the Netherlands' (and Austria's) 'natural economic integration with Germany is such that the ERM is not even necessary.'[1] This does not explain, however, the difference with other economies equally dependent on Germany, such as Belgium or Denmark, nor is it consistent with repeated devaluations of the guilder against the German mark up to 1983. Another answer, more to the point, is that – in view of this dependence – the Dutch authorities have pursued a policy linking the guilder to the German mark more consistently than others. If so, it is a question of policies as well as of economic dependence. In this chapter I shall discuss these policies as a case study of successful pegging in the Exchange Rate Mechanism of the EMS.

21.1 TRAILING THE GERMAN MARK

The Netherlands was the first country to follow a hard currency policy in the sense of an orientation of its exchange rate policy on the German mark and, after 1983, of explicitly linking the exchange rate of the guilder to the German mark. The reason for doing so was a combination of Germany's economic importance for the Netherlands, and the priority it was giving to price stability. The first manifestation of this policy can be traced back to 1961, in the days of the Bretton Woods system, when Germany took the – at the time almost unprecedented – step of revaluing the German mark's par value by 5 per cent. The guilder followed suit the same weekend. Yet it would be many years before this became a consistent policy. In the years of the snake arrangement that followed the demise of the Bretton Woods system, the guilder's central rate with the German mark remained unchanged in roughly half of the realignments that took place. This was perceived as a hard currency policy, controversial in view of the deterioration of the Netherlands' competitive position in the 1970s. If the authorities were not criticised more than was in fact the case, this was mainly due to the fact that the high exchange rate was attributed not so much to their policies but to the current account surpluses due to the export of natural gas. The phenomenon of a deteriorating competitive position associated with natural gas was often referred to as 'Dutch disease'.

Seen by the Nederlandsche Bank, the economic picture was different. From the early 1970s to the early 1980s, collective expenditure increased from 45 per cent of GDP to 67 per cent, an average annual increase of 2 per cent. Government receipts from natural gas also increased, but this windfall profit could finance only a small part of the increase in expenditure it no doubt encouraged, so that borrowing took place on a large scale. It is ironic that in the early 1980s both public gas receipts (over 5 per cent of GDP) and public sector deficits (9 per cent of GDP) simultaneously reached their maximum level. As a consequence, the public debt ratio to GDP eventually rose from 40 per cent to 80 per cent. At the same time, the collective burden increased, stimulating tax push inflation. Inflation in the mid-1970s rose to above the OECD average. Since trade unions focused on real disposable income, wage increases exceeded the rise in productivity. The resulting profit erosion pushed up unemployment. While all this went on, the current account surplus – largely due to natural gas exports – remained considerable most of this period, so that the Government had no difficulty in borrowing without having recourse to the Central Bank. The only possibility the latter had for exerting pressure was to keep the exchange rate relatively high, helped by the current account surplus. Of course this did not help the eroding competitive position. But indexation in this period had become so widespread that currency depreciation would not have improved it; the head of the largest trade union, Wim Kok, rejected proposals to correct indexation for price increases due to a deterioration of the terms of trade.[2]

Convincing the Government and the public that the central rate with the German mark should be kept unchanged was a gradual process. A welcome support was given by the two large international institutions concerned with exchange rates, the OECD and the IMF. The OECD in 1988 published eleven case studies under the title 'Why Economic Policies Change Course'. In the chapter on the Netherlands it said:

> The peg to the German mark ... proved an effective instrument for inflation control, given the consistently anti-inflationary monetary stance of the Bundesbank ... Whether this approach imposed avoidable short-term costs on the Dutch economy is perhaps debatable, though it is hard to imagine that an alternative approach would have yielded uniformly better results. It might be that a less rigorous peg, or one that focused on a basket of foreign currencies, could temporarily have alleviated somewhat the pressure on the manufacturing sector – but with a concomitant weakening of control over inflation and probably higher interest rates in the longer term. Certainly, given wage indexation and the extreme openness of the Dutch economy to trade, the squeeze on profitability and external competitiveness to which Dutch industry was exposed during the period could have been allayed only very temporarily by devaluation ... In the absence of a credible anchor for policy in the German mark peg, inflation pressures would presumably have been greater, necessitating tighter monetary policy on domestic grounds and higher interest rates on average.[3]

The International Monetary Fund also consistently supported this exchange rate policy in the regular Article IV consultations and in the reports the IMF staff wrote on the basis of the consultations.

21.2   THE LAST DEVALUATIONS (1979 AND 1983)

In September 1979 France devalued the franc against the German mark, insisting that part of the realignment should take the form of a German revaluation of 2 per cent against all other currencies (against which the Danish kroner would be devalued by 3 per cent). The Netherlands tried to resist a devaluation of the guilder against the German mark, but its position was weakened by two factors.

One was the Belgian insistence that the Belgian–Dutch exchange rate should not be adjusted. Initially the Benelux countries formed a common front opposing an adjustment of their central rates against the German mark, but in this front Belgium turned out to be the weak link when France and Germany increased the political pressure. Even more important was the fact that the Netherlands entered the discussion with a technically weak guilder, having failed to follow interest rate increases elsewhere in Europe, including Germany. Market expectations could therefore not be invoked as an argument to keep the guilder–German mark central rate unchanged.

After the realignment Deputy Director of the Nederlandsche Bank Henk Boot, who had replaced me at the meeting, analysed what had gone wrong. He concluded that in order to avoid a repetition, the main lesson to be learned from this highly unsatisfactory outcome was that it was important 'to create an undeniable political fact regarding the guilder in as far as this is possible: an unassailable position in the market, implying that next time a deviation from the German mark would not be credible.'[4] On the basis of this analysis the Executive Board of the Nederlandsche Bank agreed to change their money market policies, making a strong guilder within the fluctuation band the main policy objective. To this end we increased money market rates as soon as technical circumstances permitted, in November, and from then on deliberately kept the guilder rate close to the German mark. After some initial confusion, most market participants seemed to understand and to accept what we were trying to achieve. This was reflected in the circumstance that in the course of 1982 and the beginning of 1983 Dutch money market interest rates could be permitted to decline below German levels, at times as much as three-quarters of a per cent, while the guilder rate remained above the central rate.

Under these circumstances the decision of the new Dutch government in March 1983 to once again devalue the guilder with 2 per cent against the German mark, taken this time without any outside pressure, came as a shock to the market. In deciding to devalue the guilder against the German mark, the cabinet overruled both the Central Bank and the Finance Minister Onno Ruding, arguing that the size of the realignment, following earlier adjustments, was excessive in terms of economic fundamentals. What it failed to realise was that a devaluation of 2 per cent against the German mark would hardly have an impact on the Dutch competitive position, while the effect on confidence, and therefore on interest rates, was certain and considerable.

The Nederlandsche Bank's disagreement with the Government's decision is on record, since its advice was published by the Government at the time, as the law required: it was the only occasion that such a disagreement occurred. It is therefore surprising that more than a decade later former Prime Minister Ruud Lubbers was quoted in a newspaper saying that Central Bank President Duisenberg, though having raised objections, 'acquiesced. Had he persisted, he would of course have had his way.'[5] Duisenberg could not have been clearer in his position when the Cabinet's decision was being debated, nor did he mince his words when it was retrospectively debated a month later in the ministerial Council of Economic Affairs, calling the decision 'incomprehensible'. If the former Prime Minister implied that Duisenberg had 'acquiesced' because he did not threaten to resign, this makes the statement no less surprising. Even if he might have prevented the decision in this way, the Nederlandsche Bank would have been put in an impossible position. Imagine the effects on the market if it had become known – not unlikely in the open Dutch society – that the Cabinet 'acquiesced' in keeping the guilder's central rate with the German mark unchanged only because otherwise the Central Bank President had threatened to resign!

The Cabinet based its decision on the extent of the cumulative German mark–French franc realignment. More fundamental, however, was Prime Minister Lubbers' belief that the considerable current account surplus – due largely to natural gas – gave the authorities the option of either linking the guilder to the German mark (which he felt would worsen the Dutch competitive position) or lowering the exchange rate by cutting interest rates and thus stimulating capital exports. His preference for the latter took shape, at his initiative, in the programme of his Cabinet.[6] The Nederlandsche Bank could not convince him, until it was too late, that he could not have both a devaluation against the German mark and lower interest rates than in Germany. If the market concluded that in the next realignment the guilder might again be devalued against the German mark, German interest rates would be a floor for Dutch interest rates: Dutch rates might be higher, but not lower.

Until March 1983, while the guilder remained strong Dutch money market rates were often below German rates. Following the 1983 realignment, Dutch money market rates rose and remained considerably higher than the German ones; whenever the Nederlandsche

Bank allowed the differential to decline, the guilder weakened. It was only towards the end of the decade that confidence was regained (see the diagram overleaf). As a result, Dutch press comments and political opinion became increasingly critical of the Cabinet's decision. The Cabinet let it be known that this would not happen again. This strengthened the Nederlandsche Bank's position. From then on the Cabinet agreed with the Bank that the exchange rate objective should be an unchanged central rate of the guilder with the German mark. What remained was an ongoing difference of opinion as to whether the same objective might not be obtained at lower cost.

21.3 INTEREST RATE CONTROVERSIES

Even though after 1983 the Government was in agreement with the Bank regarding the exchange rate objective, and even though setting interest rates was the Bank's prerogative as long as the Government did not issue a directive – which was generally considered to be politically impossible – the Bank could not simply ignore the Government's yearning for lower interest rates. Any public disagreement was bound to diminish the credibility of the exchange rate policy, especially in view of the memory of the Government's 1983 decision, and would further increase the interest rate differential with Germany, hereby exposing the Bank to additional criticism. This required a delicate balance. On the one hand, whenever the guilder came under pressure early interest rate action was required, making it clear to the market that the exchange rate had priority over interest rate considerations; this would in the longer run result in lower interest rates than any other policy. On the other hand, if such policy provoked too much criticism, it would be counterproductive. For example, when immediately after the Government's decision in March 1983 to devalue the guilder against the German mark the guilder came under pressure, the Executive Board of the Nederlandsche Bank discussed raising interest rates. Though a moderate early rise was likely to make a more drastic one at a later stage unnecessary, we refrained from doing so as we realised that under the circumstances it would be interpreted as an action to spite the Government. As a matter of fact that did happen when we finally raised interest rates a few weeks later, but by then we could point to the considerable loss of reserves that had occurred in the meantime.[7]

International money market rates
three–months euro deposit–rate; monthly averages

Interest rate differential Netherlands – Germany

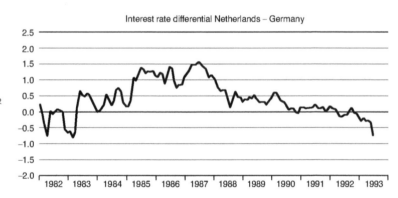

Exchange rate guilder/DM

In general we were helped by the fact that the press – and therefore also politicians – focused on the so-called official interest rate, ignoring not only money market rates but also short-term lending rates of the Nederlandsche Bank. We used a combination of 'official rate' and short-term lending rate to influence money market rates. Given the fascination of press and politicians with the former, we increasingly came to rely on the latter (like flying twin-engined airplanes on only one engine, this is less safe but sometimes inevitable). The official rate was only changed when the Bundesbank changed its rates: commentators accepted this given the exchange rate objective to maintain the central rate with the German mark. As a result it was increasingly believed that Dutch interest rate policies automatically followed those of Germany, and though comments to that effect were not always flattering, it was politically convenient. In reality, interest rate differentials between Germany and the Netherlands showed considerable variation over time, as can be seen in the Figure.

As long as it was thought we raised interest rates only if the Bundesbank did so, and followed any German cut immediately and fully, criticism of the Nederlandsche Bank was muted. Interest rates were felt to be too high, but it was the Bundesbank that was blamed, in particular when the policy mix in Germany after unification put the burden on monetary policy. We felt such criticism was unjustified, counterproductive, and in the long run dangerous since it might cause doubts on the maintenance of the link between the guilder and the German mark. We therefore tried to dissuade the Dutch government from joining British, French and other governments in criticising the Bundesbank. In this, we were only partly successful. For example, as a major Dutch newspaper revealed (*NRC Handelsblad*, 30 November 1992), the Dutch Prime Minister had sent a letter to the German Chancellor earlier that year, complaining about high German interest rates. Though ostensibly a personal letter, it was in fact a political *démarche*. We felt we had no choice but to inform the Bundesbank as well as Lubbers that we disagreed. The Prime Minister was a seasoned politician whose every action in his heyday was scrutinised for hidden meaning. In this case I am not sure there were any, and though he probably failed to realise it, it was embarrassing for all concerned. The beleaguered Bundesbank, widely criticised for doing in a difficult situation what the law required it to do, thought it could count on Dutch support. The Nederlandsche Bank did what it could to give that support, and attached great importance to the Dutch reputation of reliability and predictability in monetary matters.[8] Finance Minister Wim Kok, whatever his own feelings on interest rates cannot have relished the Prime Minister's uninvited foray into his field of competence. Chancellor Helmut Kohl had no say over the Bundesbank's policies and, since he must have assumed that Mr Lubbers was aware of this, may have wondered whether the real object of the criticism was not once again (as in November–December 1989) his own policy on German unification (see 15.3). All of them were embarrassed, as was in the end, the man who sent the letter. This also seemed to be the feeling of one of his advisers who later remarked to me that the letter did little to enhance Amsterdam's candidacy as the site of the European Central Bank. 'Or any other candidacy!' was my spontaneous reply.[9]

21.4　THE GUILDER AND THE CRISIS OF 1992

At the beginning of the 1990s confidence in the guilder, which had been shaken by the Government's decision in March 1983 to devalue the guilder against the German mark by 2 per cent, had finally been fully restored; by now, the Nederlandsche Bank could afford to let short-term interest rates decline to the German level without an immediate weakening of the exchange rate. Thus the guilder entered the turbulence of 1992–3 in a comfortable position.

Yet, the position of the Nederlandsche Bank in the summer of 1992 was not so easy as it seems in retrospect. We were increasingly aware that we had to expect an early devaluation of the lira, and this could provoke a chain reaction, starting with sterling. At the time, the Bundesbank was tightening its policies. It was aware, of course, that by doing so it caused problems elsewhere, but felt it could not afford to refrain from such a policy. The German inflation rate exceeded the EMU norm, and if a wage-price spiral developed this would impair not only the Bundesbank's credibility but also that of EMU. Moreover, long-term interest rates, surprisingly stable thanks to confidence in German monetary policies, would rise.

The Nederlandsche Bank understood these considerations and discouraged any political efforts at 'ganging up' against the Bundesbank, making clear that it would not join such efforts,[10] as I mentioned in the previous chapter (20.1). We felt that the louder the criticism of German monetary policies, the likelier were expectations in the market that the complaining countries would not be able or willing to defend their currencies with interest rate increases if this became necessary. At the same time we felt that, with the prospect of an approaching realignment and with the guilder slightly below the central rate with the German mark, we could not take risks and had to keep interest rates in line with those in Germany: failure to do so would create doubts about our determination to keep the guilder linked to the German mark. Thus when the Bundesbank increased its official rate on 16 July, the Dutch Central Bank felt we had to follow. Since the Finance Minister was opposed to interest rate increases in general, and increases of official rates in particular, and did not hesitate to make his objections clear, we only increased our short-term lending rate. In order to avoid the perception that we did not follow the Bundesbank, we took the unusual step of explaining the increase in a press communiqué. The risk that failure to follow the Bundesbank with an increase in our official rate would nevertheless be misunderstood had to be weighed against the risk that an increase in the official rate might provoke open criticism by the Government, which would have negative effects on the guilder. To make sure, we further increased the rate at the end of the month, thus eliminating the remaining negative market rate differential with Germany. These moves were carefully watched in the market, as illustrated in a comment by Reuters on 30 July: 'The Dutch Central Bank's surprise special advances money market rate hike should sweep away any doubts about its commitment to lashing the guilder to the mark, analysts said. The market was doubting slightly that this was still the Bank's policy.'

Thus treading wearily through the political minefield, we prepared for the storm. By the time it hit us, in the beginning of September, the guilder was in good shape. Its market rate was even slightly above the central rate with the German mark, enabling us to cut the official rate slightly on Black Wednesday in the hope of encouraging the British to increase theirs. For them, however it was by then too late.

21.5 GERMAN–DUTCH BILATERAL AGREEMENT

In the first half of 1993 the guilder continued to be strong, and the Nederlandsche Bank repeatedly cut interest rates, as did other EMS countries. Then, at the end of June, market sentiment abruptly changed. The German mark strengthened and the French franc found itself exposed after a series of interest rate cuts, while the political prestige the Government had invested in these cuts made it difficult to reverse them at short notice (see 20.2). The Nederlandsche Bank realised a crisis could be imminent. Dutch interest rates were again below German rates, and though the guilder rate still remained slightly above the central rate with the German mark, the Bank concluded it was time to fasten seatbelts in face of the coming turbulence that might well spell the end of the EMS. Thus, when the Bundesbank announced a cut in the discount rate on 1 July, the Nederlandsche Bank followed only partly,[11] to the irritation of the Prime Minister and the Finance Minister, who in discussing the move together disparagingly referred to the 'jellyfish at the Bank'.[12]

The full force of the storm hit the EMS in the last week of that month, after the decision of the Bundesbank Council on 29 July not to lower the official discount rate. Before the day was over, it seemed clear the EMS in its existing form was doomed. During the whole afternoon, while speculation raged and we too intervened for considerable amounts to support other currencies, there was no contact whatsoever at the management level between us and either the Bundesbank or the Banque de France. This may seem odd, the more so since Duisenberg was chairman of the Committee of Central Bank Governors. However, it reflected the reality that France and Germany disagreed on what to do, and as long as that was the case no solution was possible; this, however, is not the same as saying that anything they might agree upon would be accepted by us and by the others.

At about ten in the evening I was telephoned at home by my German counterpart Hans Tietmeyer, who was still in his office. Tietmeyer started the conversation by saying that the situation was very serious and that for the time being he saw no solution. What possibilities did I see? In reply, I started to enumerate the various options, and he commented on each of them.

'A French devaluation.'

'They exclude that.'

'A German revaluation, which necessarily would have to be a German and Dutch revaluation.'

'That would be the same thing.' (This indicated that according to his information the French – unlike earlier years – rejected any adjustment of the franc–German mark central rate, no matter how it was presented.)

'A widening of the margins.'

'What would your position be on that?'

I said I felt that we could accept that, provided it was voluntary. To his question of what I meant, I replied that only those countries that felt they had to would widen their margins. He said that it would be possible to maintain narrower margins unilaterally.

'I do not mean unilaterally. I mean maintaining the existing margins bilaterally, mutually. It would not be acceptable to us to change the arrangement between the guilder and the German mark just to suit the presentational requirements of larger countries.'

When he showed some understanding of this position, I asked whether this meant we could count on his support. 'From me personally, yes' was his reply. He added he did not know whether a widening of margins would be acceptable to the French, which I took to mean that for the time being they rejected it. In the course of our conversation I asked whether, at this juncture, Germany or France (preferably both) could do anything with their interest rates, to which – hardly to my surprise – his answer was no. He gave the clear impression that he was far from happy with the way things had been handled.[13]

Immediately after this conversation I called Wim Duisenberg, who told me he had a message to call Bundesbank President Schlesinger. Later he called me back, telling me that he had insisted even more emphatically than I had on the requirement that the guilder–German mark relationship should remain unchanged on a mutual basis. Schlesinger had not committed himself, but had told Duisenberg that a high-level German delegation would secretly visit Paris first thing in the morning. Meanwhile, interventions would be resumed. Duisenberg then called Finance Minister Kok at his holiday address in Switzerland to bring him up to date and to make sure he was in full agreement with our position.

As soon as markets opened on Friday, speculation – as expected – started again, and continued the whole day, while French–German secret talks were going on in Paris without result. In the evening the German delegation returned rather upset from its unsuccessful visit. After having reported to Chancellor Kohl, Schlesinger called Duisenberg and assured him that Germany fully agreed with our position that the German mark–guilder relationship should remain unchanged with the old fluctuation margin on the basis of mutual intervention obligations.

The Monetary Committee met in Brussels on Saturday afternoon and Sunday morning. Hans Tietmeyer proposed to widen fluctuation margins to 6 per cent, indicating that this could be done in a flexible – i.e. differentiated – way, but the French members rejected this. As far as they were concerned the markets could open on Monday, as if nothing had changed, with those countries interested continuing, in line with Balladur's letter. This of course meant Germany leaving the EMS, but that was never spelled out. The French members stated there was no French proposal. At this Tietmeyer grumbled that in that case he had apparently not paid sufficient attention earlier, the only occasion when I thought I could detect a hint of irritation on his part. From our position it followed that if that happened the guilder would leave the system too, and the Luxemburg members made it clear that, as far as they were concerned, so would Belgium–Luxemburg. It was not clear who would stay.

On Sunday afternoon ministers and governors met. Before the meeting we briefed Minister Wim Kok, still in his holiday outfit, on the Monetary Committee meeting; President Duisenberg was on his way from Amsterdam, bringing with him more suitable attire for the Minister. There was hardly any discussion on the Dutch position, but I pointed out that once it became clear that our position was causing a chain reaction, we were likely to come under heavy political pressure, as had been the case in 1979. I was not sure the Minister was sufficiently prepared for this, while he – without actually saying so – seemed to wonder why I found it necessary to insist on a point on which we were agreed. By way of explanation I remarked that, having been around for so long, I could not help remembering the occasion in 1979 when a previous minister and governor had entered a similar meeting with the best of intentions, only to yield under pressure. At this he looked at me over his reading glasses in silence for some time, then said: 'You'll realise that what you just said does not increase my inclination to yield under pressure!' I could only hope so. Later, during the meeting, he indicated to me he remembered my warning.

In the ministerial meeting it was soon clear that a differentiated widening of the fluctuation margins would not be acceptable to France. This implied that the continuation of the existing relationship between the German mark and the guilder would have to be based on a bilateral agreement between the two countries, outside any EC arrangement. France did not relish this, and for other countries it might also be awkward. In the course of the evening – the plenary meeting had been suspended and been replaced by informal talks – the Dutch delegation got the impression that the German delegation was under pressure not to enter into a bilateral agreement with the Netherlands. It is most likely that the French government was behind this. In addition, Jacques Delors was busy on the telephone at his home. According to a French source, he also contacted the Dutch Prime Minister, arguing that the EMS should continue with only Germany leaving it, and Mr Lubbers replied that he agreed but the Dutch monetary authorities did not.[14] Whether true or not, Finance Minister Wim Kok, who was aware that Delors was active on the phone, had taken the precaution of staying in close contact with his Prime Minister. At this stage of the negotiations in Brussels, Wim Kok and Wim Duisenberg indicated that they wanted to clear up the situation with the Germans before taking part in any further talks. To that end, the German and Dutch delegations withdrew in an empty meeting room, the one normally used for Monetary Committee meetings, where we drew up chairs to form a small circle next to the large conference table. Here, German Finance Minister Theo Waigel started the discussion. He said he had made it clear to others that Germany was not pressuring the Dutch either to maintain or not to maintain the link with the German mark, but he could well understand that the Dutch were not inclined to abandon a policy successfully pursued for many years; this was also a German interest. Minister Kok welcomed this attitude, and then began discussing specifics. On that basis the agreement to maintain the existing intervention points on a bilateral basis was confirmed.[15] Later, when the plenary meeting was resumed, both Duisenberg and Kok announced this agreement,[16] the German delegation obviously preferring not to rub it in. Subsequently, the Bundesbank and the Nederlandsche Bank settled the technical details of the arrangement.

We would have preferred doing this within the framework of the EMS. This would have meant differentiated fluctuation bands in the system, as had in fact existed until then (2.25 and 6 per cent bands). When France rejected this, presumably because it did not wish to be seen to be in a second class, our objective could only be realised on the basis of a bilateral exchange rate arrangement with Germany. France was not happy with this. Instead of making

Germany leave the EMS, it might find itself facing the nucleus of an arrangement similar to the old mini-snake. Germany, however, though offended by France's efforts to push it out of the EMS, did not want a European exchange rate arrangement without France. For that reason Germany might initially have preferred Dutch unilateral pegging to a formalised bilateral arrangement. It would no doubt have found it more difficult to accede to our wishes, had other countries been in a position to make similar demands at the time. However, since these were all under downward pressure during the crisis, the guilder was clearly in a different position than the other currencies.

The bilateral agreement was generally welcomed not only in the Netherlands but also in the German press, where it was seen to have prevented monetary isolation of Germany that France tried to engineer, as well as proof that criticism of German monetary policy having pushed up interest rates in neighbouring countries was unfounded. In French government circles the agreement, understandably, was deprecated. A few days after the crisis a high official at the Matignon, the Prime Minister's office, in a conversation with a Dutch Embassy representative called it evidence of national egoism; we took this as a compliment. Soon it was decided to ignore the arrangement: as another official put it, *'je connais pas, ça n'existe pas'*.[17] Our direct French counterparts showed more understanding, since they were aware that this was the result of a consistent policy on our part over many years, and they probably would not have minded a similar consistency in the policies of their own Government either. I found it gratifying that even at the emergency meeting in Brussels, during a suspension of the plenary meeting, our Banque de France colleagues solicited our views on what French interest rate policy should follow after the crisis, preparing no doubt for the battle they expected within France.[18]

21.6 ASSESSMENT

The link between guilder and German mark resulted from two factors: Dutch economic dependence on Germany, and consistent policies by the Dutch monetary authorities to establish and maintain the link. It was a policy borne out of necessity. At the beginning of the 1970s, natural gas seemed to render the Dutch economy immune from external constraints in the traditional sense of deficits on the current account of the balance of payments. As a result, public borrowing was never a problem, and political decision-making did not accept constraints on the expansion of public expenditure. The monetary authorities, i.e. the Central Bank with the support of the successive Finance Ministers, tried to impose constraints on decision-making in the form of an exchange rate objective.

Without support from the successive Finance Ministers, the policy of linking the guilder to the German mark would not have been possible. But it was equally essential that the Nederlandsche Bank, since the 1979 and 1983 devaluations, was in a position to indicate to the market, whenever interest rate decisions were taken, that the exchange rate had priority. This could not have been the case in practice if interest rate decisions were taken by the Minister of Finance, since those decisions would inevitably have been politicised. Each cut would have been made earlier, each rise postponed. The overall result would have been less confidence and therefore higher interest rates, and under those circumstances it is doubtful whether the exchange rate objective would have obtained the necessary public support in the long run. An autonomous central bank is therefore a condition for a hard currency policy.

Inevitably, the Nederlandsche Bank was influenced by the political pressure for lower interest rates. It is here that the benefits of collective decision-making in the Central Bank are clearest. The President is subject to direct political pressure, while the other members of the Executive Board are less so. While they would be reluctant to 'outvote' the President (as a matter of speech: a formal vote was never taken on policy matters in the Board in the more than twenty years that I was a member) they can stiffen his resolve, supply arguments, and perhaps even serve as an alibi. In the long run an active policy of public explanation and education can considerably strengthen the Central Bank's position. And, of course, in the long run one can judge the results: nothing succeeds like success. The seemingly effortless way in which the guilder survived the currency crises in 1992 and 1993, the fact that interest rates in the Netherlands were no longer higher, and sometimes lower, than in Germany, silenced most critics. There is a danger here, however. In its efforts to convince politicians of the correctness of its hard currency policy, the Central Bank was tempted to 'promise' low interest rates as a result. The danger is that the distinction between objective and result becomes blurred. A strong guilder is the objective, interest rates the main instrument to achieve it, and low interest rates the ultimate result. As soon as low interest rates are perceived to be more than that, an objective in their own right, credibility is at risk. The risk is further increased if the Central Bank, having 'promised' low interest rates in exchange for political support for its policies, feels obliged to deliver. Here, too, collective decision-making in the Central Bank can reduce that risk. An autonomous Central Bank implies depolitisation of interest rates. At the same time, it is essential for the Central Bank to 'think politically'. The Nederlandsche Bank would not have been successful in its exchange rate policy if it had tried simply to ignore the political pressures to which it was subjected. Thus, in addition to being consistent, its policy had to be a balancing act.

The Dutch example illustrates that even with strongly increased capital mobility, exchange rate stability is feasible. But far from following automatically and effortlessly from Dutch economic dependence on Germany, it also demonstrates the conditions that have to be fulfilled to realise it. The exchange rate has to be realistic. Its maintenance has to be generally accepted. And the policy towards that end has to be consistent and credible. This means that the exchange rate has to have priority over interest rates; in practice, only an autonomous central bank is in a position to ensure this priority, though it needs the support of the Finance Minister and the acceptance by public and Parliament of its policies. Fundamentally, these policies meant acceptance of a German mark bloc. For all their grumbling, and their periodic efforts to obtain the result without paying the costs, the Dutch government accepted the implications of a German mark bloc. It was for these reasons that the Dutch succeeded, where others failed, in keeping their currency stable against the German mark.

22 Why the Euro?

The permanent fixation of exchange rates, followed by the introduction of the Euro, will implement an intention announced by
the six founding states of the European Communities thirty years
ago, in 1969 in The Hague. It will be the culmination of a process
that started more than a decade before that, with the establishment of the Coal and Steel Community. As was the case then, the
motives for this apparently technical–economic initiative are pre-
ponderantly political. Its main movers are Germany and France,
as has been evident throughout this book. Let me summarise in
this concluding chapter their motives and the ponderous European
decision-making process with its inevitable compromises, contradictions and dilemmas.

22.1 GERMAN MOTIVES

For Germany, political integration was the main objective from an
early stage. Konrad Adenauer, the first post-war Chancellor, was
convinced that German unification could only be achieved in an
acceptable way, i.e. without putting Germany in an isolated position between East and West, in the context of a European solution. That required priority for West Germany's ties with the West,
in particular with France, since good relations between Germany
and France were at the core of European integration. When political integration suffered a severe setback as a result of the rejection
of the European Defence Community by the French Parliament,
and economic integration replaced it, Adenauer at first had misgivings. He feared economic goals would divert attention from the
main objective, Political Union. But he came to the conclusion, as
he put it, that one should not reject something that is good just
because one wants something better that is not yet attainable. Therefore he instructed the German Government to pursue economic
integration as a high political priority. But his goal remained
'achieving step by step the unification of Europe, first by economic
integration, then by political integration and finally integration in
the military sphere.'[1]

The monetary dimension was added in 1969. Monetary issues are power issues. By this time the strength of the German mark, reflecting Germany's return to the world scene as a major economic power, was becoming increasingly evident. So was French concern. German–French relations which had become cooler since Adenauer's departure were coming under strain, and European integration stagnated. For Brandt, who became Chancellor in 1969 shortly after Pompidou replaced De Gaulle, it was essential to remedy this situation. Otherwise he would have had no prospect of success in pursuing the major new item on his Government's agenda, the *Ostpolitik*. This was a major political motive to meet French concerns by agreeing to a process to establish Economic and Monetary Union. Concern that the United States might weaken its political commitment in Europe due to the Vietnam war was also a reason for deepening European integration.

The need to ensure European backing for initiatives towards the East, as well as periodic concerns about lessening US involvement in Europe, were to become recurrent themes in the two decades that followed the Summit in The Hague in 1969, encouraging the Federal Republic to bring about closer political and military cooperation in Europe, in particular with France. In principle, France agreed. Mitterrand wrote: 'The idea of Europe is inseparable from the idea of defence.' At the same time France was aware that its views on US–European relations in the sphere of defence were fundamentally different from those of Germany, and of the European partners in general. Mitterrand said, reflecting consistent French views since De Gaulle: 'Only France, in Western Europe, is autonomous in its strategic decisions.'[2] Clearly, this situation was not going to change for the time being, and no real progress could therefore be expected in this sphere. France responded to German approaches by putting monetary integration to the fore of the proposed intensified cooperation. Thus, when Helmut Schmidt's misgivings about the Carter administration's unpredictability made him intensify cooperation with Giscard d'Estaing, the result was the establishment of the European Monetary System in 1979. The closer military cooperation desired by Schmidt was postponed until after the French presidential elections. A decade later, the combined effect of the shock caused when in October 1986 in Reykjavik Reagan almost traded away the US nuclear deterrent without even consulting the European allies, and the need of support for prospective German initiatives towards the East, made Kohl and Genscher susceptible – as had been the case earlier with Willy Brandt – to French monetary initiatives. This resulted in the establishment in 1988 of the Delors Committee. By now, military cooperation was also being intensified, but when Germany proposed the establishment of a French–German Defence Council, France linked this to the establishment of a French–German Financial and Economic Council to deal with monetary issues as well. Finally, Kohl's efforts in 1989–90 to force German unification induced him to agree to Mitterrand's desire to link German unification to European integration and to accelerate preparations for EMU. Thus each time EMU received a new impetus, this was because Germany needed France and wished to reassure French concerns. There were, however, major differences in interest and view between the two countries where monetary issues were concerned.

In Germany, where there was a historically motivated, deep-seated fear of inflation among most of its population, European monetary arrangements were only acceptable if price stability was safeguarded. Consequently, the Bundesbank could always count on political support if it felt that stability was at risk. Helmut Schmidt learned this the hard way when, in his eagerness to meet French demands, he tried to brush aside the Bundesbank's objections in 1978. Helmut Kohl, who as leader of the opposition supported the Bundesbank on that occasion, took a far more cautious attitude than his predecessor when he became Chancellor. In 1985, he acceded to French wishes to insert a 'monetary dimension' into the Single European Act, but he added that German preparedness for concessions found its limits where price stability was threatened. And in the negotiations leading to the Maastricht Treaty he fully supported the German monetary authorities in their efforts to ensure that the future European Central Bank would be committed to price stability and be independent from political instructions, making this in effect a German condition for EMU. The Federal Constitutional Court, when it declared that the Maastricht Treaty was compatible with the German constitution, gave it a constitutional basis by stating that the commitment to price stability contained in the Treaty was fundamental to German participation.

On Political Union, the German attitude was and is more flexible. Like Adenauer four decades ago, Kohl regarded it as the ultimate objective, while it is also seen – by the Bundesbank and others – as a condition for the long term sustainability of EMU. EMU is seen as a means to obtain EPU rather than an objective in itself. But though trying to link EMU to EPU before Maastricht, Kohl did not insist when EPU could not be achieved on that occasion. He put his trust in the momentum EMU would create, and in the 'revision conference' – the 1996 IGC – agreed to in Maastricht. By the time the IGC was completed in Amsterdam in June 1997 Kohl's main worry seemed to be to get EMU established as scheduled in 1999.

German political considerations were presented in a paper published by the parliamentary group of the largest Government party, the CDU/CSU, on 1 September 1994, called 'Reflections on European Policy'. The paper stressed the importance for Germany of avoiding being caught once again between East and West. Since it would be the first to suffer the effects of instability in the East, it has a major interest to avoid such instability from arising.

> If (West) European integration were not to progress, Germany might be called upon, or be tempted by its own security constraints, to try to effect the stabilisation of Eastern Europe on its own and in the traditional way. However, this would far exceed its capacities and, at the same time, erode the cohesion of the European Union . . . Hence, Germany has a fundamental interest both in widening the Union to the East and in strengthening it through further deepening. Indeed, deepening is a precondition for widening.

The paper went on to argue that 'Monetary Union is the cornerstone of Political Union.' In a speech shortly after publication of the paper, its main author, Karl Lamers, explained that this was because Monetary Union has the most supranational character of the various arrangements in the Treaty: 'In Maastricht we arranged perfectly the monetary part, but the rest was incomplete.'[3]

22.2   FRENCH MOTIVES

From an early stage, money was a central element of European integration for French policy makers. There is a much-quoted statement attributed to Jacques Rueff, later De Gaulle's Economic Adviser: *'L'Europe se fera par la monnaie ou ne se fera pas.'* (Europe will be made by money, or it will not be made.) Some four decades later it was echoed by President Mitterrand who stated

that without a common monetary system there is no Europe.[4]
The European Commission shared this view; it was probably not by
chance that the monetary portfolio in the Commission has almost
permanently been in French hands.

More than almost any other country, France regarded monetary
policy as part of its Government's foreign and domestic policy. During
the presidencies of De Gaulle and Pompidou, France was engaged
in confrontational policies regarding the United States, whose dominance over Europe it resented. When De Gaulle took power he
felt that in the post-war years the United States had been permanently dominating French foreign policy, allowed to do so by French
dependence on Marshall Aid, by its military dependence on NATO
and by its lack of political stability. From now on, France wished
to take its affairs in its own hands and have its own policies.[5] While
there was no way he could compete with a superpower in the military domain, De Gaulle recognised the US balance of payments
deficits – which had been increasing as a result of the effects of
the Vietnam war – as a chink in its armour which he could try to
exploit, and endeavoured to weaken the dollar's international
position. But even here the only prospect of successfully standing
up to the United States was if France could do so with Europe
behind it, in particular Germany with its increasing monetary strength.
Organising coordinated policies vis-à-vis the dollar under French
leadership with the aim of reducing the dollar's global role, and
establishing Europe as a counterweight to the United States,
became the early objective of French European monetary policy.

With German economic power steadily increasing the emphasis
shifted. A common policy towards the dollar remained desirable,
but the motive became increasingly domestic. Strict German monetary policies tended to force an appreciation of European currencies against the dollar, threatening French competitive position
and economic growth. And even apart from the dollar, as a result
of Germany's importance for France, strict German monetary
policies imposed a severe constraint on French domestic policy by
limiting economic growth to less than what was desired on the
basis of domestic considerations which tended to give priority to
employment even at the risk of inflation. Attempts to ignore these
constraints would result in pressure on the franc, eventually forcing a reversal of domestic policies, or open or disguised devaluation. Concern on this point is amply documented by statements
made by French officials and politicians. The EMS failed to provide

France with influence on monetary decision-making, the lack of which had made it leave the snake. The rules of behaviour agreed in Basle and Nyborg accentuated French dependence, and were initially rejected in 1986 by Daniel Lebègue, Director of the *Trésor*, for precisely that reason (see 8.2). In the end, in 1987 they had to be accepted, since speculation threatened the continued existence of the EMS, but former Minister Jean-Pierre Chevènement argued:

> France cannot accept, under the pretext of coordination of economic policies, to have its growth permanently limited by that of Germany ... The Germans should know that France is not condemned to only one possible policy. In order to achieve progress in the EMS, it should be realised that we can, if necessary, leave it.'[6]

Basically, this view was widely shared in France. But the alternative to the EMS as a German mark bloc was not seen in leaving it, but in transferring monetary decision-making to the European level. Getting rid of the EMS' constraints was presented by former Prime Minister Michel Rocard as one of the main virtues of EMU: 'It is of this kind of archaism, obstacle to growth, that the single currency will finally liberate us.'[7] As Banque de France Governor Jacques de Larosière put it: 'Only collective management of a single currency inside a well-balanced and independent institution will allow France to participate fully in the European monetary decision-making process and provide the best guarantee for the exercise of national monetary sovereignty.'[8] France wanted European monetary arrangements that would enable it to pursue relatively expansionary domestic monetary policies without being constrained by balance of payments deficits, i.e. without being placed in a position where reserve losses resulting from these policies would end up by forcing it either to adopt German policy priorities or to let its currency depreciate. Such arrangements would of course force Germany to pursue more expansionary policies than it would itself have preferred.

Thus France was engaged in a power struggle, initially mainly with the United States in which it needed German support, and later with Germany. In both cases it needed some form of common monetary decision-making in Europe to ensure French influence. At first it was felt this could be established by introducing a common currency that need not be a single currency: it would be used for international transactions but – notwithstanding French endorsement of the Werner Report of 1970 – need not replace national currencies. Decisions at a European level regarding the common currency (notably on interventions to support the dollar) would put German monetary policy under pressure to expand, while France would not have to give up the franc and could thus keep its monetary sovereignty (to the extent that it exists). It was probably only towards the end of the 1980s that France came to the conclusion that this approach was unpromising and the only way to influence monetary decision-making was by completely transferring it from the national to the European level, establishing a single currency and a common monetary policy pursued by a European Central Bank. According to Aeschimann and Riché, the issue was debated within the French government as late as January 1991. They quote President Mitterrand as stating on this occasion that he had long rejected a European Central Bank, but had come to the conclusion that France would be better able to influence the policies of the ECB than those of the Bundesbank.[9]

Mitterrand, however, publicly expressed his regrets at the cost of this. In order to attain its objective, France had to acquiesce in the future ECB's independence from political instructions and its commitment to price stability as its priority objective. Earlier these issues had been left open. By now the Bundesbank's policies' success had contributed to make this an issue widely supported domestically in Germany, and Germany's increased strength enabled it to insist on this as a condition for EMU. But while France had no choice but to accept this, it insisted on language in the Treaty that would enable it to raise the issue in the future.

France agrees with Germany that European integration should be extended beyond the monetary domain. But far more than Germany it regards EMU as desirable in itself, to be established whether integration takes place in other fields or not. And though it desires political cooperation, in the French view this will have to be mainly intergovernmental. In this respect the French view resembles the British one. Unlike Britain, however, France wants permanent, institutionalised and not *ad hoc* cooperation.

22.3 THE DECISION-MAKING PROCESS

The main motives for establishing Economic and Monetary Union are political rather than economic. This is borne out by the close involvement of the Heads of State or Government, in particular the German Chancellor and the French President (even when, as in the case of Helmut Kohl and François Mitterrand, they were not particularly noted for their personal interest in economics). In 1969, when EMU was first announced as an objective, as well as in 1988, when the Delors Committee was established to make proposals for its implementation, the initiatives came from the highest political level. Heads of State or Government can initiate; in fact, in these cases only they could do so. But they cannot implement. For that, they need the monetary authorities: the Finance Ministries and the Central Banks. On both occasions, Heads of State or Government carefully refrained from entering into specifics, confining themselves in essence to indicating that the action was to take place in the monetary sphere, and what its direction might be. Negotiations, including those on the definition of the objective, took place at the level of the monetary authorities.

There were good reasons for this division of decision-making. For one thing the perspective at the level of the monetary authorities is different from the rarefied atmosphere at the summit, if only because central bankers are more aware than politicians are that no arrangement is sustainable that is not credible to the market. Even more important, central banks – notably the more independent ones – attach a high priority to price stability. And the Bundesbank in particular has sufficient political backing in Germany to ensure that its views cannot easily be brushed aside, whatever the German Chancellor might be prepared to concede. This became clear in 1978 on the only occasion that the European Council, at the insistence of Schmidt and Giscard d'Estaing, tried to fix the specifics of the European Monetary System before involving 'the experts'. Though Schmidt was prepared to meet French demands to make the EMS more 'symmetrical' than the snake had been, he was not able to deliver. Something similar happened at the Rome Summit in October 1990 after Kohl appeared to concede the establishment of a European Central Bank at the start of the second stage.

Thus, when asked to make proposals for the implementation of what had – usually with great publicity – been announced from the summit, the monetary authorities did not usually confine themselves to trying to fathom what the Heads of State or Government might have had in mind. After the Schmidt–Giscard initiative to replace the snake by the EMS, for example, the Committee of Governors had an initial discussion on its implementation following the European Council Meeting in Bremen in July 1978. My Belgian counter-part, who was then chairman of the alternates who had to prepare the Governors' meetings on the subject, complained about the lack of information of the summit's intentions. Bundesbank President Emminger retorted that it was the Central Banks' job to provide a sensible *(vernünftige)* interpretation. And Dutch President Zijlstra (himself a former Prime Minister!) added that the only way to find out what the Heads of Government had in mind would be to make Messrs Schmidt and Giscard d'Estaing honorary members of the subcommittee of foreign exchange officials. Since this did not seem practicable, it was up to us to agree what it was they should have had in mind![10]

Results tended to differ from announcements owing partly to this two-tier decision-making, partly to the fact that Heads of State or Government were sometimes only vaguely aware of the implica-tions of their intentions and, once these became clearer, were not really willing or able to accept them, and partly to market devel-opments. This would in time lead to new initiatives at the highest level. The announcement in 1969 to establish EMU within a dec-ade resulted not in EMU but in the snake, which France and others subsequently had to leave due to pressure on the franc resulting from differences in macroeconomic policy priorities which the po-litical initiatives had hardly tackled, let alone reduced. To restore European monetary cooperation, Schmidt and Giscard in 1978 took the initiative to replace the snake with the EMS. This was pre-sented as being fundamentally different but, as it finally emerged from the negotiations, in fact was not. The same, still unresolved, policy differences that had wrecked the snake in its original form now strained the EMS. But France felt it could not leave the new system as it had the old. Devaluations (however disguised) tended to increase in frequency and did not offer an acceptable solution. Thus French dependence on the Bundesbank's policies became increasingly manifest. And since this was not satisfactory to France, in 1988 the European Council took the initiative to revive EMU. The shifting of action from the highest political level to that of the monetary authorities where the approach is different, market reac-tions to unresolved policy differences, limiting progress towards vaguely defined objectives, and the shift back again as the political summit takes fresh initiatives, are all features of the European monetary decision-making process. So too is the fact that the results of such a process can only be compromises.

22.4 CONTRADICTIONS

Compromises comprise contradictions. Both France and Germany are facing them. For France, the construction of Europe is first and foremost the way to safeguard French influence in both Europe and the world. In 1994 Prime Minister Edouard Balladur put it as follows: 'First something evident: the organisation of Europe is, for France, an additional element of strength and influence. My Government has demonstrated that Europe could serve the interests of France, if the latter's political will is expressed without ambiguity.'[11] Can France really rely on the emerging European Union, with EMU at its core, to serve this purpose?

EMU is, for France, the way to obtain influence on monetary decision-making in Europe. But Germany attached conditions to EMU which France had no choice but to accept. If genuinely respected, these will prevent the French government from exerting influence on monetary decision-making in EMU. Article 107 expressly forbids governments from influencing the ECB's decisions. Does this not defy the purpose?

German unification added an unexpected urgency to European integration. Not being in a position to stop or delay unification, France insisted on linking it to accelerating the process of European integration. Until then there had been a precarious balance between the two countries in so far as France, which had been one of the occupying powers in Berlin, as well as a nuclear power and a member of the UN Security Council, still felt it had a political status that to some extent compensated for German economic strength. This balance is now destroyed. Would not the European Union be dominated by Germany, rather than as France hopes by a duumvirate?

The problem of imbalance is aggravated by the European Union's prospective expansion. In the article quoted above, Balladur pointed out that expansion – to which France had earlier been decidedly cool – was unavoidable. But in a European Union expanding first to the North and then to the East, France – he wrote – risked being marginalised. 'Deepening' is seen to be one way to avoid this, but can it really do so?

The fundamental contradiction in the eyes of those who challenge this policy seems to be that France, in order to safeguard its strength and influence as a country, seeks European integration, which by definition implies partial loss of sovereignty.

Despite doubts and contradictions, successive French governments have persisted on the road to Monetary Union. Edouard Balladur, Jacques Chirac and Lionel Jospin all expressed misgivings when out of office. Once in office, however, all came to the conclusion that France had no alternative. Only by continuing the French policy of pursuing Monetary Union could they hope to ensure a leading role for France in Europe.

The difference with Britain is striking. Britain also aspires to a leading role in Europe, but divisions over Europe have run right through the main political parties in the post-war years. Historically Britain followed a fairly consistent policy of abstaining from participation in any major initiative for European integration so long as it might fail, only to join once that did not happen. There are perfectly understandable reasons for this attitude, which is rooted in geography, history and economics. It is more surprising that this insular policy in no way seemed to diminish British aspiration to leadership in Europe. In the 1960s, when Britain belatedly decided to enter the Common Market but was kept out by De Gaulle, Foreign Secretary George Brown reportedly told Willy Brandt: 'Willy, you must get us in so that we can take the lead!' Nor did John Major see any contradiction between insisting on the British opt-out and claiming to put Britain in the heart of Europe. This is essentially also the attitude taken by Tony Blair's Labour Government: 'If the single currency is established and if it is a success, then Great Britain . . . in the long run should join.'[12] This meant, as Chancellor of the Exchequer Gordon Brown made it clear in the House of Commons on 27 October 1997 that the United Kingdom might join EMU after the year 2002, or it might not. On the basis of this open-minded attitude he feels entitled to participate in any 'inner circle' that EMU participants may establish.

Thus, while France believes it can only ensure a leading role in Europe by playing a leading role in its construction, influencing it as much as possible and therefore being closely involved and vulnerable if things turn out differently, the British approach is just the opposite. Britain feels it can afford to stay aloof, joining only once it turns out to be a success, and still claim a leading role. In the past this did not work. Whether it will in the future, only time will tell.

Like France, Germany is facing contradictions. For reasons discussed before, it wants Political Union. Yet it is odd to reflect that if Political Union, implying genuinely common foreign and security policy, had existed in 1989, it is doubtful whether German unification – a major German policy objective – would have come about, given the partners' manifest lack of enthusiasm.

As it is, EMU appears to be a condition that has to be fulfilled to obtain Political Union. There is a widespread awareness that Monetary Union is a major German concession. At a parliamentary hearing in Bonn in September 1991 I pointed out in my concluding remarks that, unlike other participants, Germany will really relinquish monetary sovereignty. This was repeatedly quoted in the German press. At the hearing the next speaker, Hans Tietmeyer, prefaced his prepared statement with the remark that he might take it easy, confining his contribution to merely stating 'that's right!'[13] But Germany did not succeed in its efforts to link the establishment of EMU to a commitment to EPU, and prospects to attain the latter seem, if anything, to have diminished.

Moreover, there is increasing doubt in Germany whether the conditions Germany attached for relinquishing the German mark are really being fulfilled. It was mainly at German insistence that the convergence criteria, in particular the requirement that only those countries that have their public finances sustainably under control can participate in EMU, were written into the Treaty. The intention of strictly interpreting this requirement was announced by both Government and Parliament, and received the blessing of the Constitutional Court. However, with the date of decision approaching it became increasingly clear that a strict interpretation as intended at the time would mean postponement. Kohl's Government refused to contemplate this for fear that postponing EMU would mean abandoning it.

Thus Germany finds itself in a position that having accepted to establish EMU as the price for obtaining EPU, it now insists on paying the price without any certainty that the goods will be delivered, and is prepared to waive strict adherence to the conditions attached at its own demand.

Despite widespread misgivings in Germany, which pose a potential domestic political threat of which Chancellor Helmut Kohl must undoubtedly have been aware, he and his Government have come to the conclusion that Germany could not afford to endanger the establishment of Monetary Union. EMU has become the centrepiece of European integration. If the establishment of EMU became uncertain, the whole process of European integration would be thrown into disarray. Widening would also become uncertain, with possibly destabilising effects on Germany's eastern borders. French–German relations would come under strain. The German government could not take the risk of allowing such a situation, with its unpredictable consequences, to arise.

Thus, neither France nor Germany is realising its objectives in EMU as agreed at present. Yet both want to proceed, since there is no viable alternative. In doing so each no doubt hopes that once EMU is established its own preference will in the end prevail. Germany expects monetary integration will force integration in other respects (a 'monetarist' view it once disputed), while France presumably hopes that in a large EMU it will be able to muster sufficient support for its views.

22.5 DILEMMAS

Even though the motives for establishing Economic and Monetary Union are political rather than economic, its objectives – political as well as economic – can only be realised if EMU functions well. Fundamental to the Maastricht Treaty is the view that Monetary Union can only be sustainable if based on Economic Union. It is with this in mind that the convergence criteria have been agreed. Sustainable control of public finances is at the core of Economic Union and of the convergence criteria. The Stability Pact is meant to make it operational. Only if public sector deficits were to be reduced sufficiently below the 3 per cent ceiling would member states be able to continue to respect the ceilings without being obliged to resort to counter-cyclical measures whenever an economic downturn sets in. Firm control of public finances is necessary in order to allow automatic stabilisers to take effect.

In the course of 1997, if not before, it became evident that even Germany and France had considerable difficulties in reducing their public sector deficits to 3 per cent of GDP. Prospects for a further reduction, in accordance with the Stability Pact, appeared slim, with the risk that the Pact would loose its credibility right at the start. If governments that had earlier indicated their intention to interpret the criteria strictly maintain that position, EMU would have to be postponed. Though the Treaty does not provide for this, neither does it provide for the possibility that participants would not respect the convergence criteria.

In view of the expectations created, however, and in view of the political as well as economic risks of postponement, towards the end of 1997 most member states seemed to have rejected the possibility of postponement. This meant a less than strict interpretation of the convergence criteria in the case of Germany and France. Moreover, since it is felt to be politically awkward to admit Germany and France despite doubts regarding their performance, while at the same time rejecting the participation of other countries, then it was decided the other countries had to be admitted as well.

This implied a further watering down of the interpretation of the convergence criteria, particularly in the case of Italy, and to a lesser extent, Belgium. The convergence report of the European Monetary Institute, which had to be produced as part of the process of assessing which countries fulfilled the criteria in effect pointed out that the Italian public sector deficit in 1997 was 2.7 per cent of GDP due only to one-off measures in the order of 1 per cent GDP. The debt-to-GDP ratio was far above the 60 per cent reference value, and significant and persistent overall fiscal surpluses were rapidly needed to be able to forcefully reduce the ratio to 60 per cent, in order to make Italy comply with the criteria.[14] The Bundesbank in its report was even more explicit. It expressed 'considerable doubt' on the sustainability of the public finance situation in the longer run, even taking into account plans for further measures known at the time, and stated that the existing 'serious concerns' could only be met if Belgium and Italy accepted substantial further obligations.[15] The Nederlandsche Bank expressed similar concerns. Italy – mainly under pressure initiated by the Dutch – did undertake to effectuate additional measures, but these fell far short of the 'significant and persistent overall surpluses' deemed necessary by the European Monetary Institute.

At the meeting on 2 May 1998, however, where the Heads of State or of Government had to confirm which countries qualified for participation in EMU, the question hardly played a part since it had in fact been settled earlier. The meeting was dominated by the appointment of the first President of the European Central Bank. By threatening to veto the Dutch candidate W.F. Duisenberg, who was supported by the overwhelming majority, French President Jacques Chirac secured an understanding that Duisenberg would retire before the end of his term and would be succeeded by a French national, Jean-Claude Trichet. The French felt that establishing a large EMU – including Italy – from the start in which German views are less likely to dominate than would be the case in a small core group, as well as securing the early prospect of a French ECB President was essential to counterbalance the perceived threat of German domination and thus to establish a more acceptable balance of power in EMU. Immediately after the meeting, President Chirac referred explicitly to French national interests regarding the ECB presidency. French Minister for European Affairs Pierre Moscovici shortly afterwards stated that 'having a French head take over reasonably early in the new bank in Frankfurt does fit the pattern of a broad equilibrium in top European jobs that is healthy for the French–German relationship and the outlook for integration.'[16]

Yet there are considerable risks both for participants and for the outside world in starting EMU with members that do not really comply with their commitments. Tensions between governments and the ECB, as well as between governments themselves, are to be expected. If the ECB would control the money supply in accordance with the priority it has to give to price stability, interest rates would rise, causing problems in a number of countries. If it yields to political pressure, price stability would be threatened as a result and this would cause problems for Germany where the priority for price stability embodied in the Treaty is seen as the basis for German participation. EMU would thus become a source of discord instead of unifying participants, as intended. In the end, such a situation might even threaten the continued existence of EMU, though liquidating it once it has started would be such a traumatic event that all would try to avoid it if at all possible.

In its relations to the outside world, an EMU subject to internal disagreements and tensions would be destabilising, since it would become inward-looking and rigid in its external positions. US Deputy Secretary Larry Summers' warning 'that European policy-makers will have to avoid being overly preoccupied with building and refining the architecture of Monetary Union' can only be heeded if Monetary Union is based on a well-functioning Economic Union, i.e. if participating countries genuinely respect their budgetary commitments and sustain control of their public finances.[17]

There is a dilemma because Germany and France agree that EMU has to be part of a wider process of European integration, but they do not agree either on its substance or form. Starting EMU without agreement on what is a fundamental political issue implies considerable risk, but it is felt that no agreement is likely so long as EMU is not in place.

A major dilemma confronting many governments is that they are committed to what is a major change affecting all citizens without real backing from a large part of the public. Merging national currencies is both a complex technical question and a highly political issue. It requires that the public understands what it implies and why it is done. As yet, it does neither. Convincingly explaining an operation situated in the borderland of technique and politics is not easy, nor is it made easier by the inevitable compromises and resulting contradictions. Yet acquiring the backing of the public for major political issues is the basis of democracy, and it will be indispensable once EMU is in place and unpopular measures are necessary. Explaining what they are trying to achieve, and why, is therefore one of the most urgent tasks still facing governments.

To summarise the dilemmas facing governments: EMU's success depends on proper policies and popular acceptance. A successful EMU can encourage continued integration and contribute to stability in Europe, while failure will have the opposite effect. Having made EMU the centrepiece of European integration, however, Germany and France could not allow it to be postponed, even though doubts remain whether the conditions for its success are fulfilled.

22.6 CONCLUSION

Establishing Economic and Monetary Union is a major political enterprise undertaken primarily for political reasons. Germany and France both take the view that French–German cooperation is essential for stability in Europe, and that such cooperation should not be purely bilateral but requires a European framework. In order to be acceptable to France this framework has to contain monetary arrangements, since it is in the monetary sphere that German dominance has become increasingly manifest since the late 1960s. For Germany, aware of the implications of its size and its location in the centre of Europe, and with its recent history in mind, further development towards a Political Union seems imperative. To that end, it is prepared to merge its successful German mark into a single European currency, the Euro, provided its stability is safeguarded by an independent European Central Bank committed to price stability, and by arrangements ensuring that participating countries will avoid, or correct, excessive public sector deficits. In its view Economic and Monetary Union is a condition that has to be fulfilled in order to create the momentum necessary for further integration.

Germany and France both believe that the European framework necessary to ensure their cooperation has to extend beyond the monetary sphere, and they probably also agree that in order for it to be permanent it has to go beyond purely intergovernmental co-operation. Both concur that agreement on substance and form of what has to be added can only be expected once EMU is established.

In introducing the Euro, member states are taking risks. All major political enterprises carry risks. They also present opportunities. From a monetary point of view, the establishment of EMU will take place at a time when important lessons have been learned: few still believe that anticyclical government policies and pump-priming can ensure stability and prosperity. These lessons enabled member states to agree on a Treaty obliging them to avoid excess-ive budget deficits and establishing a European Central Bank whose main task will be to pursue price stability. Of course price stability and balanced public finances by themselves do not ensure success. But they are conditions for success. From a political point of view the end of the cold war and of the artificial divide running through Europe requires the establishment of new relationships within Europe. An enlarged European Union will provide the framework for these relationships. This framework should promote political stability, essential for Europe and for the world. Monetary and budgetary stability cannot ensure political stability, though the re-verse may well be true. But they can make a vital contribution.

Notes

1 The Political Background to European Integration

1. The Schumann Declaration, 9 May 1950. Reprinted in A.G. Harryvan and J. van der Harst, 1997, p. 61.
2. Ibid., p. 65ff.
3. Ibid., p. 92.
4. Anthony Gorst and Lewis Johnman, 1997, p. 152.
5. W. Scott Lucas, 1991, pp. 292ff, 314, 324ff.
6. Georges-Henri Soutou, 1996, pp. 60–1.
   Robert Rhodes James, 1986, p. 578.
7. Colette Barbier, 1993, p. 109.
   Jan Reifenberg, *Frankfurter Allgemeine Zeitung*, 28 August 1995.
8. Robert Marjolin, 1989, pp. 284ff.
9. Georges-Henri Soutou, 1996, p. 62.
10. Harold Macmillan, 1971, pp. 164, 176.
    Harold James, in his admirable book on IMF history, does mention US support to Britain, but ignores the earlier obstruction.
    Harold James, 1996, pp. 102–3.
11. Georges-Henri Soutou, 1996, p. 59ff.
12. Anthony Gorst and Lewis Johnman, 1997, pp. 152, 160.
13. Anthony Eden's predecessor Winston S. Churchill in *The Gathering Storm*, p. 518.

2 The Rome Treaty (1958) and the Barre Plans (1968–9)

1. Robert Marjolin, 1989, p. 325.
2. Robert Marjolin, 1965.
3. Dutch Parliamentary Record, 2nd Chamber, 9 February 1965, 1964–5, p. 1096.
4. These schools of thought are also dubbed 'behavioralist' and 'institutionalist', Lorenzo Bini-Smaghi *et al.*, 1994, pp. 11–12.
5. M.W. Holtrop, 1956.
6. M.W. Holtrop, 1963.
7. Robert Marjolin, 1989, p. 363.
8. This report was not published. But in its eleventh Annual Report which was published the Monetary Committee pointed to the difference in inflation rates between member states and argued in general terms that coordination could not be confined to monetary policies. (Paragraphs 17 and 18.)
9. M.W. Holtrop, 1956.

3 **Economic and Monetary Union: The Hague Summit of 1969**

1. Reprinted in *Compendium of Community Monetary Texts*, European Communities, Monetary Committee, 1974, pp. 14–15.
2. Communiqué of the Ministers of Finance and Central Bank Presidents of the Group of Ten of 2 October 1963. The Group of Ten consisted of Belgium, Canada, the Federal Republic of Germany, France, Italy, Japan, the Netherlands, Sweden, the United Kingdom and the United States.
3. George P. Shultz and Kenneth W. Dam, 1977, p. 121.
4. The meeting is described in some detail in Robert Solomon, 1977, pp. 143–8.
5. Harold James, 1996, p. 231.
6. Harold Wilson, 1971, p. 91ff.
7. De Gaulle in particular protested against what he called in a much quoted phrase the exorbitant privilege (*privilège monumentalement abusif*) of the United States to finance their deficits by creating more of their own currency, a complaint echoed by Debré and Couve de Murville. But since he realised that France could never share in this privilege he was bent on making the United States lose it rather than creating a European currency to share in it. Charles de Gaulle, 1971, p. 202. Michel Debré, 1993, p. 160. Maurice Couve de Murville, 1971, pp. 52–3.
8. Maurice Couve de Murville, 1971, p. 53, 264ff.
9. Hermann Kusterer, 1995, p. 164.
10. Robert Marjolin, 1989, p. 281.
11. Hermann Kusterer, 1995, p. 201.
12. Pierre Servent in *Le Monde*, 25 January 1993, quoting Alfred Grosser: *Les Occidentaux*.
13. Pierre Servent, ibid.
14. Michel Debré, 1993, p. 262.
15. Hermann Kusterer, 1995, p. 334.
16. Otmar Emminger, 1986, p. 146. This was also the view of Charles Coombs, senior Vice-President of the Federal Reserve Bank of New York, who gives an amusing description of the Bonn meeting. Charles Coombs, 1976, p. 182ff.
17. Otmar Emminger, 1986, p. 143.
18. The next day, 24 November, De Gaulle explained his decision in a short speech over the radio, blaming *cette odieuse spéculation* (this odious speculation) for the problems and announcing both the re-introduction of exchange controls that had recently been abolished, and budget cuts. Charles de Gaulle, 1970, p. 385ff.
19. Michel Debré, 1993, p. 324.
20. Ibid., p. 326.
21. Ibid., p. 262.
22. Ibid., p. 325.
23. Willy Brandt, 1976, p. 319.
24. Henry Kissinger, 1979, pp. 409–10.
25. Peter Bender, 1986, 1995, p. 138ff.
26. Egon Bahr, 1994, p. 7.

27. Henry Kissinger, 1979, p. 409.
28. Ibid., p. 408.
29. Ibid., p. 410.
30. Ibid., p. 422.
31. Eric Roussel, 1984, p. 407.
32. Gerhard Stoltenberg, 1997, pp. 193, 208.
33. Willy Brandt, 1976, p. 339. Stoltenberg also states 'that Brandt wanted to make his *Ostpolitik* more secure (*absichern wollte*) by deepening European unification, also in view of the possibility of a reduced US political engagement that was feared as a result of the Vietnam war.' Gerhard Stoltenberg, 1997, p. 229.
34. Ibid., p. 321.
35. Ibid., p. 321.
36. Georges-Henri Soutou, 1996, p. 317. According to Stoltenberg, Barzel would even have been prepared to vote in favour of the Treaties, but was defeated on the issue in his party by Franz-Joseph Strauss. Gerhard Stoltenberg, 1997, pp. 208–9.

4 The Werner Report (1970)

1. Decision of the Council of 6 March 1970 regarding the procedure in the matter of economic and monetary cooperation. *Compendium of Community Monetary Texts*, European Communities, Monetary Committee, 1974, p. 17.
2. *Compendium of Community Monetary Texts*, European Communities, Monetary Committee, pp. 20–3.
3. Hans Tietmeyer, 1994, p. 24.

5 The Snake

1. Letter of 12 June 1970 of Pierre Werner to Hubert Ansiaux. Werner Report, Annex 5.
2. Annex 5 to the Report of the Werner Committee.
3. Second Chamber of Parliament, 25 May 1971, p. 84.
4. Meeting of the Council of Finance Ministers in Brussels on 11 March 1973; author's diary, 13 March 1973.
5. Letter dated 4 August 1975 to the Dutch Minister of Finance.
6. Press release of 22 September 1975.
7. Philippe Jurgensen, 1991, p. 32.
8. France was consistent in this attitude over time. Once the European Monetary System had replaced the snake it opposed association with Austria pending membership negotiations of the European Community, no doubt for similar reasons. It was therefore somewhat surprising that the French Minister of Finance Jacques Delors stated in an interview published in *Euromoney* in October 1983 that he was in favour of association with the EMS by Sweden and Austria, adding: 'Perhaps one day even the Swiss may find it sensible not to have a currency which goes its own way'.
9. *Bulletin of the European Communities*, no. 9, 1974.

10. Valéry Giscard d'Estaing, 1988, p. 139ff.
11. Author's notes of the meeting of Ministers of Finance and Central Bank Governors of the countries participating in the snake held in Brussels on 14 March 1976. See also Ludlow, 1982, p. 33.
12. Author's diary, 16 and 18 March 1976.
13. Margevernauwing in de EEG, *Bank- en Effectenbedrijf*, February 1971, pp. 45–8.

6 The European Monetary Cooperation Fund

1. Willy Brandt, 1976, p. 322.
2. In the French text: 'un Fonds de réserve auquel devrait aboutir une politique économique et monétaire commune.'
3. Regulation (EEC) no. 907/73 of the Council of 3 April 1973 establishing a European Monetary Cooperation Fund, Compendium, 1974, p. 81.
4. Commission des Communautés européennes: Interpretation de l'article 4 du règlement no 907/73 du Conseil du 3 avril 1973 instituant le Fonds Européen de Coopération Monétaire, 5 juillet 1973.
5. Decision of the representatives of the governments of the member states of 24 July 1973 on the provisional location of the European Monetary Cooperation Fund, 73/208/EEC, Compendium, 1974, p. 88.

7 The Making of the European Monetary System (1978)

1. For a very good study of the making of the EMS see Peter Ludlow, 1982.
2. Valéry Giscard d'Estaing, 1988, p. 132. Egon Bahr in his memoirs also quotes Schmidt's remark about Carter's lack of strategic notion, adding that Schmidt repeated it so often that it could not remain a secret. Egon Bahr, 1996, p. 505.
3. Valéry Giscard d'Estaing, 1988, p. 136.
4. *Der Spiegel*, nr 1/1979, p. 48.
5. Valéry Giscard d'Estaing, 1988, p. 142.
6. In principle it was the same as had been the case under the Bretton Woods system, though these interventions had in practice been confined to the dollar.
7. Author's notes of a ministerial meeting of the snake countries on 21 January 1974 in Brussels.
8. Helmut Schmidt, 1987, p. 196.
9. Helmut Schmidt, 1990, p. 219ff.
10. To quote just a very few of Schmidt's many earlier statements, made when Finance Minister: 'monetary commitments will not be taken without parallel steps toward harmonising the national economic plans. This provision was particularly dear to our hearts, for we recognised that you can't link currencies closely if you're going to permit the economies ... to veer apart.' Interview with *Newsweek*, 21 August 1972. 'We could certainly not keep the 'snake' alive by creating new credit mechanisms or by pooling reserves. By doing so we might merely establish a new dangerous inflationary mechanism. The only theoretical

and practical possibility to maintain stable exchange rates and narrow fluctuation bands within Europe consists of a better coordination of economic and financial policy objectives of participating countries . . .' Statement in the Bundestag, 23 October 1973. As late as 8 April 1976 he warned in the Bundestag against 'currency gimmicks' (*Währungspolitische Kunstgriffe*) and the inflationary danger this might pose for Germany.

11. Roy Jenkins, 1989, p. 246.
12. Author's diary, 18 April 1978.
13. James Callaghan, 1987, p. 492.
14. Author's diary, 8 July 1978.
15. Compendium, 1986, p. 41.
16. Peter Ludlow, 1982, p. 291. According to Ludlow, Schmidt had to spend 'at least 200 hours coaxing and cajoling a predominantly sceptical and in many cases hostile domestic constituency into acceptance of his ideas', p. 135.
17. Resolution of the European Council on the establishment of the European Monetary System (EMS) and related matters. Brussels, 5 December 1978. Compendium, 1986, p. 43ff.
18. Helmut Schmidt, 1990, pp. 164, 173.
19. Author's diary, 1 August 1973.
20. Roy Jenkins, 1989, p. 244. The incident was also noted by the Dutch Foreign Minister. C.A. van der Klaauw, 1995, p. 252.
21. *Bulletin des Presse- und Informationamtes der Bundesregierung*, 8 December 1978.
22. For the last days of Schmidt's chancellorship see Klaus Bölling, 1983. Hans Tietmeyer as Lambsdorff's collaborator played an important role in the fall of Schmidt's government. How this rankled can be deduced from Schmidt's attack, fourteen years later, on Tietmeyer's alleged opposition to Monetary Union. In a lengthy article in *Die Zeit* of 8 November 1996, Schmidt enumerated the catalogue of what he considered Tietmeyer's errors of economic and political judgement, starting with the so-called Lambsdorff Paper of 1982 of which he was the author.
23. *Financial Times*, 14 April 1988.
24. Helmut Schmidt, 1990, pp. 202–3, 222ff.
25. Egon Bahr – who had been asked by Schmidt to continue to take charge of the informal communication channel between the German Chancellor and Leonid Brezhnev, started under Brandt – relates a very odd incident. In his presence, Schmidt one day used the channel to inquire what the Soviet reaction would be, should the Federal Republic wish to transfer part of the Bundesbank's international reserves from the United States to Moscow. Brezhnev's reaction was positive, but Schmidt did not revert to the issue even though the Soviets inquired once or twice what the next step would be. (Egon Bahr, 1996, p. 507). If this really, improbable as it seems, happened, it is unlikely to have been more than an impulse, Schmidt being a moody person. But it would seem to reflect both his feelings on the Carter administration and his tendency to assume that he could impose his

wishes on the Bundesbank. Both factors played a role in determining Schmidt's attitude in the making of the EMS.
26. Helmut Schmidt, speech in Berlin on 27 October 1978. *Bulletin des Presse- und Informationamtes der Bundesregierung*, 9 November 1978.

8 The Working of the European Monetary System in the Period 1979–87

1. Jacques Attali: *Verbatim*, 1993.
2. *Frankfurter Allgemeine Zeitung*, 15 March 1983. *Le Monde*, 16 March 1983.
3. Jacques Attali, 1993, p. 413.
4. The link between Mitterrand's decision in 1983 to keep the franc in the EMS and his policy aiming at European integration in the years that followed is stressed by several authors, for instance: Favier and Martin-Roland, 1990, pp. 443, 586. Aeschimann and Riché, 1996, pp. 29, 171.
5. *The Times*, 19 March 1983.
6. 'C'est une loi à laquelle nul n'échappe: un pays dont la hausse des prix dépasse celle de ses voisins est condamné à dévaluer d'une façon ou d'une autre. Telle est la vérité. Je devais vous la dire sans chercher d'excuses trompeuses.' *Le Figaro*, 24 March 1983.
7. Possible lessons from past realignments. Note presented by Mr Szász, 6 June 1986, II/300/86–EN.
8. Later published by Piet Korteweg, 1984.
9. When I attended one of President Duisenberg's weekly meetings on 12 January 1983 with Finance Minister Ruding and Treasurer-General Piet Korteweg in order to prepare for the realignment we expected, I proposed that the Minister should ask the Monetary Committee to discuss the issue, which he subsequently did. The letter, we agreed on that occasion, was to be a follow-up of this initiative. Author's diary, 6 March 1983.
10. Author's diary, 13 January 1987.
11. D.H. Boot, Internal memorandum, 17 March 1987.
12. The report was released after a ministerial meeting in Kolding, Denmark, on 22 May 1993. For the text see Paul Temperton (ed), 1993, Appendix 1, p. 299ff.
13. This explains why they are emphasised in the literature. Tsoukalis, for instance, does not even mention the rules of conduct. Loukas Tsoukalis, 1993, p. 202. Nor are they mentioned by former French Treasury official Philippe Jurgensen, 1991.
14. Daniel Gros and Niels Thygesen, 1992, p. 95.

9 Promoting the ECU

1. The transfer of liquidity creation to the EMF, note transmitted to the Monetary Committee by the Dutch members, 28 December 1979.
2. Compendium, 1986, pp. 41, 43.
3. Meeting of Ministers of Finance in Brussels on 18 December 1978.
4. *Ecu News Letter*, May 1983.

5. *Institutional Investor*, March 1982.
6. Author's note to files, 27 February 1985.

10 The Single European Act (1985–6)

1. In this chapter extensive use has been made of Age Bakker's dissertation on the liberalisation of capital movements in Europe.
2. W.F. Duisenberg, 1985.
3. *Die Zeit*, 15 March 1985.
4. Age F.P. Bakker, 1996, p. 184.
5. *Financial Times*, 15 January 1985.
6. Notes of Dutch participants.
7. Draft of 5 November 1985, II/582/85. Earlier drafts had been circulated informally.
8. Margaret Thatcher, 1993, p. 552ff, 741.
9. *Financial Times*, 8 June 1985. If one compares Kohl's objectives as formulated here with those advanced a decade later, the consistency is remarkable, and his use of the expression 'second pillar' almost suggests an uncanny foresight. One must conclude that Thatcher had little understanding of German policies when she wrote in her memoirs that it was only since German unification that Kohl has struck out with a distinctive German foreign policy, being willing for most of the 1980s 'to subordinate German interest to French guidance, since this reassured Germany's neighbours.' (Margaret Thatcher, 1993, p. 552.)
10. *Frankfurter Allgemeine Zeitung*, 4 December 1985.
11. Hans van den Broek, 1985.
12. Note to files, 27 November 1985. Author's diary, 27 November 1985.
13. Note to files, 29 November 1985. Author's diary, 30 November 1985.
14. Age F.P. Bakker, 1996, pp. 168, 179–81.

11 French–German Tussle: Monetary Union Revived (1987–8)

1. Er erörtert regelmässig die Währungspolitik beider Länder im nationalen, europäischen und internationalen Bereich mit dem Ziel einer möglichst weitgehenden Abstimmung. *VWD-Finanz- und Wirtschaftsspiegel*, Eschborn, 25-1-1988.
2. Jacques Attali, 1995, p. 390.
3. *Le Monde*, 8 January 1988.
4. The new right-wing government under Prime Minister Jacques Chirac evidently wanted an early devaluation while they could still blame their socialist predecessors. See Jacques Attali, 1995, pp. 235–6.
5. *Le Monde*, 11 February 1987, also 14 February.
6. Jacques Attali's diary first mentions a European Central Bank when recording a conversation on 4 September. Jacques Attali (1995), p. 382.
7. *European Affairs*, Amsterdam/Brussels, no 1/1987.
8. *Frankfurter Allgemeine Zeitung*, 11 February 1988, Europäische Notenbank nur längerfristig möglich. Stoltenberg: 'Das Pferd nicht vom Schwanz her aufzäumen.'
9. *Frankfurter Allgemeine Zeitung*, 19 September 1987.

10. *Handelsblatt*, 21 January 1988.
11. Gerhard Stoltenberg: 'Zur weiteren Entwicklung der währungspolitischen Zusammenarbeit in Europa', 15 March 1988. In his memoirs Stoltenberg states that Genscher had consulted neither the Chancellor nor himself. And as far as substance was concerned, he calls Genscher's contribution 'problematic' since, deviating from the official German position, guaranteeing by treaty that EMU participants' economic and fiscal policy would pursue stability 'was no issue for him'. Gerhard Stoltenberg, 1997, p. 329.
12. David Marsh, 'Bonn sees Monetary Union as far-off goal', *Financial Times*, 25 January 1988.
13. Press conference in Brussels after a visit to the European Commission, Reuters, 11 May 1988.
14. 'Die deutsch–französische Vereinbarung wurde natürlich von beiden Partnern in einer eindeutig europäischen Perspektive geschlossen. Sie soll zur Verwirklichung der Europäischen Wirtschafts- und Währungsunion beitragen, die das Ziel dieser Bundesregierung bleibt. Dazu gehört auch eine enge Integration der Währungen. Wir werden die politische Einigung Europas nur erreichen, wenn wir auch eine gemeinsame Währung für dieses Europa schaffen mit einer Europäischen Zentralbank, die unabhängig von Weisungen anderer Institutionen die Verantwortung für diese Währung wahrnimmt, die ihren Umlauf kontrolliert und ihre Stabilität sichert. Dafür gilt es die Voraussetzungen zu schaffen. Die Bundesregierung wird diese Entwicklung aktiv mitgestalten.' Helmut Kohl, speech in Bonn on 15 March 1988, Deutsche Bundesbank, *Auszüge aus Presseartikeln*, nr 19, 17 March 1988.
15. Valéry Giscard d'Estaing, 1988, p. 136. Helmut Schmidt, 1990, pp. 170–1.
16. Georges-Henri Soutou, 1996, p. 382.
17. Philip H. Gordon, 1993, pp. 147–9, 1995, p. 21.
18. Georges-Henri Soutou, 1996, p. 391.
19. Julius W. Friend, 1993, pp. 165–6.
20. Reuters, 27 June 1989.

12 The Delors Report

1. Nigel Lawson (1992), p. 903. According to a French source, Kohl and Mitterrand had agreed a week before the Hanover meeting to entrust the task to central bankers: Kohl in order to commit the Bundesbank, Mitterrand to exclude Finance Ministry opposition. Aeschimann and Riché, 1996, p. 87.
2. Margaret Thatcher (1993), pp. 740–1.
3. Ibid., p. 708.
4. Author's note to files, 11 May 1988. Pöhl himself later confirmed that he would have preferred outsiders to be entrusted with the task, arguing that the Bundesbank would then not have been committed to the result. Karl Otto Pöhl, 1996, p. 197.
5. She was not the only one to expect this. For precisely the same reason, former German Chancellor Helmut Schmidt criticised the composition of the group, calling it too full of 'technicians to make

much progress towards setting up a European Central Bank', according to David Marsh in the *Financial Times* of 5 July 1988.

6. Karl Otto Pöhl, 1996, pp. 196–7.
7. The German and Dutch Central Bank Presidents did not consult their governments, taking them at their word regarding their personal capacity. In the Netherlands, however, we kept the Finance Ministry informed of developments. I realised how unpleasant it would have been for them if, in their regular contacts with their British and French counterparts, the latter were fully informed while they themselves knew nothing. Moreover, I pointed out to my German counterpart Gleske that, once this episode was over and the Intergovernmental Conference would start, the boot would be on the other foot, and we would not be in a position to complain about not being fully informed if we would have failed to inform the Finance Ministry ourselves.
8. Reuters, 8 January 1989.
9. Favier and Martin-Roland 1996, p. 163. Aeschimann and Riché, 1996, p. 88.
10. Paragraph 53 of the Delors Report. A paper by Governor De Larosière on the European Reserve Fund is published in the collection of papers that are annexed to the report.
11. *International Herald Tribune*, 29 September 1988; *Les Echos*, 16 December 1988; *Financial Times*, 30 December 1988.
12. Report on Economic and Monetary Union in the European Community, 1989, paragraph 19. Italics in the original.
13. Ibid., paragraph 21.
14. Ibid., paragraph 30.
15. Ibid., paragraph 32.
16. Ibid., paragraph 39.
17. Ibid., paragraph 62.
18. Ibid., paragraph 29.
19. The parallel currency strategy was introduced in the European integration debate by the so-called 'All Saints' day manifesto for European Monetary Union', published in *The Economist* of 1 November 1975 and backed by what was called nine prominent European economists. One of them was Niels Thygesen, now a member of the Delors Committee.

13 British Opposition

1. Nigel Lawson, 1992, p. 908.
2. Margaret Thatcher, 1993, p. 708.
3. She had – as we have seen – redefined EMU, but not even her then Chancellor of the Exchequer took this seriously, pointing out that 'Monetary Union had a clearly defined meaning.' Nigel Lawson, 1992, p. 904.
4. Quoted in Nigel Lawson, 1992, p. 910.
5. Nigel Lawson, 1989:2.
6. Nigel Lawson, 1992, pp. 924–5.
7. Ibid., p. 925.

8. Ibid., 1992, p. 898.
9. Ibid., pp. 889, 903.
10. Margaret Thatcher, 1993, p. 559.
11. Ibid., p. 539.
12. Geoffrey Howe, 1994, p. 701.
13. Geoffrey Howe, in the *Financial Times* of 23–4 October 1993.
14. Margaret Thatcher, 1993, p. 718ff., 1995, 483ff.
15. Margaret Thatcher, 1993, p. 700.
16. Margaret Thatcher, 1993, pp. 690–1. In this, she was probably right.
17. Ibid., p. 698.
18. Ibid., p. 913.
19. Geoffrey Howe, 1994, p. 577.
20. Author's diary, 8 May 1989, 29 May 1989.
21. Ibid., 23 May 1989.
22. Roy Jenkins, 1991, p. 496.
23. Margaret Thatcher, 1993, p. 765.
24. Ibid., p. 765.
25. Ibid., p. 727.
26. Ibid., p. 552.
27. Margaret Thatcher, 1995, p. 483.
28. Delors Report, paragraph 39.
29. Nigel Lawson, 1992, p. 914.

14 The Madrid Summit (June 1989) and its Follow-up

1. Report on the Principal Questions Raised by the Implementation of Economic and Monetary Union (Gigou Report), *Europe Documents*, 9 November 1989, p. 1580.
2. Wilhelm Schönfelder/Elke Thiel, 1994. Lorenzo Bini-Smaghi, Tommaso Padoa-Schioppa and Francesco Papadia, 1994.
3. Bini-Smaghi *et al.*, pp. 32–3.
4. Speech in Amsterdam on 27 November 1991.
5. *The Wall Street Journal*, 30 October 1990.
6. Margaret Thatcher, 1993, pp. 765–7.

15 German Unification (1989–90)

1. Philip Zelikow and Condoleezza Rice, 1995, p. 87. The full text of the East German record of the conversation is reproduced in Hans-Hermann Hertle, 1996, pp. 462–82.
2. Timothy Garton Ash, 1997, pp. 158–9. According to a former Soviet Ambassador in Bonn, the Soviets had had misgivings as early as 1975 about the GDR's increasing financial dependence on West Germany. They did not see a clear alternative, however, and therefore did not press their view, allowing East German Party boss Erich Honecker to ignore their criticism. Julij Kwizinskij, 1993, pp. 258ff.
3. Philip Zelikow and Condoleezza Rice, 1995, p. 104.
4. Bundesbank President Karl Otto Pöhl at the meeting of EC Governors in Basle on 13 February 1990. Author's notes, 15 February 1990.

5. 'Kommt die Dmark, bleiben wir,
   Kommt sie nicht, gehen wir zu ihr.'
   Helmut Kohl, 1996, p. 259.
6. Philip Zelikow and Condoleezza Rice, 1995, p. 79. Helmut Kohl, 1996,
   p. 69.
7. The presentation of the Ten Points was timed to precede the meeting
   in Malta of Gorbachov with Bush on 1 December, the announcement
   of German Monetary Union came days before Kohl's visit to Gorbachov
   on 10 February.
8. Philip Zelikow and Condoleezza Rice, 1995, p. 79.
9. Favier and Martin-Roland, 1996, p. 197.
10. Since Adenauer the German Federal Republic had rejected neutral-
    isation as a price for reunification. Yet according to former Soviet
    Ambassador in Bonn Kwizinskij, it would have chosen to leave NATO,
    or at least its military structure (as France had done) if firmly put
    before the choice between unification and NATO. However, it did
    not need to make that choice since the GDR had by now lost the will
    to fight for its existence as a separate state: 'Once it was prepared to
    envisage Monetary Union with the Federal Republic and swallowed
    the sweet bait of the Deutsche mark, its fate was sealed.' Jurij Kwizinskij,
    1993, p. 22.
11. Margaret Thatcher, 1993, p. 796.
12. Favier and Martin-Roland, 1996, p. 203.
13. François Mitterrand, 1996, p. 85.
14. Favier and Martin-Roland, 1996, p. 206.
15. Helmut Kohl, 1996, pp. 195–7. Kohl mentions in particular Margaret
    Thatcher's deep mistrust of Germans. Regarding Ruud Lubbers he
    adds, that the Dutch position was also determined by war memories.
    Kohl's adviser Horst Teltschik, in his diaries published in 1991, does
    not mention any unpleasantness on this occasion but quotes Kohl earlier
    telling him after a summit dinner in Paris on 18 November 1989 that,
    unlike most others, Thatcher and Lubbers had been decidedly cool.
    (Horst Teltschik, 1991, p. 38.)
16. Margaret Thatcher, 1993, p. 797. In a press interview almost a decade
    later, Lubbers insisted that contrary to allegations he had never opposed
    German unification, but had argued in favour of recognition of Poland's
    western frontier to which Kohl objected at the time. *NRC-Handelsblad*,
    22 August 1997.
17. Horst Teltschik, pp. 14, 99, 104.
18. Favier and Martin-Roland, 1996, pp. 243–6.
19. Her former Chancellor of the Exchequer, in his memoirs, calls it 'her
    pathological hostility to Germany and the Germans which in the end
    came to dominate her view of the European Community,' and else-
    where 'her gut anti-German mode, which was never far from below
    the surface.' Nigel Lawson, 1992, pp. 275, 656.
20. Margaret Thatcher, 1995, p. 342.
21. Margaret Thatcher, 1993, pp. 796–7.
22. Ibid., pp. 554–6.
23. Ibid., p. 798.

24. Ibid.
25. François Mitterrand, 1996, p. 43.

16 Monetary Union

1. De Nederlandsche Bank, Annual Report 1989.
2. Nigel Lawson, 1992, pp. 868–9.
3. James M. Buchanan: 'Democracy within Constitutional Limits', lecture given in the Netherlands in the early 1990s.
4. *Le Nouvel Economiste*, no. 655–5/8/88, p. 50.
5. Quoted in Deutsche Bundesbank, *Auszüge aus Presseartikeln*, 9 September 1992, no. 61.
6. Idem, 25 February 1994, no. 13.
7. In the law on the Nederlandsche Bank of 1948, the Minister of Finance was empowered to issue instructions to the Executive Board of the Bank if he deemed this necessary for the coordination of the Government's and the bank's policy. Such instructions were meant to be an *ultimum remedium* in case of a major conflict. They would trigger a procedure carefully described in the law, according to which both the Bank's objections and the Government's reasons to overrule them would be published. Thus, the conflict was certain to cause maximum publicity and parliamentary debate, embarrassing for the Government – in the Netherlands always a coalition – as well as for the Nederlandsche Bank. In practice, such instruction had never been issued, but the fact that it could be done made the Finance Minister politically responsible in Parliament for the Nederlandsche Bank's policies.
8. Parliamentary Committee meeting, 6 December 1989, 21 300 V, no. 70.
9. *Nederlandsche Staatscourant*, 2 April 1991.
10. Reuters, 7–8 May 1990. *NRC/Handelsblad*, 8 May 1990.
11. Bérégovoy, 1988: 2.
12. *Le Monde*, 12 October 1996.
13. Reuters, 27 June 1989.
14. *Le Monde*, 14 December 1996.

17 Economic Union

1. A. Lamfalussy, 1989, p. 91ff.
2. Delors Report, paragraph 30.
3. Communication publiée à l'issue du Conseil des Ministres du 5 décembre 1990, Les progrès vers l'Union Économique et Monétaire.
4. Intervention of Pierre Bérégovoy at the Intergovernmental Conference on 28 January 1991, published by the French Finance Ministry on 29 January 1991.
5. Schönfelder and Thiel, 1994, pp. 82, 91–2.
6. For Germany, see Schönfelder and Thiel, 1994, p. 82.
7. Voorhoeve and Hoogervorst, 1988.
8. A similar view was expressed by Bundesbank President Hans Tietmeyer in a press interview. *Die Woche*, 5 September 1997.

9. He did so at a Conference in Vaals, the Netherlands, in February 1996.
10. Bini-Smaghi *et al.* state as their objection to the proposal the absence of a meaningful commitment to EMU, pp. 17–18. But it is unlikely that Italy's prospects of fulfilling the requirements would have played no role in the Italian objections. At the time, the objections concerned mainly the different speeds.
11. *Financial Times*, 10 September 1991. Crawford comments that Kok's decision 'to disown his own department's paper . . . (had) the embarrassing implication that he had not read it before its submission, or had read it but not understood it.' Malcolm Crawford, 1993, 1996, p. 151. Dutch newspapers at the time also contained some critical comments, e.g. *NRC Handelsblad*, 11 September 1991.
12. According to the OECD, 'structural deficits would have to be reduced to the range of 1 to 1½ per cent of GDP in most countries, and to lower levels in some, in order to keep actual deficits within the 3 per cent limit in a "typical" recession.' *OECD Economic Outlook* 62, December 1997, p. 24.
13. Helmut Kohl in *Handelsblatt*, 31 December 1991.
14. Der Vertrag von Maastricht war daher für die Bundesregierung nur mit einer Revisionsklausel akzeptabel, die einen festen Termin zum Weiterbau des europäischen Hauses vorsieht. *Börsen-Zeitung*, Frankfurt am Main, 31 December 1994. Accordingly, the Maastricht Treaty stipulated in Article N, paragraph 2 that a conference of the representatives of the governments of the member states would be convened in 1996. Oddly, former Prime Minister Ruud Lubbers, who chaired the Maastricht Meeting, later denied that it had been agreed in Maastricht to convene an intergovernmental conference in 1996. Interview in *NRC-Handelsblad*, 22 August 1997.

18 Ratification (1992–3)

1. Note of 17 June 1992 by Central Bank Governor Erik Hoffmeyer to his EC colleagues.
2. *NRC Handelsblad*, 24 June 1994.
3. I do not, however, agree with the view that 'U.K. negotiators masterfully forced a dilution of solutions, weakened in exchange for the mere hope that Britain would sign in the end.' Bini-Smaghi *et al.*, 1994, p. 42.
4. The Dutch Parliament ensured a similar commitment on the part of the Dutch Government.
5. Ruling of the Federal Constitutional Court, announced on 12 October 1993. The quotes are from a translation prepared by the Federal Foreign Ministry.
6. Author's notes of a meeting in the Cabinet Room in The Hague on Economic and Monetary Union on 16 May 1990. I happened to leave the Cabinet Room together with the Minister of Economic Affairs, and remarked to him that what struck me most was the Prime Minister's doubts whether politicians knew what they were doing. 'They've no idea! No idea!' the Minister, himself a former Professor of Economics, replied. Author's diary, 20 May 1990.

19 Black September (1992)

1. *OECD Economic Outlook* 59, June 1996, Annex table 43.
2. Carlo Santini, 1993, p. 236.
3. Ibid., p. 238.
4. Ibid., p. 243.
5. Author's Diary, 3 and 4 July 1992.
6. Author's diary, 13 September 1992.
7. Margaret Thatcher, 1993, p. 723.
8. Ibid., p. 831.
9. For instance in a speech in London, 20 October 1986. See also Philip Stephens, 1996, p. 67.
10. Author's Diary, 24 August 1987.
11. *European Affairs*, Special issue on the European Finance Symposium, 1989, pp. 119–22 and 124–8.
12. 'Britain's Failure to Consult Angers System Partners', *Financial Times*, 8 October 1990.
13. Bank of England Governor Robin Leigh-Pemberton later said he had disagreed with the Government over the timing of the cut. *Financial Times*, 17 December 1990. According to Philip Stephens, officials in the Treasury also felt it was a mistake. Philip Stephens, 1996, pp. 169, 172.
14. Norman Lamont, speech for the European Policy Forum on 10 July 1992.
15. Margaret Thatcher, 1993, p. 724.
16. *The Economist*, 8 August 1992. See also: Philip Stephens, 1996, pp. 218–19.
17. Author's Diary, 8 September 1992.
18. Under the title 'Crisis? What Crisis?' *The Economist* pointed out that while for other countries 'interest rate rises are as much part of the routine of membership (of the ERM) as interest rate cuts', Britain was the only member country that did not once increase its rates in this period, having cut it nine times with five percentage points in total earlier. Author's Diary, 29 August 1992.
19. Author's Diary, 8 September 1992.
20. Author's Diary, 4 August 1993.
21. The communiqué was issued, as usual, on behalf of Ministers and Central Bank Governors, who had been repeatedly raised out of their beds by telephone by their people in the Committee in the course of the night. There was nothing their physical presence in Brussels could possibly have added to the outcome, apart from further dramatising the situation and adding to rumours of discord. But the Monetary Committee's all-night session, with an army of journalists in attendance, attracted extensive publicity, and with a number of ministers – being politicians – this rankled. Some announced to journalists that in future they themselves would take a hand. By the time of the next adjustment this was conveniently forgotten. (Author's diary, 24 November 1992.)
22. Reuters, 21 October 1992.

23. Robin Leigh-Pemberton, 1993, p. 287.
24. Ibid., p. 291.
25. Ibid., p. 289.
26. George Brock: 'Major Forced to Tread Warily in Wake of a Blundering Lamont', *The Times*, 30 September 1992.
27. Philip Stephens, 1996, p. 271.
28. *The Times*, 2 October 1992.
29. Reproduced in Paul Temperton, 1993, p. 299ff.

20 The Collapse of the Old EMS (1993)

1. *Le Monde*, 27 June 1991: an article by François Renard, 'Les marchés doutent', put the amount at French franc 50 billion, a figure contested by Finance Minister Pierre Bérégovoy.
2. *Wall Street Journal*, 5 November 1991.
3. 'Bérégovoy kritisiert deutschen egoismus', *Frankfurter Allgemeine Zeitung*, 27–28 December 1991.
4. Author's diaries, 3 July, 6 July, 8 July 1992. Eric Aeschimann and Pascal Riché mention a secret visit by Sapin to The Hague in order to organise a coordinated rate cut by countries other than Germany, pp. 140–1.
5. Radio interview on 22 (or 23) September 1992, Eric Aeschimann and Pascal Riché, 1996, p. 154. One year later I alluded to this in a speech in London. My comments were summarised by a Dutch newspaper with the quote 'Since the guillotine is no longer available, central banks have to use interest rates.' *NRC-Handelsblad*, 18 September 1993.
6. Author's diary, 26 October 1992.
7. *Financial Times*, 26 June 1993.
8. Deutsche Bundesbank, *Auszüge aus Presseartikeln*, 16 June 1993, no. 42.
9. Dow Jones, 24 June 1993, Eric Aeschimann and Pascal Riché, 1996, pp. 208–9.
10. Author's Diary, 30 June 1993.
11. 'Weighing up the anchor', *The Economist*, 10 July 1993.
12. *NRC/Handelsblad*, 25 August 1992.
13. Author's Diary, 23 September 1992. Also mentioned in Eric Aeschimann and Pascal Riché, p. 156.
14. In September, in a London speech (mentioned in footnote 5), I mentioned governments' impatience to lower interest rates as an important factor triggering the crisis. The *Financial Times* commented that this was taken by some as criticism of Edmond Alphandéry. 'Pressed for elucidation, the Delphic Szász said he would "never presume" to give Alphandéry any advice. Any similarity between persons criticised in his speech and what he called "living characters" was "purely coincidental"', *Financial Times* of 16 September 1993, article entitled 'Living Banker'.
15. Various Dutch and German papers, 16 February 1990. On the same day, Minister Kok wrote a soothing letter to Parliament, assuring it that Dutch policy would remain linking the guilder to the strongest

currency in the EMS, i.e. the German mark, given the consensus on price stability existing in Germany.
16. Author's Diary, 18 February 1990.
17. *OECD Economic Outlook*, June 1996, Annex table 42.

21 The Guilder: A Case Study of a Hard Currency Policy

1. John Laughland in the *Wall Street Journal*, 14 September 1995.
2. W. Kok: *Vakbondskrant*, 5 July 1979.
3. 'Why Economic Policies Change Course, Eleven Case Studies', OECD, Paris, 1988, pp. 96–7.
4. D.H. Boot, 1992, pp. 161–2. On Henk Boot's 60th anniversary in 1992 the Nederlandsche Bank decided to compile for internal circulation his internal papers and memoranda written over a number of years. During the summer we had to decide which papers to select. As one of the editors I made sure that this analysis was among them. By now I was the only member of the Executive Board who had had that function back in 1979, and I wanted to make sure the lessons then learned were not lost on my colleagues during the turbulence I expected.
5. *De Volkskrant*, 7 September 1996.
6. *Bijgewerkte kanttekeningen van fractievoorzitters bij het rapport van de Werkgroep A*, 26 October 1982.
7. Author's diary, 6 and 7 April, 5 May 1983.
8. It so happened that a few days later Vice Prime Minister and Finance Minister Wim Kok had a speaking engagement in Brussels that he could not keep, and the Ministry asked me to help them out. This was an unsought opportunity to express in public, in the Government's time so to speak, our support for the Bundesbank's policies, without of course mentioning the letter. Author's diary, 28 January, 12 February 1992.
9. Author's diary, 21 May 1992.
10. Author's Diary, 3 July 1992, 6 July 1992.
11. At the monthly meeting in Basle, on 12 July, I explained our policy to my EC counterparts: 'Press comments often use the word "cautious" when discussing our policies. This is what we intended. Each single interest rate measure is meant to convey to the market the message: "the exchange rate first!"' I pointed out that this message had to be repeated from time to time, and that it implied certain rules of the thumb. As long as the guilder was below the central rate with the German mark, interest rate differentials with Germany should be positive. If the guilder rate was above the central rate, interest rate differentials might decline and even become negative, but we tried to keep it under firm control. (Speaking notes for the meeting of the Alternates of the EC Governors on 12 July 1993 in Basle.) The purpose of this explanation was to inspire similar caution in others. But for that it was now too late.
12. Author's Diary, 9 July 1993. The Dutch word they used, one of their collaborators who was present told me, was *angsthazen*.
13. Author's Diary, 29 July 1993. During the afternoon, in conversations

first with President Duisenberg and then with the Finance Ministry, I had stressed the importance of maintaining unchanged the existing fluctuation band between guilder and German mark on the basis of mutual intervention obligations. Any perceived change might induce the market, in its disturbed state, to test the guilder as it had other currencies. In a paper surveying our options, received earlier that day from the Ministry, this option had been lacking. We agreed that this should be our priority.

14. Eric Aeschimann and Pascal Riché, 1996, p. 232.
15. Minister Kok summarised the agreement in political terms, stating that our mutual policies would remain unchanged. Feeling that this lacked technical precision, I intervened to state that this implied that the existing upper and lower limits for the two currencies would remain in force. To my consternation, Bundesbank President Schlesinger hesitated, saying that he was not sure this was possible. But Hans Tietmeyer, who in the Bundesbank Board was responsible for foreign exchange, brushed these doubts aside, saying that of course it was possible, and Schlesinger agreed. It was in these terms that the Dutch delegation announced the bilateral agreement in a brief written statement issued to the press after the conference was completed. The statement was added to the communiqué.
16. At an early stage of the meeting, Minister Kok made it clear, as we had in the Monetary Committee, that the Netherlands was not prepared to change the existing relationship between guilder and German mark, meaning the 2.25 per cent band based on mutual intervention obligations; this had therefore to become part of any agreed conclusion. Towards the end, he and President Duisenberg informed the meeting that the existing guilder-German mark relationship would be maintained on the basis of a bilateral agreement. Aeschimann and Riché write erroneously in their book that the Dutch opened the discussions by announcing, that the guilder had to follow the German mark, if the latter left the ERM, since the two currencies were linked within a band of 1 per cent on the basis of a secret agreement. No such statement was made, nor did any secret agreement exist. Eric Aeschimann and Pascal Riché, 1996, p. 231.
17. Author's diary, 5 August 1993. At times I could not help reflecting that we might have found it more difficult to get the German government to ignore French objections, had the high-level German delegation visiting Paris on 30 July found more understanding, and received red carpet treatment instead of – as rumour had it – being transported through the rush hour traffic in a minibus. *Financial Times*, 23 December 1993.
18. Author's diary, 4 August 1993.

22 Why the Euro?

1. Konrad Adenauer, 1967, pp. 13, 14, 27, 254ff.
2. François Mitterrand, 1986, p. 101.
3. *De Volkskrant*, 17 November 1994.

4. 'Sans système monétaire commun, il n'y a pas d'Europe'. *Le Monde*, 30 March 1993.
5. M. Couve de Murville, 1971, pp. 18–19, 52–3. Couve de Murville was De Gaulle's first Foreign Minister; in July 1968 he became Prime Minister.
6. Interview in *Le Monde*, 24 September 1987.
7. *Le Monde*, 24 April 1992.
8. Covering letter by the Governor to the Annual Report over 1991, page VII. The French authorities reacted irritably to anything that tended to emphasise the EMS' character as a German mark bloc, for instance when Belgian Prime Minister Wilfried Martens announced on television on 16 June 1990 that henceforth the Belgian franc would be linked to the German mark.
9. Eric Aeschimann and Pascal Riché, 1996, p. 91.
10. Author's diary, 11 July 1978.
11. Article in *Le Monde*, 30 November 1994.
12. Foreign Secretary Robin Cook, quoted in *Le Monde*, 15 May 1997.
13. I shall remember this Hearing for an amusing incident. The first witness, Banque de France Governor Jacques de Larosière, who announced at the outset that he was speaking as a 'technician' and not as a politician, commented in his statement on the growing German fiscal deficit. If Germany would enter the road of durable deficit spending in order to finance German unification, he sternly warned, this would concern not only Germany but also its EC partners: EMU was not only about common monetary policy, but also affected the main features of budgetary policy. This admonition, coming from a Frenchman, was the last thing German MPs expected. As a result, when I followed as the next speaker I had to speak over a buzz of excited conversation that only stopped when I cracked a joke. This always works: those who listen laugh, the others hear the laughter and stop talking, hoping not to miss the next joke. Author's diary, 18 September 1991.
14. European Monetary Institute, Convergence Report, March 1998.
15. Deutsche Bundesbank, Stellungnahme des Zentralbankrates zur Konvergenzlage in der Europäischen Union im Hinblick auf die Dritte Stufe der Wirtschafts- und Währungsunion, 26 March 1998.
16. Interview in the *International Herald Tribune* of 14 May 1998.
17. Larry Summers, 'Personal View, American Eyes on EMU', *Financial Times*, 22 October 1997.

Bibliography

Adenauer, Konrad, *Erinnerungen*, Stuttgart.
(1965) 1945–53
(1966) 1953–5
(1967) 1955–9
(1968) 1959–63
Aeschimann, Eric and Pascal Riché (1996), *La guerre de sept ans, Histoire secrète du franc fort 1989–1996*, Paris.
Amouroux, Henri (1986), *Monsieur Barre*, Paris.
Ash, Timothy Garton (1997), *The File: A Personal History*, London.
Attali, Jacques, *Verbatim*, Fayard.
(1993) I 1981–6
(1995) II 1986–8
(1995a) III 1988–91
Bahr, Egon (1994), *Ostpolitik en Wende, Duitsland voor en na 1989/90*, Vrije Universiteit, Amsterdam.
Bahr, Egon (1996), *Zu meiner Zeit*, Munich.
Bakker, Age, Henk Boot, Olaf Slijpen and Wim Vanthoor (eds) (1994), *Monetary Stability through International Cooperation*, Amsterdam.
Bakker, Age F.P. (1996), *The Liberalisation of Capital Movements in Europe, The Monetary Committee and Financial Integration*, 1958–1994, Dordrecht.
Balladur, Edouard (1995), *Deux ans à Matignon*, Paris.
Barbier, Colette (1993), 'The French Decision to Develop a Military Nuclear Programme in the 1950s', *Diplomacy & Statecraft*, Vol. 4, No. 1, March 1993, London.
Baring, Arnulf (1982), *Machtwechsel, Die Ära Brandt-Scheel*, Stuttgart.
Bauchard, Philipe (1986), *La guerre des deux roses, du rêve à la réalité, 1981–1985*, Paris.
Bender, Peter (1986), *Die 'Neue Ostpolitik' und ihre Folgen, Vom Mauerbau zur Vereinigung*, Nördlingen.
Bérégovoy, Pierre (1988:1), 'The Need for a Common Monetary Policy', Interview in *International Herald Tribune*, 29 September 1988.
Bérégovoy, Pierre (1988:2), Pour une gestion monétaire à deux niveaux, *Les Echos*, 16 December 1988.
Bini-Smaghi, Lorenzo, Tommaso Padoa-Schioppa and Francesco Papadia (1994), *The Transition to EMU in the Maastricht Treaty*, Princeton, New Jersey.
Bölling, Klaus (1983), *Die letzten 30 Tage des Kanzlers Helmut Schmidt, ein Tagebuch*, Hamburg.
Boot, D.H. (1992), *Achter de coulissen van het beleid, Geselecteerde notities en verslagen 1970–92*, Amsterdam.
Boot, Henk (1994), 'Techniques for Stability', in Bakker, Boot *et al.*, *Monetary Stability through International Cooperation*, Amsterdam.
Brandt, Willy (1976), *Begegnungen und Einsichten 1960–1975*, Hamburg.

Broek, Hans van den (1985), 'De Europese verdragen kunnen een opknapbeurt goed gebruiken', *NRC/Handelsblad*, 25 May 1985.

Brouwer, Henk J., and Bernard ter Haar (1994), 'Economic Policy Coordination and the Role of Fiscal Targets', in: Age Bakker, Henk Boot *et al.* (eds): *Monetary Stability through International Cooperation*, Amsterdam.

Callaghan, James (1987), *Time and Change*, London.

Compendium (1974), Monetary Committee of the European Communities, *Compendium of Community Monetary Texts*, Brussels.

Compendium (1986), Monetary Committee of the European Communities, *Compendium of Community Monetary Texts*, Brussels.

Connolly, Bernard (1995), *The Rotten Heart of Europe, The Dirty War for Europe's Money*, London.

Coombs, Charles A. (1976), *The Arena of International Finance*, New York.

Crawford, Malcolm (1993, 1996), *One Money for Europe? The Economics and Politics of Europe*, London.

Couve de Murville, Maurice (1971), *Une politique étrangère 1958–1969*, Paris.

Dalgaard, Henning (1994), 'The Exchange Rate Mechanism after the Basle–Nyborg Agreement', in Age Bakker, Henk Boot *et al.* (eds): *Monetary Stability through International Cooperation*, Amsterdam.

Debré, Michel (1993), *Gouverner autrement, Mémoires 1962–1970*, Paris.

Dell, Edmund (1996), *The Chancellors: a History of the Chancellors of the Exchequer 1945–1990*, London.

Delors Report (1989), *Report on Economic and Monetary Union in the European Community, Committee for the Study of Economic and Monetary Union*, Brussels.

Dini, Lamberto (1994), 'Turbulence in the foreign exchange markets: old and new lessons', in: Age Bakker, Henk Boot *et al.* (eds): *Monetary Stability through International Cooperation*, Amsterdam.

Dormael, Armand van (1997), *The Power of Money*, New York.

Duchêne, François (1994), *Jean Monnet: The First Statesman of Interdependence*, New York, London.

Duisenberg, Wim F. (1985), Steps towards international monetary order, Speech in Berlin on 24 January 1985.

Eden, Anthony (1960), *The Memoirs of Anthony Eden*, Full Circle, London.

Eisenhower, Dwight D. (1965), *The White House Years 1956–1961, Waging Peace*, Guildford and London.

Emerson, Michael, and Christopher Huhne (1991), *Een Europa, een munt, Invloed en betekenis van de ECU*, Leiden.

Emminger, Otmar (1986), *D-Mark, Dollar, Währungskrisen, Erinnerungen eines ehemaligen Bundesbank-präsidenten*, Stuttgart.

Fabius, Laurent (1995), *Les blessures de la vérité*, Flammarion.

Favier, Pierre, and Michel Martin-Roland, *La décennie Mitterrand*, Paris.
(1990) 1. *Les ruptures* (1981–4)
(1991) 2. *Les épreuves* (1984–8)
(1996) 3. *Les défis* (1988–91)

Friend, Julius W. (1993), 'U.S. Policy toward Franco–German Cooperation', in McCarthy, Patrick (ed.), *France–Germany 1983–1993*.

Gaulle, Charles de (1970), *Discours et messages*, Plon.

Gaulle, Charles de, *Mémoires d'Espoir*, Plon.
    (1971) *L'effort 1962–. . . .*
    (1970a) *Le renouveau 1958–1962*
Genscher, Hans-Dietrich (1987), 'Genscher befürwortet Stärkung der Europäischen Gemeinschaft', *Frankfurter Allgemeine Zeitung*, 19 September 1987.
Genscher, Hans-Dietrich (1988), *Diskussionsgrundlage, Memorandum für die Schaffung eines europäischen Währungsraumes und einer europäischen Zentralbank*, 26 February 1988, Bonn.
Genscher, Hans-Dietrich (1995), *Erinnerungen*, Berlin.
George, Stephen (1991), *Britain and European Integration since 1945*, Oxford.
Giscard d'Estaing, Valéry (1978), 'La conférence de presse du président de la république', *Le Monde*, 23 November 1978.
Giscard d'Estaing, Valéry (1988), *Le pouvoir et la vie*, Compagnie 12.
Gorbatchev, Mikhail (1995), *Memoirs*, London.
Gordon, Philip H. (1993), 'The Franco-German Security Partnership', in McCarthy, Patrick (ed.), *France–Germany 1983–1993*.
Gordon, Philip H. (1995), *France, Germany and the Western Alliance*, Boulder, Colorado.
Gorst, Anthony, and Lewis Johnman (1997), *The Suez Crisis*, London.
Grauwe, Paul de, and Lucas Papademos (1990), *The European Monetary System in the 1990s*, London.
Griffiths, R.T. (ed.) (1990), *The Netherlands and the Integration of Europe 1945–1957*, Amsterdam.
Gros, Daniel and Niels Thygesen (1992), *European Monetary Integration: From the European Monetary System to European Monetary Union*, Harlow.
Gütgemann, Annette-Victoria (1997), *Italien und die Europäische Währungsunion, Zur politischen und wirtschaftlichen Diskussion in Italien auf dem Wege zur EWWU*, Arbeitspapier, Konrad Adenauer Stiftung, Sankt Augustin.
Hannoun, Hervé (1994), 'The Merits of Stable Exchange Rates', in Age Bakker, Henk Boot *et al.* (eds): *Monetary Stability through International Cooperation*, Amsterdam.
Harryvan, A.G. and J. van der Harst (eds) (1997), *Documents on European Union*, London.
Hertle, Hans-Hermann (1996), *Der Fall der Mauer, Die unbeabsichtigte Selbstauflösung des SED-Staates*, Opladen.
Hoffmeyer, Erik (1992), *The International Monetary System: An Essay in Interpretation*, North-Holland.
Hoffmeyer, Erik (1994), 'European Exchange Rate Cooperation', in: Age Bakker, Henk Boot *et al.* (eds): *Monetary Stability through International Cooperation*, Amsterdam.
Holtrop, M.W. (1956), 'Monetaire aspecten van de economische integratie', in *De Economist jrg.* 104, no. 12, 1956.
Holtrop, M.W. (1963), 'Monetaire problematiek in Benelux en EEG', in *De Economist*, jrg. 111, no. 1/2, 1963.
Howe, Geoffrey (1994), *Conflict of Loyalty*, London.
Issing, Otmar (1995), 'Geld stiftet noch keine Staatlichkeit', *Frankfurter Allgemeine Zeitung*, 15 July 1995.

James, Harold (1996), *International Monetary Cooperation since Bretton Woods*, New York, Oxford.

James, Robert Rhodes (1986), *Anthony Eden*, London.

Jehee, M.C.J., J.A. de Koning, J.W. Sap (1996), *De Frans-Duitse as: tiranniek of sympathiek?*, Groningen.

Jenkins, Roy (1989), *European Diary 1977–1981*, London.

Jenkins, Roy (1991), *A Life at the Centre*, London.

Johnson, Christopher (1996), *In With the Euro, Out With the Pound: The Single Currency for Britain*, London.

Juppé, Alain (1996), *Entre nous, Mesnil-sur-l'Estrée*, Paris.

Jurgensen, Philippe (1991), *Écu, naissance d'une monnaie*, J.-C. Lattès.

Kees, Andreas (1994), 'The Monetary Committee as a promoter of European integration', in: Age Bakker, Henk Boot *et al.* (eds): *Monetary Stability through International Cooperation*, Amsterdam.

Kissinger, Henry (1979), *White House Years*, Boston.

Kissinger, Henry (1994), *Diplomacy*, New York.

Klaauw, C.A. van der (1995), *Een diplomatenleven, Memoires*, Amsterdam.

Kohl, Helmut (1996), 'Ich wollte Deutschlands Einheit', with Kai Diekmann and Ralf Georg Reuth, Berlin.

Köhler, Horst and Kees, Andreas (1996), 'Die Verhandlungen zur Europäischen Wirtschafts- und Währungsunion', in Theo Waigel (ed.): *Unsere Zukunft heisst Europa*.

Korteweg, Piet (1984), 'Het EMS, het internationale monetaire stelsel en de weg naar monetaire en wisselkoersstabiliteit', in *Zicht op Bancaire en Monetaire Wereld*, Leiden/Antwerpen.

Kusterer, Hermann (1995), *Der Kanzler und der General*, Stuttgart.

Kwizinskij, Jurij A. (1993), *Vor dem Sturm. Erinnerungen eines Diplomaten*, Berlin.

Lamfalussy, Alexandre (1994), 'Macro-economic performance and the international monetary system', in: Age Bakker, Henk Boot *et al.* (eds): *Monetary Stability through International Cooperation*, Amsterdam.

Lamfalussy, Alexandre (1989), 'Macro-coordination of fiscal policies in an Economic and Monetary Union in Europe', appendix to Committee for the study of Economic and Monetary Union (Delors Committee), *Report on Economic and Monetary Union in the European Community*, Brussels.

Lamont, Norman (1995), *Sovereign Britain*, London.

Lawson, Nigel (1989:1), Speech at the Royal Institute for International Affairs on 25 January 1989 in London.

Lawson, Nigel (1989:2), House of Commons, Treasury and Civil Service Committee, Fourth Report, The Delors Report, 19 June 1989, H.C. 341.

Lawson, Nigel (1992), *The View from No. 11, Memoirs of a Tory Radical*, London.

Leigh-Pemberton, Robin (1993), 'A UK Perspective', in Paul Temperton (ed.), *The European Currency Crisis*.

Lucas, W. Scott (1991), *Divided We Stand: Britain, the US and the Suez Crisis*, London.

Ludlow, Peter (1982), *The Making of the European Monetary System: A case study of the politics of the European Community*, London.

Macmillan, Harold (1971) *Riding the Storm 1956–1959*, London.
Marjolin, Robert (1965), 'Le chemin à suivre', *Communauté Européenne*, no. 1, January 1965, Brussels.
Marjolin, Robert (1986, 1989), *Architect of European Unity, Memoirs 1911– 1986*, London.
Marsh, David (1992), *The Bundesbank: The Bank that Rules Europe*, London.
Marsh, David (1994), *Germany and Europe: The Crisis of Unity*, London.
McCarthy, Patrick (ed.) (1993), *France–Germany 1983–1993: The Struggle to Cooperate*, New York.
Meerssche, P. van de (1978), *Europese integratie en desintegratie 1945–heden*, Antwerpen.
Mitterrand, François (1986), *Réflexions sur la politique extérieure de la France*, Paris.
Mitterrand, François (1996), *De l'Allemagne, de la France*, Paris.
Pöhl, Karl Otto (1996), 'Der Delors–Bericht und das Statut einer Europäischen Zentralbank', in Waigel, Theo (ed.), *Unsere Zukunft heisst Europa*.
Prate, Alain (1987), *La France et sa monnaie, Essai sur les relations entre la Banque de France et les gouvernements*, Paris.
Rey, Jean-Jacques (1994), 'Pros and Cons of a Two-speed Monetary Integration', in Age Bakker, Henk Boot *et al.* (eds): *Monetary Stability through International Cooperation*, Amsterdam.
Roussel, Eric (1984), *Georges Pompidou*, J-C. Lattès.
Santini, Carlo (1993), 'An Italian Perspective' in Paul Temperton (ed.), *The European Currency Crisis*.
Schmidt, Helmut (1985), *A Grand Strategy for the West*, New Haven and London.
Schmidt, Helmut (1987), *Menschen und Mächte*, Berlin.
Schmidt, Helmut (1990), *Die Deutschen und ihre Nachbarn*, Berlin.
Schönfelder, Wilhelm, and Elke Thiel (1994), *Eine Markt – Eine Währung, Die Verhandlungen zur Europäischen Wirtschafts- und Währungsunion*, Baden-Baden.
Shultz, George P. and Kenneth W. Dam (1977), *Economic Policy Beyond the Headlines*, New York.
Solomon, Robert (1977), *The International Monetary System 1945–1976: An Insider's View*, New York.
Soutou, Georges-Henri (1996), *L'alliance incertaine. Les rapports politico-stratégiques franco-allemands, 1954–1996*, Fayard.
Stephens, Philip (1996), *Politics and the Pound: The Conservatives' Struggle with Sterling*, London.
Stoltenberg, Gerhard (1988), 'Zur weiteren Entwicklung der währungspolitischen Zusammenarbeit' in *Europa*, 15 March 1988, Bonn.
Stoltenberg, Gerhard (1997), *Wendepunkte, Stationen deutscher Politik 1947 bis 1990*, Berlin.
Taylor, Christopher (1995), *EMU 2000? Prospects for European Monetary Union*, London.
Teltschik, Horst (1991), *329 Tage. Innenansichten der Einigung*, Berlin.
Temperton, Paul (ed.) (1993), *The European Currency Crisis: What Chance Now for a Single European Currency?* Cambridge.

Thatcher, Margaret (1993), *The Downing Street Years*, London.

Thatcher, Margaret (1995), *The Path to Power*, London.

Thompson, Helen (1996), *The British Conservative Government and the European Exchange Rate Mechanism 1979–1994*, London.

Tietmeyer, Hans (1994), 'The Relationship between Economic, Monetary and Political Integration' in Age Bakker, Henk Boot *et al.*, *Monetary Stability through International Cooperation*.

Tsoukalis, Loukas (1977), *The Politics and Economics of European Monetary Integration*, London.

Tsoukalis, Loukas (1993), *The New European Economy: The Politics and Economics of Integration*, Oxford.

Tsoukalis, Loukas (1997), *The New European Economy Revisited*, Oxford.

Vanthoor, Wim F.V. (1996), *European Monetary Union since 1848: A Political and Historical Analysis*, Cheltenham, UK.

Voorhoeve, J.J.C., and H. Hoogervorst (1988), 'Naar een Europese Centrale Bank', *Economisch–Statistische Berichten*, 1 June 1988.

Waigel, Theo, and Manfred Schell (eds.) (1994), *Tage, die Deutschland und die Welt veränderten, Vom Mauerfall zum Kaukasus, Die deutsche Währungsunion*, Munich.

Waigel, Theo (ed.) (1996), *Unsere Zukunft heisst Europa, der Weg zur Wirtschafts- und Währungsunion*, Düsseldorf.

Weizsäcker, Richard von (1997), *Vier Zeiten, Erinnerungen*, Berlin.

Wellink, Nout (1994), 'The Economic and Monetary Relation between Germany and the Netherlands', in Age Bakker, Henk Boot *et al.* (eds): *Monetary Stability through International Cooperation*, Amsterdam.

Werner Report: *Rapport au Conseil et à la Commission concernant la réalisation par étapes de l'Union Economique et Monétaire dans la Communauté*, Luxemburg, 8 October 1970.

Wilson, Harold (1971), *The Labour Government 1964–1970: A Personal Record*, London.

Young, John W. (1993), *Britain and European Unity 1945–1992*, London.

Zelikow, Philip, and Condoleezza Rice (1995), *Germany Unified and Europe Transformed: A Study in Statecraft*, Cambridge, Mass.

Zijlstra, Jelle (1994), 'Central Bank and Government', in: Age Bakker, Henk Boot *et al.* (eds): *Monetary Stability through International Cooperation*, Amsterdam.

Index

Ingram Content Group UK Ltd.
Milton Keynes UK
UKHW012108090423
419778UK00002B/28